Avotaynu Monograph Series

Jewish Vital Records, Revision Lists and Other Jewish Holdings in the Lithuanian Archives

compiled by
Harold Rhode & Sallyann Amdur Sack

Avotaynu, Inc. • Teaneck, NJ
1996

Avotaynu, Inc.
P.O. Box 900
Teaneck, NJ 07666

Printed in the United States of America

First Printing

Map 1 courtesy of U. S. Library of Congress, map 2 courtesy of Yad Vashem, map 3 courtesy of National Geographic Society.

ISBN 1-886223-02-5

How to Use This Monograph

Lithuanian Jews—known as Litvaks—belonged to a highly sophisticated culture which was known throughout the Jewish and non-Jewish world for having produced some of the most brilliant scholars and works of learning. Some of these Jews and their descendants immigrated mostly to the U.S., South Africa, and to what was to become Israel. Approximately 95% of those who stayed behind were murdered during World War II, some by the Nazis but more by local henchmen. As a result, almost seven centuries of vibrant Lithuanian-Jewish culture effectively came to an end.

Most of what remains of that culture is its documentary legacy, much of which is kept in the Lithuanian archives. This monograph is an index to the late 18th-, 19th- and early 20th-century documents regarding those Litvaks who lived in Kovna, Vilna and Suvalki guberniyas (defined below). From the end of the 18th century until World War I, this territory belonged to the Russian Empire. Lithuania, as a country name, was not used during that time period.

Typed inventories of 19th century Jewish vital records (birth, marriage, divorce and death) held in the State Historical Archives of Lithuania in Vilnius were given to the Jewish Genealogy Society of Greater Washington by Laima Tautvaisaite, director of this institution, when she was guest of honor at the 14th Summer Seminar on Jewish Genealogy held in Washington, D.C., June 26–30, 1996.

We have organized and computerized these lists; they form the bulk of this monograph. To them have been added other databases compiled and donated by FAST Genealogical Service and by Yakov Shadevich. Most records are held in the Lithuanian State Historical Archives in Vilnius, but some are stored in a branch archives in Kaunas; a few are at the Academy of Science Library in Vilnius.

Data is presented geographically by town where the documents were created. Town names are rendered in the spelling currently used by Lithuanian archivists. Where known, alternative names are given in parentheses. *Fond, opis* and file (*delo*) numbers are given for all of the vital records and many other types of records. These terms are archival designations of the record storage system that enable an archivist to retrieve records, much as a librarian relies upon a cataloging system. A *fond* corresponds to a record group; an *opis* is an inventory of a subset of records within a specific fond and a *delo* is a file within an opis. Each file may consist of many pages or simply a single sheet of paper.

Boundaries

Country boundaries have changed frequently over the past two centuries in that part of the world. So also have administrative districts within countries. Provenance determines where records are to be kept. That is, international archival standards mandate that records be held in the archives of the country that today governs the land where they were created.

For example, some records created during the 19th century in what was then Kovno, Suvalki and Vilna guberniyas are today held in archives in Belarus or Poland. Revision lists from four *uyezds* (the term, uyezd, will be described below) that once were part of what was historically known as Lithuania (Disna, Lida, Oshmiany and Vileika) are now in a branch of the State Historical Archives of Belarus in Grodno. Other records, especially from former areas of Suvalki *guberniya* now in Poland, are held in the Polish Archives of Ancient Acts in Warsaw. (The address is 6 Dluga St., Warsaw. Many have been microfilmed by the Genealogical Society of Utah, the acquisition arm of the LDS (Mormon) Family History Library and may be accessed through the LDS Family History Centers.) Nevertheless, some of the holdings of the Lithuanian State Historical Archives in Vilnius listed in this monograph were created in towns that today are part of Belarus, Latvia or Poland, yet are held by the Lithuanian State Historical Archives. During the last century, the Russian Czarist Empire ruled over all the countries listed here.

Wars, revolutions, fire, neglect and plain human error have taken their toll on the records from this area. Many have been lost. Others are not found where one expects them to be. Although revision lists from former Lithuanian *uyezds* are in archives in Belarus, some Jewish vital records from the same areas are held in the Vilnius archives and are listed in this monograph. Researchers in this area must discard any notion that record keeping is an exact science. Many a slip has occurred between an official plan for record storage and what actually can be found today.

Historical Geography

Some geographical terms used in this monograph must be defined. During the latter part of the 19th century, what is present-day Lithuania was divided administratively among three *guberniyas*, which were similar in size and function to provinces or states in Western countries. The three *guberniyas*—Kovno, Suvalki and Vilna—were named after the largest city in each of these *guberniyas*. Each *guberniya* was itself subdivided into *uyezds*, territorial units that corresponded roughly in size and function to what we in the West know as counties. Today they often are referred to in English-language writings as districts. The principle of naming an administrative unit after its largest population concentration held here as well. Hence, each *uyezd* was given the name of its largest community.

Sometimes records of interest may be found in a collection for an entire *uyezd* (as in the case of those for Vilnius County), rather than in records listed under the name of the town of interest. Be sure to check these county registers as well. For this reason, it is important to know not only the *uyezd* in which a town was located, but also the history of the boundary and name changes for that area. A typical example is that of the town of Braslav, today in Belarus. Prior to 1838, Braslav was the administrative center of an *uyezd* by that name. At that time, it belonged to the Lithuanian guberniya. After Kovno and Vilna were created as separate *guberniyas* in 1843, the new *uyezd* of Novo-Aleksandrovsk was created and Braslav became part of Novo-Aleksandrovsk *uyezd* of Kovno *guberniya*. Today, Novo-Aleksandrovsk is called *Zarasai*, as is the district in which it is located. A thorough researcher seeking 19th century records from Braslav must check both the town records of Braslav, and the uyezd records for Novo-Aleksandrovsk.

There were other, smaller, territorial units as well. One was *valscius* (*volost* in Polish) which was the smallest governmental unit of the 19th century Russian Empire. It corresponded roughly to a township in Western countries. Another was an *okrug*, a Russian word often used during the last century, which simply means an undefined region or neighborhood. A parish or religious community (*obshchestvo*) was composed of all individuals served by the same church or synagogue. The *Pale of Settlement*, the western area of the Russian Empire, was the only territory where most Jewish inhabitants were permitted to live during the last century. Much of this land was acquired during the three partitions of Poland in 1772, 1775 and 1795.

In 1981, the Soviet archival expert Patricia Kennedy Grimsted wrote:

> By the late nineteenth century, the territories that now constitute the Soviet republics of Estonia. Latvia, Lithuania and Belarussia, were divided among eleven different guberniyas, none of which coincide with present republic boundaries....Archival jurisdiction is determined along territorial lines by the provenance of the records involved. Thus, according to present Soviet archival regulations, earlier records generally fall under the jurisdiction of the state historical archive in the present-day republic occupying the territory where the records were created....In practice, given present Soviet archival regulations, many former guberniya records are now often divided between archives in several different locations. In the case of records from the uyezd level and from cities or smaller administrative levels, the present location of the uyezd center or of the city or district in question determined the present archival jurisdiction.[1]

Grimsted notes that many changes of administrative-territorial divisions occurred over the last century. For a researcher, the question is not who rules a given town today, but rather, who ruled it during the 19th century.

Uyezds of the Three Lithuanian Guberniyas during the 19th Century
(19th Century Russian Name/Modern Lithuanian, Polish or Belarussian Name)

Kovno (created in 1842/43 from Vilna *Guberniya*)
Kovno / Kaunas, Lithuania
Novo-Aleksandrovsk (Prior to 1839, this was called Braslav *uyezd*; today the town and its county

---

[1] *Grimsted, Patricia Kennedy, *Archives and Manuscript Repositories in the USSR: Estonia, Latvia, Lithuania and Belorussia* (Princeton, New Jersey: Princeton University Press, 1981).

have been renamed Zarasai.)
Ponevezh (Upita) / Panevezys, Lithuania
Rossieny / Raseiniai, Lithuania
Shavli / Siauliai, Lithuania
Telshi / Telsiai, Lithuania
Vilkomir / Ukmerge, Lithuania

Suvalki (created in 1866/67 from Avgustov Guberniya)
Avgustov / Augustow, Poland
Kalvaria / Kalvarija, Lithuania
Mariampol / Marijampole, Lithuania
Seiny / Sejny, Poland
Suvalki / Suwalki, Poland
Vladislavov / Kudirkos Naumiestis, Lithuania
Volkovyshki / Vilkaviskis, Lithuania

Vilna (annexed from Poland in 1795; from 1796–1801 it was part of Lithuanian guberniya)
Disna / Dzisna, Belarus
Lida / Lida, Belarus
Oshmiany / Ashmyany, Belarus
Sventsiany / Svencionys, Lithuania
Troki / Trakai, Lithuania
Vileika / Vileyka, Belarus
Vilna / Vilnius, Lithuania

Records Defined

All genealogists know about the value of so-called "vital" records—the accounts of births, marriages, divorces and deaths. They and the *reviskie skazki* (fiscal censuses) are well known to most Jewish genealogists. Less well known, but often equally valuable are other categories of records, many of which are alien to Westerners not accustomed to totalitarian rule. A multitude of them were created in 19th century czarist Russia. Following are the categories of records listed in this monograph. Just because a particular record is not listed in the monograph does not necessarily mean that it does not exist; it may mean only that the records has not yet been located.

Vital Records

Vital Records are birth, marriage, divorce and death records. Only in 1826, did the czarist government issue a requirement that rabbis keep registration books of births, marriages, divorces and death. After that date, Jews were required to go to the synagogue to which they were assigned to register vital events. Once a year, the authorities went to the synagogues to copy these registers. The materials stored in archives today are all copies; original records, kept in synagogues, no longer exist. They were destroyed no later than 1942, primarily by the Germans.

Often a range of dates is given. Because we have not personally inspected every record listed, we cannot definitely say what is in them. It is known, however, that a range of dates does not necessarily mean that every date in between is represented in the collection, only that the earliest and latest date are know to be present. We assume, however, that several dates in between also exist. Any given file may include records for more than one year, and the records for a single year may be spread over a number of files.

Reviskie Skazki

Reviskie skazki (often called revision lists) were a series of ten censuses designed for taxation and conscription purposes begun by czarist authorities in the middle of the 18th century. The Imperial Czarist Empire of Russia had almost no Jewish inhabitants before the three partitions of Poland. Revision lists were first drawn up in the Lithuanian *guberniyas* only in 1795, the year that Jews first appeared in these lists. The *reviskie skazki* were organized by family and listed (by name and age) the head of the household, spouse and children. Jewish revision lists were created separately from Christian lists. Because the lists were used for conscription, and army service was an especially onerous ordeal for the Jews, every effort was made by these families to keep males from being recorded. This was especially true during the reign of Nicholas I (1825–55), during which Jewish boys as young as eight years of age were drafted for as long as 25 years. Revisions V (1795), VI (1811) and VII (1815) are known to be especially inaccurate, with many missing males (but only males were recorded in the sixth revision). (For excellent descriptions of the *reviskie skazki*, see, "Information for Jewish Genealogists in the State Archive of Zhitomir Oblast", *Avotaynu*, XII/1/14; "What May Be Learned from 19th Century Czarist Jewish Birth Records and Revision Lists," *Avotaynu*, X/3/05; and "Vital Statistics in Czarist Russia," *Avotaynu*, V/3/06). Because information about revision lists in this monograph was obtained from private researchers, the *fond*, *opis* and file information was not always available.

Finally, we believe that the reviskie skazki for the towns were usually kept in registers drawn up for entire uyezds. This means that researchers should examine the registers for the uyezd for the town in question, especially if revision lists do not appear in this monograph under then town entry in question.

Kupah Tax

Kupah Tax, called *koroboçhny* in Russian, has also been called the box tax in some English-language writings. According to Professor Dov Levin, author of the recently published *Pinkas Hakehillot-Lithuania*, the box in question was most likely what is called a *pushke* in Yiddish; the blue and white Jewish National Fund boxes that once were found in almost every Jewish home is an example of a *pushke*. Certain items, such as Sabbath candles and/or kosher salt were indispensable items for every Jewish household; it was on these items, therefore, that the tax to support the *kehillah* (Jewish community) was levied. Typically, the rabbi's wife had a monopoly on the sale of such items, and it was she who was responsible for collecting the tax. Banks were rare or nonexistent in Czarist Russia during most of the 19th century, so when a tax was collected, it was put into a special box, a *pushke* or (in Hebrew) *kupah*. Thus, a list of payers of a *kupah* tax is, for all intents and purposes, a census of the total Jewish community.

Other Records

Sprinkled throughout the monograph are notations of other categories of records listed only as financial, police, military, etc. As we went to press, the value of another, previously-unknown category of record came to light; these are records of postal savings accounts, popular in the Pale of Settlement at the end of the last century. Apparently, the authorities demanded extensive documentation of those with accounts—including parents' names, birth places, etc. Without inspecting each file, the exact nature of these miscellaneous categories of records cannot be known precisely. What is known, however, is that some researchers of Jewish genealogy have found valuable information in them. Listed below are the abbreviations used to denote the various categories of records:

ai	alphabetical index	el	elections
al	alphabetical list	fin	financial
b	births	fl	family list
bdm	births, deaths, marriages	g	former residents of Griniskis
bdmv	births, deaths, marriages, divorces	hev	house estimated value
can	candle tax	hol	homeowner's list
cen	census	jcl	Jewish community list
cr	cemetery records—Jewish	jh	Jewish hospital
crl	city resident list	jkjc	joining Kovna Jewish community
ct	communal taxes	k	*kupah* tax
d	deaths	m	marriages
dc	draftee collecting & planning	m/r	merchants/residents
de	Duma elections	mer	merchants
dl	draftee list	misc	miscellaneous records
dl-j	draft list—Jews	ml	military list

ol	owners list	tcdr	tax collection & distribution records
p	police	tpl	taxpayers list
pbr	postal bank records	tpl-a	apartment tax payers list
pib	passport issuance book	tpl-l	land tax payer tax
prb	passport registration book	tpl-r	real estate tax payers list
rc	real estate as collateral	txp	land tax planning
resl	resident's list	v	divorces
rs	*reviskie skazki*	var	various
ta	town administration	vl	voters list
		vl-j	voters list—Jews

How to Access Records

As we go to press, the Mormons are slowly microfilming at the State Historical Archives in Vilnius. No Jewish records have yet appeared in Salt Lake City, and none are expected in the near future. For now, therefore, researchers have only three options for accessing the records listed in this monograph:

1. Write directly to the Lithuanian State Historical Archives, Gerosios Vilties 10, Vilnius 2015, fax: 65-23-14, and inquire about the possibility of obtaining copies of files or records of interest. Be sure to ask about fees and estimated time for completion of the task.

2. Hire a private genealogical search service. This may be the only available option in the case of records for which no *fond*, *opis* and *delo* number is given. Two researchers with experience in Lithuania, and were contributors to this book are: Yakov Shadevich; 10412 Parthenon Court; Bethesda, MD 20817; fax, 301-365-5719; e-mail, yakov@inter.net. Boris Feldblyum; FAST Genealogy Service; 8510 Wild Olive Drive; Potomac, MD 20854; e-mail, bfeldbly@capaccess.org.

3. Research in person at the archives in Vilnius or Kaunas. This is likely to be the most unpredictable and/or unproductive course of action—unless the services of an on-site Lithuanian researcher with known experience searching Jewish records are engaged in advance.

Some records are noted as being physically located in Kaunas at the time of this writing. However, a plan has existed for several years to move some of the records to the archives in Vilnius. If you plan to go, be sure to inquire in advance if records of interest are still in Kaunas.

* Some *reviskie skazkie* are listed without *fond*, *opis* and file numbers. They were obtained from a private researcher and, at the time of writing could be accessed only through FAST Genealogy Service or through Yakov Shadevich. Although most are believed to be in the Vilnius archives, a few unidentified *reviskie skazki* records (including some from Kelme) are known to be held at the National Library.

Bibliographical Sources

In past years, *Avotaynu*, The International Review of Jewish Genealogy, has published articles relevant to Lithuanian archival research. Following is a list of the most important ones. Following the name of the article are the volume/issue/page numbers:

"Association of Lithuanian Jews in Israel," III/1/24.

"Missing YIVO Records May Be Found," V/2/26.

"Letter from Jewish Community of Kaunas," V/4/21.

"Book on Lithuanian Jewish Communities Delayed," VI/1/41.

"Vital Records of Lithuanian Jewry Found," VI/2/03.

"News of Marijampole Society," VI/3/39.

"Jewish Vital Statistic Records in Lithuanian Archives," VI/4/04.

"Book on Lithuanian Jewish Communities to be Published," VI/4/63.

"A Genealogical Trip to Lithuania: the Host's Perspective," VII/1/03.

Book Review, *Lithuanian Jewish Communities*, VII/3/36.

"Numerous Photographic Essays of Jewish Lithuania Planned," VIII/2/57.

"Explains 1795 Revision List," VIII/3/66.

"Lithuania Reluctant to Allow Microfilming of Jewish Documents," VIII/4/03.

"Dvinsk Genealogy and Post-Holocaust Questions," VIII/4/06.

"A Trip to Skoudas, Kavarskas and Ukmerge," VIII/4/09.
"More About the Lithuanian Archives," IX/1/65.
"Relates Experience with Lithuanian Archives," IX/1/65.
"Poses Theory for Vanished Cemeteries," IX/3/65.
"SIG for Northwest Lithuania Formed," X/2/65.
"Recommends Lithuanian Researcher Located in Vilnius," X/2/65.
"Reports on Jewish State Museum of Lithuania in Vilnius,"X /2/66.
"Notes Difference in Response Between Lithuanian SSR Archives and Republic of Lithuania Archives," X/4/80.
"Lithuanian Archivist Heads Speakers at Washington Seminar," XI/1/21.
"New Archival Finds from Lithuania," XI/2/10.
"Archival Sources in Lithuanian State Archives," XI/3/03.
"Using Litvak Naming Patterns to Derive Names of Unknown Ancestors," XI/3/22.

Description of Columns on Listing

Year(s) Year(s) for which a record exists.

Type Record Type (See the introduction for the abbreviations for the various types of documents listed.)

Fond/File(s)/Op (Fond/File(s)Opis). Archival Location. See the introduction for detailed description of the terms.

A Archival Location (If nothing appears in this column, the record is located in the Lithuanian State Historical Archives in Vilnius. "K" indicates that the record is now located in the Kaunas branch of this archive. At some future date, much of this material is scheduled to be transfered to the archives in Vilnius. "A" indicates that the record is located in the Academy of Science Library in Vilnius.

F Flag. Additional information supplied about records. See inidividual town descriptions of towns.

Notes Additional information about the records.

Map 1 — The Lithuanian State Before the Partitions (1772–1793)

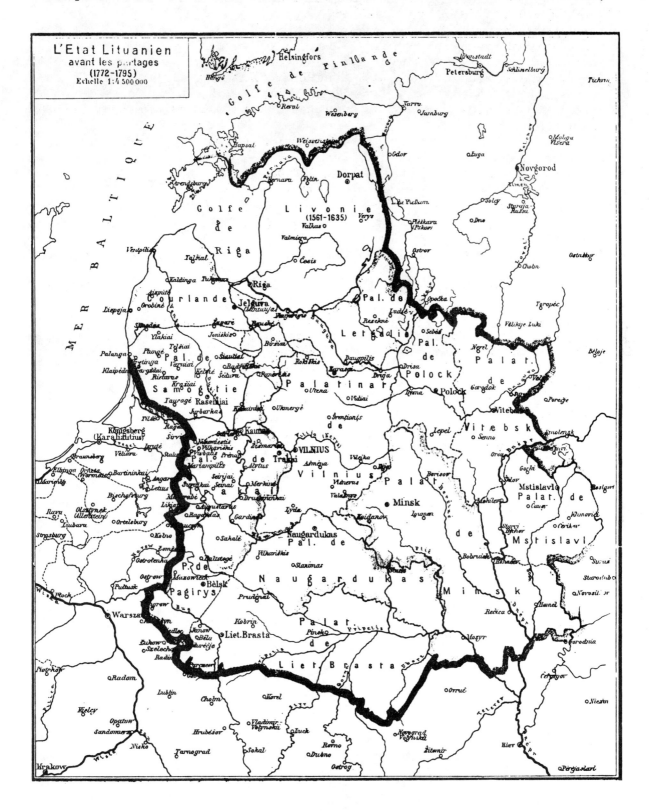

Map 2 — 1918-1940 Independent Lithuania

LATVIA

BELARUSSIA
(from September, 1939)

EAST PRUSSIA
GERMANY

POLAND

BALTIC SEA

1918-1940 INDEPENDENT LITHUANIA
A MAP OF THE JEWISH COMMUNITIES

Lithuania in mid-1939

Vilna Region captured by Poland
in 1920 and annexed to Lithuania
in October, 1939

Memel Region annexed to Germany
in March, 1939

Annexed from Soviet Belarussia
to Lithuania in 1940

Map 3 — Contemporary Lithuania

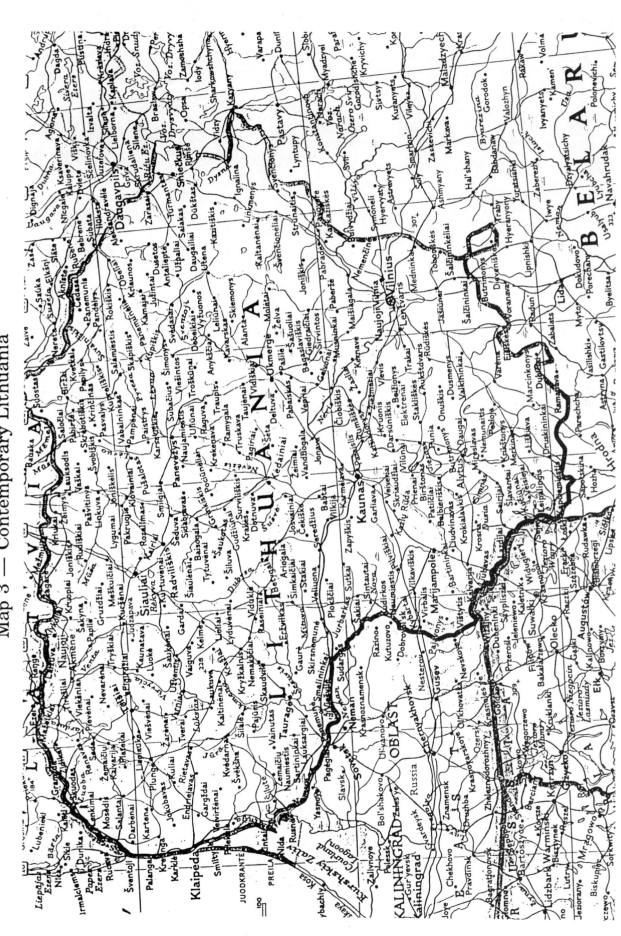

Year(s)	Type	Fond	File(s)	Op	A	F	Notes	Page 1

Akmene (Akmene)

Year(s)	Type	Fond	File(s)	Op	A	F	Notes
1858	rs						
1862	rs						
1866	rs						
1875–1894	rs	670	41	1			crl
1895	cen						

Akniste, Latvia

Year(s)	Type	Fond	File(s)	Op	A	F	Notes
unclear	prb	209				K	Novo-Aleksandrovsk (Zarasai) County

Aleksotas

Year(s)	Type	Fond	File(s)	Op	A	F	Notes
1875	resl	670	41	1			Permanent Resident Register
1914	dl	1–58	42	1			family members listed

Alsedziai

Year(s)	Type	Fond	File(s)	Op	A	F	Notes
1912–1916	tpl-r					K	

Alytus (Alyta)

This town is divided into two parts by a river. Until 1918, the western part belonged to Kalvaria/Kalvarija County of Suvalki guberniya (identified in the listings below with a *K* in the Flag column). The eastern part belonged to Troki/Trakai County of Vilna guberniya (identified in the listings below with a *T* in the Flag column). Records for each part were kept in separate registers.

Year(s)	Type	Fond	File(s)	Op	A	F	Notes
1858	rs	515	110–122	25		T	srs
1858–1905	rs	515				T	
1859	rs	515	123	25		T	srs
1860	rs	515	124	25		T	srs
1861	rs	515	124	25		T	srs
1862	rs	515	124	25		T	srs
1863	rs	515	124	25		T	srs
1864	rs	515	125–126	25		T	srs
1865	rs	515	127	25		T	srs
1867	rs	515	128	25		T	srs
1868	rs	515	128–129	25		T	srs
1869	rs	515	129–130	25		T	srs
1870	rs	515	130–131	25		T	srs
1871	rs	515	132	25		T	srs
1872	rs	515	133	25		T	srs
1873	rs	515	133	25		T	srs
1874	rs	515	133	25		T	srs
1905–1908	rs	515	144	25		T	srs
1852	b	1108	9	1		K	
1853	b	1108	9	1		K	
1854	b	1108	9	1		K	
1854	d	728	118	1		T	
1854	b	728	38	1		T	
1854	m	728	53	1		T	
1854	v	728	81	1		T	
1855	b	1108	9	1		K	
1855	b	728	125	1		T	
1855	m	728	161	1		T	
1855	v	728	176	1		T	
1855	d	728	186	1		T	
1856	b	1108	9	1		K	
1856	b	728	215	1		T	
1856	v	728	253	1		T	
1856	d	728	258	1		T	
1857	b	1108	9	1		K	
1857	b	728	294	1		T	
1858	b	1108	9	1		K	
1858	b	728	360	1		T	
1858	m	728	365	1		T	
1858	v	728	390	1		T	
1858	d	728	400	1		T	
1859	b	1108	9	1		K	
1859	b	728	433	1		T	
1859	m	728	463	1		T	
1859	v	728	470	1		T	
1859	d	728	499	1		T	
1860	b	1108	9	1		K	
1860	b	728	512	1		T	
1860	m	728	547	1		T	
1860	v	728	548	1		T	
1860	d	728	570	1		T	
1861	b	1108	9	1		K	
1861	b	728	614	1		T	
1861	d	728	676	1		T	
1862	b	1108	9	1		K	
1862	m	728	725	1		T	
1862	d	728	747	1		T	
1863	b	1108	9	1		K	
1863	b	728	782	1		T	
1863	d	728	853	1		T	
1864	b	1108	9	1		K	
1864	b	728	701	3		T	
1864	m	728	702	3		T	
1864	d	728	703	3		T	
1865	b	1108	9	1		K	
1865	b	728	704	3		T	
1865	d	728	706	3		T	

Alytus (Alyta) continued

Year(s)	Type	Fond	File(s)	Op	A	F	Notes
1866	b	1108	9	1		K	
1866	b	728	707	3		T	
1866	m	728	708	3		T	
1866	d	728	710	3		T	
1867	b	1108	9	1		K	
1867	b	728	711	3		T	
1867	m	728	712	3		T	
1867	d	728	714	3		T	
1868	b	1108	9	1		K	
1868	b	728	715	3		T	
1868	m	728	716	3		T	
1868	d	728	717	3		T	
1869	b	1108	9	1		K	
1869	m	728	718	3		T	
1869	d	728	720	3		T	
1870	b	1108	9	1		K	
1870	b	728	721-722	3		T	
1870	m	728	723-724	3		T	
1870	d	728	726	3		T	
1871	b	1108	9	1		K	
1871	b	728	727-728	3		T	
1871	m	728	729-730	3		T	
1871	d	728	732	3		T	
1872	b	1108	9	1		K	
1872	b	728	733-734	3		T	
1872	m	728	735-736	3		T	
1872	d	728	738-739	3		T	
1873	b	1108	9	1		K	
1873	m	1236	991	3		T	
1873	b	728	740-741	3		T	
1873	m	728	742-743	3		T	
1873	d	728	745	3		T	
1874	b	1108	9	1		K	
1874	b	728	147, 746	3		T	
1874	m	728	747-748	3		T	
1875	b	1108	9	1		K	
1875	b	728	750-751	3		T	
1875	m	728	752-753	3		T	
1875	d	728	755	3		T	
1876	b	1108	9	1		K	
1876	m	1236	991	3		K	
1876	b	728	1245	3		T	
1876	m	728	1250-1251	3		T	
1876	d	728	1257	3		T	
1876	b	728	321	4		T	
1877	b	1108	9	1		K	
1877	b	728	1246-1247	3		T	
1877	d	728	1258	3		T	
1878	b	728	1248	3		T	
1879	b	728	1249	3		T	
1879	m	728	1255	3		T	
1880	m	1236	991	3		K	
1880	m	728	1256	3		T	
1880	b	728	321	4		T	
1881	m	1236	991	3		K	
1881	b	728	321	4		T	
1881	d	728	322	4		T	
1882	m	1236	991	3		K	
1882	b	728	321	4		T	
1882	d	728	322	4		T	
1883	b	728	321	4		T	
1883	d	728	322	4		T	
1884	m	1236	991	3		K	
1884	b	728	321	4		T	
1884	d	728	322	4		T	
1885	d	728	322	4		T	
1886	d	728	322	4		T	
1887	b	728	321	4		T	
1888	m	1236	991	3		K	
1888	b	728	321	4		T	
1889	m	1236	991	3		K	
1890	b	728	321	4		T	
1890	d	728	322	4		T	
1891	b	728	321	4		T	
1891	d	728	322	4		T	
1892	b	728	321	4		T	
1893	m	1236	991	3		K	
1893	b	728	321	4		T	
1893	d	728	322	4		T	
1894	m	1236	991	3		K	
1895	m	1236	991	3		K	
1896	m	1236	991	3		K	
1896	b	728	321	4		T	
1896	d	728	322	4		T	
1897	m	1236	991	3		K	
1897	b	728	321	4		T	
1897	d	728	322	4		T	
1898	m	1236	991	3		K	

Year(s)	Type	Fond	File(s)	Op	A	F	Notes

Alytus (Alyta) continued

Year(s)	Type	Fond	File(s)	Op	A	F	Notes
1898	b	728	321	4		T	
1898	d	728	322	4		T	
1899	m	1236	991	3		K	
1899	b	728	321	4		T	
1899	d	728	322	4		T	
1900	m	1236	991	3		K	
1900	b	728	321	4		T	
1900	d	728	322	4		T	
1901	m	1236	991	3		K	
1901	b	728	321	4		T	
1901	d	728	322	4		T	
1902	m	1236	991	3		K	
1902	b	728	321	4		T	
1902	d	728	322	4		T	
1903	m	1236	991	3		K	
1903	b	728	321	4		T	
1903	d	728	322	4		T	
1904	m	1236	991	3		K	
1904	b	728	321	4		T	
1904	d	728	322	4		T	
1905	m	1236	991	3		K	
1905	d	728	322	4		T	
1906	m	1236	991	3		K	
1906	b	728	321	4		T	
1907	m	1236	991	3		K	
1907	b	728	321	4		T	
1908	m	1236	991	3		K	
1908	b	728	321	4		T	
1908	d	728	322	4		T	
1909	m	1236	991	3		K	
1909	b	728	321	4		T	
1909	d	728	322	4		T	
1910	m	1236	991	3		K	
1910	b	728	321	4		T	
1911	m	1236	991	3		K	
1911	b	728	321	4		T	
1911	d	728	322	4		T	
1912	m	1236	991	3		K	
1912	b	728	321	4		T	
1913	m	1236	991	3		K	
1913	d	728	322	4		T	
1914	m	1236	991	3		K	
1914	b	728	321	4		T	
1914	d	728	322	4		T	

Antakalnis (Antokol) Was a suburb of Vilnius. Those items with a Flag code of "7" are in the Vilnius County Register.

Year(s)	Type	Fond	File(s)	Op	A	F	Notes
1816-1818	rs	515	288	25	K	7	Jews
1834	rs	515	298	25	K	7	Jews
1843-1849	rs	515	306	25	K	7	Jews
1849	rs	515	312	25	K	7	Jews
1850-1854	rs	515	273	25	K	7	Jews
1858	rs	515	285	25	K	7	Jews
unknown	rs						
unknown	rs	515	299	25	K	7	Jews
unknown	rs	515	320	25	K	7	Jews
1854	b	728	159, 160	3			
1854	m	728	40-41	2			
1854	d	728	42	2			
1855	b	728	68	2			
1855	b	728	69	2			
1855	m	728	70-71	2			
1855	v	728	72	2			
1855	d	728	73	2			
1855	d	728	74	2			
1856	b	728	103	2			
1856	b	728	104	2			
1856	m	728	105-106	2			
1856	v	728	107	2			
1856	d	728	108, 127	2			
1857	b	728	138	2			
1857	b	728	139	2			
1857	m	728	140-141	2			
1857	v	728	142-143	2			
1857	d	728	144-145	2			
1858	b	728	177	2			
1858	b	728	178	2			
1858	m	728	179-180	2			
1858	v	728	181	2			
1858	d	728	182-183	2			
1859	b	728	217	2			
1859	b	728	218	2			
1859	m	728	219-220	2			
1859	m	728	220	2			
1859	v	728	221	2			
1859	d	728	222-223	2			
1860	b	728	260	2			
1860	b	728	261	2			

|---------|------|------|---------|----|----|----|-------|--------|
Antakalnis (Antokol) continued								
1860	m	728	263-264	2				
1860	d	728	265-266	2				
1861	b	728	320	2				
1861	m	728	321	2				
1861	d	728	322	2				
1862	b	728	323	2				
1862	b	728	324	2				
1862	m	728	325-326	2				
1863	m	728	161	3				
1863	b	728	352	2				
1863	b	728	353	2				
1863	m	728	354	2				
1864	m	728	162	3				
1864	b	728	379	2				
1864	b	728	380	2				
1864	m	728	381	2				
1865	b	728	163	3				
1865	b	728	164	3				
1865	m	728	165-166	3				
1866	b	728	164, 167	3				
1866	m	728	168-169	3				
1867	b	728	164, 170	3				
1867	m	728	171-172	3				
1868	b	728	164, 173	3				
1868	m	728	174-175	3				
1869	b	728	164, 176	3				
1869	m	728	177-178	3				
1870	b	728	179, 180	3				
1870	m	728	181-182	3				
1871	b	728	179, 183	3				
1871	m	728	184	3				
1872	b	728	179, 185, 193, 1032	3				
1872	m	728	186-187	3				
1873	b	728	188, 189	3				
1874	b	728	190, 191	3				
1875	b	728	192	3				
1876	b	728	1033	3				
1876	m	728	1072-1073	3				
1877	b	728	1040	3				
1877	m	728	1077, 1077A	3				
1878	b	728	1048	3				
1878	m	728	1083	3				
1879	b	728	1051, 1117	3				
1879	m	728	1079	3				
1880	b	728	1104, 1117	3				
1881	b	728	1062, 1047	3				
1882	b	728	1047, 1064	3				
1883	b	728	1068, 1165	3				
1884	b	728	1068, 1165	3				
1885	b	728	1068, 1168	3				
1886	b	728	1122, 1171	3				
1887	b	728	1175, 1421	3				
1888	b	728	1421, 1424	3				
1889	b	728	1421, 1429	3				
1890	b	728	1437, 1439	3				
1891	b	728	1447	3				
1892	b	728	1453	3				
1893	b	728	1459	3				
1894	b	728	1466	3				
1895	b	728	1473	3				
Antaliepte								
1882	rs							
Anyksciai								
	rs	1262	21	1				
1853 or 1856	rs	525	845	2				
1858	rs	1262	16	1				
1865	rs	525	856	2			Inventory	
1866	rs							
1872-74	rs	1262	17	1				
1874	rs							
1879	rs							
1893	rs							
1895	rs	768					Census, Includes surrounding area	
1897	rs	768					Population Lists of Kaunas Guberniia	
1809-1813?	ml	497					Ukmerge County Draft Commission Records	
1827-1918	fin	715					Property	
1843-1917	p	J-50		1		K	Chancellory of Kaunas Guberniia Civil Governor, "On Issuing Foreign Passports:	
1863-1870	ml	1252					Ukmerge County Military Commander	
1863-1917	ta	J-347				K	Financial Ledgers	
1865-1917	p	J-34				K	Ukmerge County Police Headquarters, 900 files	
1897		768						
1900-1914	p		34	1		K	Ukmerge Okrug Police Heaquarters	
1901-1912	p	1227					People Under Surveillance - Kovna Guberniia Gendarmie Heaquarters	

Anyksciai continued

1905-1917	p	J-39		1	K		Elections, index of 5th Police Ward	

Ariogala

Year(s)	Type	Fond	File(s)	Op	A	F	Notes
1816	rs						
1851	rs						
1874	rs	I-61	1644	1	K		Alphabetic - Jews
1868	dl-j				K		
1868	dl	61		1	K		Jews
1870-1874	k				K		
1871	dl				K		Jews
1887	fl	I-201	4	1	K		Alphabetic - Jews
Early 20th Cent.	fl	2101			K		

Asmena

Year(s)	Type	Fond	File(s)	Op	A	F	Notes
1795-1831	rs	515	1032	15	K		All Social Classes including Jews

Aukstadvaris (Visokidvor) Listed as Stakliskes-Aukstadvaris.

Year(s)	Type	Fond	File(s)	Op	A	F
1881	b	728	331	4		5
1881	m	728	332	4		5
1881	d	728	333	4		5
1881	v	728	333	4		5
1882	b	728	331	4		5
1882	m	728	332	4		5
1882	d	728	333	4		5
1882	v	728	333	4		5
1883	b	728	331	4		5
1883	m	728	332	4		5
1883	d	728	333	4		5
1883	v	728	333	4		5
1884	b	728	331	4		5
1884	m	728	332	4		5
1884	d	728	333	4		5
1884	v	728	333	4		5
1885	b	728	331	4		5
1885	m	728	332	4		5
1885	d	728	333	4		5
1885	v	728	333	4		5
1886	b	728	331	4		5
1886	m	728	332	4		5
1886	d	728	333	4		5
1887	b	728	331	4		5
1887	m	728	332	4		5
1887	d	728	333	4		5
1888	m	728	332	4		5
1889	b	728	331	4		5
1889	m	728	332	4		5
1889	d	728	333	4		5
1889	v	728	333	4		5
1890	b	728	331	4		5
1890	m	728	332	4		5
1890	d	728	333	4		5
1890	v	728	333	4		5
1891	b	728	331	4		5
1891	m	728	332	4		5
1891	d	728	333	4		5
1891	v	728	333	4		5
1892	b	728	331	4		5
1892	m	728	332	4		5
1892	d	728	333	4		5
1892	v	728	333	4		5
1893	b	728	331	4		5
1893	m	728	332	4		5
1893	d	728	333	4		5
1894	m	728	332	4		5
1894	d	728	333	4		5
1894	v	728	333	4		5
1895	b	728	331	4		5
1895	m	728	332	4		5
1895	d	728	333	4		5
1895	v	728	333	4		5
1896	b	728	331	4		5
1896	m	728	332	4		5
1896	d	728	333	4		5
1896	v	728	333	4		5
1897	b	728	331	4		5
1897	m	728	332	4		5
1897	v	728	333	4		5
1898	m	728	332	4		5
1898	d	728	333	4		5
1899	b	728	331	4		5
1899	m	728	332	4		5
1899	d	728	333	4		5
1900	b	728	331	4		5
1900	m	728	332	4		5
1900	d	728	333	4		5
1901	b	728	331	4		5
1901	m	728	332	4	F	5
1902	b	728	331	4		5

Year(s)	Type	Fond	File(s)	Op	A	F	Notes
Aukstadvaris (Visokidvor) continued							
1902	m	728	332	4		5	
1902	d	728	333	4		5	
1903	b	728	331	4		5	
1903	m	728	332	4		5	
1903	d	728	333	4		5	
1904	b	728	331	4		5	
1904	m	728	332	4		5	
1904	d	728	333	4		5	
1905	b	728	331	4		5	
1905	m	728	332	4		5	
1905	d	728	333	4		5	
1906	b	728	331	4		5	
1906	m	728	332	4		5	
1906	d	728	333	4		5	
1907	b	728	331	4		5	
1907	m	728	332	4		5	
1907	d	728	333	4		5	
1908	b	728	331	4		5	
1908	m	728	332	4		5	
1908	d	728	333	4		5	
1909	m	728	332	4		5	
1910	b	728	331	4		5	
1910	m	728	332	4		5	
1910	d	728	333	4		5	
1911	b	728	331	4		5	
1911	m	728	332	4		5	
1911	d	728	333	4		5	
1912	b	728	331	4		5	
1912	m	728	332	4		5	
1912	d	728	333	4		5	
1913	b	728	331	4		5	
1913	m	728	332	4		5	
1913	d	728	333	4		5	
1914	b	728	331	4		5	
1914	m	728	332	4		5	
Avgustov							
	var						
Babtai (Bobt)							
1858	rs	196			K		Jews
1858-1880	rs	196			K		Jews
1874	rs	I-61	1645	1	K		Alphabetic - Jews
1858-1880	cen				K		Jews
1870-1874	k				K		
1875	b	1226	1339	1			
1875	m	1226	1340	1			
1875	d	1226	1341	1			
1876	b	1226	1339	1			
1876	m	1226	1340	1			
1876	d	1226	1341	1			
1877	b	1226	1339	1			
1877	m	1226	1340	1			
1877	d	1226	1341	1			
1878	b	1226	1339	1			
1878	m	1226	1340	1			
1878	d	1226	1341	1			
1879	b	1226	1339	1			
1879	m	1226	1340	1			
1879	d	1226	1341	1			
1880	b	1226	1339	1			
1880	m	1226	1340	1			
1880	d	1226	1341	1			
1881	b	1226	1339	1			
1881	m	1226	1340	1			
1881	d	1226	1341	1			
1882	b	1226	1339	1			
1882	m	1226	1340	1			
1882	d	1226	1341	1			
1883	m	1226	1340	1			
1883	d	1226	1341	1			
1883	b	1226	1342	1			
1884	m	1226	1340, 1962	1			
1884	d	1226	1341, 1962	1			
1884	b	1226	1342, 1962	1			
1884	v	1226	1962	1			
1885	m	1226	1340, 1962	1			
1885	b	1226	1342, 1962	1			
1885	d	1226	1343, 1962	1			
1885	v	1226	1962	1			
1886	m	1226	1340, 1962	1			
1886	b	1226	1342, 1962	1			
1886	d	1226	1343, 1962	1			
1886	v	1226	1962	1			
1887	m	1226	1340, 1962	1			
1887	b	1226	1342, 1962	1			
1887	d	1226	1343, 1962	1			
1887	v	1226	1962	1			

Babtai (Bobt) continued

Year(s)	Type	Fond	File(s)	Op	A	F	Notes
1888	b	1226	1342, 1962	1			
1888	d	1226	1343, 1962	1			
1888	m	1226	1962	1			
1888	v	1226	1962	1			
1889	b	1226	1342, 1962	1			
1889	d	1226	1343, 1962	1			
1889	m	1226	1962	1			
1889	v	1226	1962	1			
1890	b	1226	1342, 1962	1			
1890	d	1226	1343, 1962	1			
1890	m	1226	1962	1			
1890	v	1226	1962	1			
1891	b	1226	1342, 1962	1			
1891	d	1226	1343, 1962	1			
1891	m	1226	1962	1			
1891	v	1226	1962	1			
1892	d	1226	1343, 1962	1			
1892	b	1226	1962	1			
1892	m	1226	1962	1			
1892	v	1226	1962	1			
1893	d	1226	1343, 1962	1			
1893	b	1226	1962	1			
1893	m	1226	1962	1			
1893	v	1226	1962	1			
1894	b	1226	1962	1			
1894	d	1226	1962	1			
1894	m	1226	1962	1			
1894	v	1226	1962	1			
1895	b	1226	1962	1			
1895	d	1226	1962	1			
1895	m	1226	1962	1			
1895	v	1226	1962	1			
1896	b	1226	1962	1			
1896	d	1226	1962	1			
1896	m	1226	1962	1			
1896	v	1226	1962	1			
1897	b	1226	1962	1			
1897	d	1226	1962	1			
1897	m	1226	1962	1			
1897	v	1226	1962	1			
1898	b	1226	1962	1			
1898	d	1226	1962	1			
1898	m	1226	1962	1			
1898	v	1226	1962	1			
1899	b	1226	1962	1			
1899	d	1226	1962	1			
1899	m	1226	1962	1			
1899	v	1226	1962	1			
1900	b	1226	1962	1			
1900	d	1226	1962	1			
1900	m	1226	1962	1			
1900	v	1226	1962	1			
1901	b	1226	1962	1			
1901	d	1226	1962	1			
1901	m	1226	1962	1			
1901	v	1226	1962	1			
1902	b	1226	1962	1			
1902	d	1226	1962	1			
1902	m	1226	1962	1			
1902	v	1226	1962	1			
1903	b	1226	1962	1			
1903	d	1226	1962	1			
1903	m	1226	1962	1			
1903	v	1226	1962	1			
1904	b	1226	1962	1			
1904	d	1226	1962	1			
1904	m	1226	1962	1			
1904	v	1226	1962	1			
1905	b	1226	1962	1			
1905	d	1226	1962	1			
1905	m	1226	1962	1			
1905	v	1226	1962	1			
1906	b	1226	1962	1			
1906	d	1226	1962	1			
1906	m	1226	1962	1			
1906	v	1226	1962	1			
1907	b	1226	1962	1			
1907	d	1226	1962	1			
1907	m	1226	1962	1			
1907	v	1226	1962	1			
1908	b	1226	1962	1			
1908	d	1226	1962	1			
1908	m	1226	1962	1			
1908	v	1226	1962	1			
1909	b	1226	1962	1			
1909	d	1226	1962	1			
1909	m	1226	1962	1			
1909	v	1226	1962	1			

Babtai (Bobt) continued

Year(s)	Type	Fond	File(s)	Op	A	F	Notes
1910	b	1226	1962	1			
1910	d	1226	1962	1			
1910	m	1226	1962	1			
1910	v	1226	1962	1			
1911	b	1226	1962	1			
1911	d	1226	1962	11			
1911	m	1226	1962	1			
1911	v	1226	1962	1			
1912	b	1226	1962	1			
1912	d	1226	1962	1			
1912	m	1226	1962	1			
1912	v	1226	1962	1			
1913	b	1226	1962	1			
1913	d	1226	1962	1			
1913	m	1226	1962	1			
1913	v	1226	1962	1			
1914	b	1226	1962	1			
1914	d	1226	1962	1			
1914	m	1226	1962	1			
1914	v	1226	1962	1			
1935-1938	bdmv	1226	1344	1			Extracts

Bagaslaviskis (Bogoslavishok) Those items with a Flag code of "2" are in the Vilnius County 2nd Okrug Registers.

Year(s)	Type	Fond	File(s)	Op	A	F	Notes
1854	b	728	26, 27	1			
1854	m	728	60	1			
1854	d	728	97-98	1			
1855	b	728	130	1			
1855	m	728	149	1			
1855	d	728	191	1			
1856	m	728	228	1			
1856	d	728	272	1			
1857	b	728	284	1			
1857	m	728	297	1			
1858	b	728	346-347	1			
1858	m	728	372-373	1			
1858	d	728	404-405	1			
1859	b	728	422-423	1			
1859	m	728	441, 453	1			
1859	d	728	479-480	1			
1860	b	728	521-522	1			
1860	m	728	528-529	1			
1860	d	728	586-587	1			
1861	b	728	610, 616	1			
1861	m	728	626-627	1			
1861	d	728	669-670	1			
1862	b	728	689-690	1			
1862	d	728	759-760	1			
1863	b	728	767, 771	1			
1863	m	728	807-808	1			
1863	d	728	837-838	1			
1864	b	728	860, 874	1			
1864	m	728	900-901	1			
1864	d	728	938, 940	1			
1865	b	728	202-203	3			
1865	m	728	204	3			
1865	d	728	205	3			
1866	b	728	206-207	3			
1866	m	728	208	3			
1866	d	728	209-210	3			
1867	b	728	211-212	3			
1867	m	728	213-214	3			
1867	d	728	215-216	3			
1868	b	728	216-217	3			
1868	m	728	219-220	3			
1868	d	728	221-222	3			
1869	b	728	223-224	3			
1869	m	728	225-226	3			
1869	d	728	227-228	3			
1870	b	728	229-230	3			
1870	m	728	231-232	3			
1870	d	728	233-234	3			
1871	b	728	235-236	3			
1872	b	728	237-238	3			
1872	m	728	239-240	3			
1872	d	728	241-242	3			
1873	b	728	1030	3	2		
1873	m	728	142, 144	3	2		
1873	d	728	146	3	2		
1873	d	728	146	3	2		
1874	b	728	148-149	3	2		
1874	m	728	150-151	3	2		
1874	d	728	152, 341	3	2		
1874	d	728	152, 341	3	2		
1875	b	728	153-154	3	2		
1875	m	728	155-156	3	2		
1875	d	728	157-158	3	2		
1875	d	728	157-158	3	2		
1876	b	728	1035	3	2		

Bagaslaviskis (Bogoslavishok) continued

Year(s)	Type	Fond	File(s)	Op	A	F
1876	m	728	1074, 1074A	3		2
1876	d	728	1124	3		2
1876	d	728	1124	3		2
1877	b	728	1041	3		2
1877	m	728	1075-1076	3		2
1877	m	728	1075-1076	3		2
1877	d	728	1128	3		2
1877	d	728	1128	3		2
1878	b	728	1049	3		2
1878	m	728	1078	3		2
1878	m	728	1078	3		2
1878	d	728	1134	3		2
1878	d	728	1134	3		2
1890	m	728	1481	3		2
1891	b	728	1445	3		2
1891	m	728	1482	3		2
1891	m	728	1482	3		2
1892	b	728	1484	3		2
1893	b	728	1491	3		2
1893	m	728	1495	3		2
1893	m	728	1495	3		2
1894	b	728	1498, 1501	3		2
1894	m	728	1504	3		2
1894	m	728	1504	3		2
1895	m	728	1481	3		2
1895	b	728	1510	3		2
1895	m	728	1514	3		2
1896	m	728	10	4		2
1896	b	728	9	4		2
1897	b	728	23	4		2
1897	m	728	23	4		2
1898	b	728	40	4		2
1898	m	728	41	4		2
1898	v	728	42	4		2
1899	b	728	56	4		2
1899	m	728	57	4		2
1900	b	728	68	4		2
1900	m	728	69	4		2
1900	d	728	75	4		2
1901	d	728	75, 83	4		2
1901	b	728	81-82	4		2
1902	b	728	96	4		2
1902	m	728	97	4		2
1902	d	728	98	4		2
1903	b	728	109	4		2
1903	m	728	110	4		2
1903	d	728	111	4		2
1904	b	728	122	4		2
1904	m	728	123	4		2
1904	d	728	124	4		2
1905	b	728	135	4		2
1905	m	728	136	4		2
1905	v	728	137	4		2
1905	d	728	75	4		2
1906	b	728	147	4		2
1906	m	728	148	4		2
1906	v	728	149	4		2
1906	d	728	75	4		2
1907	b	728	159	4		2
1907	d	728	75	4		2
1908	m	728	170	4		2
1908	d	728	75	4		2
1909	b	728	181	4		2
1909	m	728	182	4		2
1909	v	728	183	4		2
1909	d	728	75	4		2
1910	b	728	195	4		2
1910	m	728	196	4		2
1911	b	728	209	4		2
1911	m	728	210	4		2
1912	m	728	223	4		2
1913	m	728	236	4		2
1914	b	728	249	4		2
1914	m	728	250	4		2

Baisogala

Year(s)	Type
1858	rs
1866	rs

Balbieriskis (Balbirishok)

Year(s)	Type	Fond	File(s)	Op
1808	b	1236	6	4
1809	b	1236	6	4
1810	b	1236	6	4
1811	b	1236	7	4
1812	b	1236	7	4
1813	b	1236	8	4
1814	b	1236	8-9	4
1815	b	1236	9	4

Year(s)	Type	Fond	File(s)	Op	A	F	Notes	Page 10

Balbieriskis (Balbirishok) continued

Year(s)	Type	Fond	File(s)	Op
1816	b	1236	10	4
1817	b	1236	10	4
1818	b	1236	11	4
1818	d	1236	12	4
1819	b	1236	13	4
1822	b	1236	291	4
1823	b	1236	14	4
1824	b	1236	15-16	4
1825	b	1236	17	4
1826	b	1236	19	4
1826	d	1236	19	4
1826	m	1236	19	4
1827	b	1236	21	4
1827	d	1236	21	4
1827	m	1236	21	4
1828	b	1108	1	1
1828	d	1108	1	1
1828	m	1108	1	1
1829	b	1236	22	4
1829	d	1236	22	4
1829	m	1236	22	4
1830	b	1236	24	4
1830	d	1236	24	4
1830	m	1236	24	4
1831	b	1236	24	4
1831	d	1236	24	4
1831	m	1236	24	4
1832	b	1236	24	4
1832	d	1236	24	4
1832	m	1236	24	4
1833	b	1236	24	4
1833	d	1236	24	4
1833	m	1236	24	4
1834	b	1236	24	4
1834	d	1236	24	4
1834	m	1236	24	4
1835	b	1236	24	4
1835	d	1236	24	4
1835	m	1236	24	4
1836	b	1236	27	4
1836	d	1236	27	4
1836	m	1236	27	4
1837	b	1236	28	4
1837	d	1236	28	4
1837	m	1236	28	4
1838	b	1236	30	4
1838	d	1236	30	4
1838	m	1236	30	4
1839	b	1236	32	4
1839	d	1236	32	4
1839	m	1236	32	4
1840	b	1236	34	4
1840	d	1236	34	4
1840	m	1236	34	4
1841	b	1236	36	4
1841	d	1236	36	4
1841	m	1236	36	4
1842	b	1236	38	4
1842	d	1236	38	4
1842	m	1236	38	4
1843	b	1236	40	4
1843	d	1236	40	4
1843	m	1236	40	4
1844	b	1236	41	4
1844	d	1236	41	4
1844	m	1236	41	4
1845	b	1236	42	4
1845	d	1236	42	4
1845	m	1236	42	4
1846	b	1236	44	4
1846	d	1236	44	4
1846	m	1236	44	4
1847	b	1236	47	4
1847	d	1236	47	4
1847	m	1236	47	4
1858	b	1236	55	4
1858	d	1236	55	4
1858	m	1236	55	4
1859	b	1236	56	4
1859	d	1236	56	4
1859	m	1236	56	4
1860	b	1236	57	4
1860	d	1236	57	4
1860	m	1236	57	4
1861	b	1236	58	4
1861	d	1236	58	4
1861	m	1236	58	4
1862	b	1236	59	4

Balbieriskis (Balbirishok) continued

Year(s)	Type	Fond	File(s)	Op
1862	d	1236	59	4
1862	m	1236	59	4
1863	b	1236	60	4
1863	d	1236	60	4
1863	m	1236	60	4
1864	b	1236	61	4
1864	m	1236	61	4
1865	b	1236	62	4
1865	d	1236	62	4
1865	m	1236	62	4
1866	b	1236	63	4
1866	d	1236	63	4
1866	m	1236	63	4
1867	b	1236	64	4
1867	d	1236	64	4
1867	m	1236	64	4
1868	b	1236	65	4
1868	d	1236	65	4
1868	m	1236	65	4
1869	d	1236	67	4
1869	m	1236	67	4
1870	b	1236	69	4
1870	d	1236	69	4
1870	m	1236	69	4
1871	b	1236	71	4
1871	m	1236	71	4
1871	d	1236	72	4
1872	b	1236	72	4
1872	m	1236	72	4
1873	b	1236	73	4
1873	d	1236	73	4
1873	m	1236	73	4
1889	b	1226	1405	1
1889	d	1226	1405	1
1889	m	1226	1405	1
1903	b	1226	2089	1
1903	d	1226	2089	1
1903	m	1226	2089	1

Batakiai (Batak)

Year(s)	Type	Fond	File(s)	Op
1816	rs			

Bezdonys (Bezdany) Items for this town are in the Vilnius County 4th Okrug Registers.

Year(s)	Type	Fond	File(s)	Op
1885	m	728	353	4
1886	m	728	353	4
1887	d	728	1478	3
1887	m	728	353	4
1887	b	728	364	4
1888	d	728	1478	3
1888	m	728	353	4
1888	b	728	364	4
1889	d	728	1478	3
1889	m	728	353	4
1889	b	728	364	4
1890	d	728	1478	3
1890	b	728	1479	3
1890	m	728	1480	3
1890	m	728	353	4
1890	b	728	364	4
1891	b	728	1446	3
1891	d	728	1478	3
1891	m	728	1483	3
1891	m	728	353	4
1891	b	728	364	4
1892	d	728	1478	3
1892	b	728	1486, 1553	3
1892	m	728	1487, 1488, 1554	3
1892	v	728	1489	3
1892	m	728	353	4
1892	b	728	364	4
1893	d	728	1478	3
1893	b	728	1490, 1553	3
1893	m	728	1494, 1554	3
1893	v	728	1496	3
1893	m	728	353	4
1893	b	728	364	4
1894	b	728	1499, 1553	3
1894	m	728	1505, 1554	3
1894	v	728	1516	3
1894	m	728	353	4
1894	b	728	364	4
1895	b	728	1508, 1553	3
1895	m	728	1513, 1556	3
1895	v	728	1519	3
1895	v	728	3	4
1895	m	728	353	4
1895	b	728	364	4
1896	b	728	13, 364	4

Year(s)	Type	Fond	File(s)	Op	A	F	Notes
Bezdonys (Bezdany) continued							
1896	m	728	14, 353	4			
1896	b	728	1553	3			
1896	m	728	1556	3			
1897	b	728	28-29, 364	4			
1897	m	728	30, 353, 437	4			
1897	d	728	32	4			
1898	b	728	28, 45, 364	4			
1898	d	728	32	4			
1898	m	728	46, 353, 437	4			
1899	b	728	28, 60, 364	4			
1899	v	728	3	4			
1899	d	728	32	4			
1899	m	728	61, 353, 437	4			
1900	v	728	3	4			
1900	b	728	72, 364	4			
1900	m	728	73-74, 353, 437	4			
1900	d	728	75	4			
1901	v	728	3, 88	4			
1901	d	728	75	4			
1901	b	728	86, 364	4			
1901	m	728	87, 353, 437	4			
1902	m	728	102, 353, 438	4			
1902	d	728	103, 439	4			
1902	b	728	364	4			
1903	b	728	114-115, 364	4			
1903	m	728	116, 353, 438, 444	4			
1903	d	728	117, 439	4			
1904	b	728	127, 364	4			
1904	m	728	128, 353, 438	4			
1904	d	728	129, 439	4			
1905	b	728	139, 364	4			
1905	m	728	140, 353, 438	4			
1905	d	728	75, 141, 439	4			
1906	b	728	151, 364, 441	4			
1906	m	728	152, 353	4			
1906	d	728	75, 153	4			
1907	b	728	161, 364, 441	4			
1907	m	728	162, 353	4			
1907	v	728	3	4			
1907	d	728	75	4			
1908	b	728	172, 364, 441	4			
1908	v	728	3, 173	4			
1908	m	728	353	4			
1908	d	728	75	4			
1909	b	728	187, 364	4			
1909	v	728	3, 188	4			
1909	m	728	353, 442	4			
1909	d	728	75	4			
1910	b	728	199, 364	4			
1910	v	728	3, 200	4			
1910	m	728	353, 443	4			
1911	b	728	213, 364	4			
1911	m	728	214, 353	4			
1911	v	728	215	4			
1912	b	728	226, 364	4			
1912	m	728	227-228, 353	4			
1913	b	728	239, 364	4			
1913	m	728	240, 353	4			
1914	b	728	253, 364	4			
1914	m	728	253-254, 353	4			
1914	v	728	255	4			
1915	m	728	353	4			
1915	b	728	364	4			
1916	b	728	364	4			
1917	b	728	364	4			
1917	b	728	364	4			
1918	b	728	364	4			
1919	b	728	364	4			
1920	b	728	364	4			
1921	b	728	364	4			
Birzai (Birzh)							
1816	rs						
1818	rs						
1834	rs						
1848	rs						
1852	b	728	25	1			
1861	b	728	598	1			
1861	v	728	647	1			
1861	d	728	657	1			
1862	b	728	695	1			
1862	m	728	710	1			
1862	d	728	750	1			
1863	b	728	774	1			
1863	v	728	828	1			
1863	d	728	836	1			
1864	m	728	894-895	1			
1864	d	728	943	1			

Birzai (Birzh) continued

Year(s)	Type	Fond	File(s)	Op	A	F	Notes
1865	b	1226	376	1			
1865	m	1226	377	1			
1865	v	1226	378	1			
1865	d	1226	379	1			
1866	b	1226	380	1			
1866	m	1226	381	1			
1866	v	1226	382	1			
1866	d	1226	383	1			
1867	b	1226	384	1			
1867	m	1226	385	1			
1867	v	1226	386	1			
1867	d	1226	387	1			
1868	b	1226	388	1			
1868	m	1226	389	1			
1868	v	1226	390	1			
1868	d	1226	391	1			
1869	b	1226	392	1			
1869	m	1226	393	1			
1869	v	1226	394	1			
1869	d	1226	395	1			
1870	m	1226	396	1			
1870	v	1226	397	1			
1870	d	1226	398	1			
1871	b	1226	399	1			
1871	m	1226	400	1			
1871	v	1226	401	1			
1871	d	1226	402	1			
1872	b	1226	403	1			
1872	m	1226	404	1			
1872	v	1226	405	1			
1872	d	1226	406	1			
1873	b	1226	407	1			
1873	m	1226	408	1			
1873	v	1226	409	1			
1873	d	1226	410	1			
1874	b	1226	411	1			
1874	m	1226	412	1			
1874	v	1226	413	1			
1874	d	1226	414	1			
1875	b	1226	415	1			
1875	m	1226	416	1			
1875	v	1226	417	1			
1875	d	1226	418	1			
1876	m	1226	1028	1			
1876	v	1226	1033	1			
1876	d	1226	1037	1			
1876	b	1226	1314	1			
1877	m	1226	1029	1			
1877	v	1226	1034	1			
1877	d	1226	1038	1			
1877	b	1226	1314	1			
1878	m	1226	1030	1			
1878	v	1226	1035	1			
1878	d	1226	1039	1			
1878	b	1226	1314	1			
1879	b	1226	1026	1			
1879	m	1226	1031	1			
1879	d	1226	1040	1			
1880	b	1226	1027	1			
1880	m	1226	1032	1			
1880	v	1226	1036	1			
1880	d	1226	1041	1			
1881	b	1226	1314	1			
1881	m	1226	1960	1			
1881	d	1226	1961	1			
1882	b	1226	1314	1			
1882	m	1226	1960	1			
1882	d	1226	1961	1			
1883	b	1226	1314	1			
1883	m	1226	1960	1			
1883	d	1226	1961	1			
1884	b	1226	1314	1			
1884	m	1226	1960	1			
1884	d	1226	1961	1			
1885	b	1226	1314	1			
1885	m	1226	1960	1			
1885	d	1226	1961	1			
1886	b	1226	1314	1			
1886	m	1226	1960	1			
1886	d	1226	1961	1			
1887	b	1226	1314	1			
1887	m	1226	1960	1			
1887	d	1226	1961	1			
1888	m	1226	1960	1			
1888	d	1226	1961	1			
1889	m	1226	1960	1			
1889	d	1226	1961	1			
1890	m	1226	1960	1			

Birzai (Birzh) continued

Year(s)	Type	Fond	File(s)	Op	A	F	Notes
1890	d	1226	1961	1			
1891	m	1226	1960	1			
1891	d	1226	1961	1			
1891	b	728	985	1			
1892	m	1226	1960	1			
1892	d	1226	1961	1			
1893	b	1226	1314	1			
1893	m	1226	1960	1			
1893	d	1226	1961	1			
1894	b	1226	1314	1			
1894	m	1226	1960	1			
1894	d	1226	1961	1			
1895	b	1226	1314	1			
1895	m	1226	1960	1			
1895	d	1226	1961	1			
1896	b	1226	1959	1			
1896	m	1226	1960	1			
1896	d	1226	1961	1			
1897	b	1226	1959	1			
1897	m	1226	1960	1			
1897	d	1226	1961	1			
1898	b	1226	1959	1			
1898	m	1226	1960	1			
1898	d	1226	1961	1			
1899	b	1226	1959	1			
1899	m	1226	1960	1			
1900	b	1226	1959	1			
1900	m	1226	1960	1			
1901	b	1226	1959	1			
1901	m	1226	1960	1			
1902	b	1226	1959	1			
1902	m	1226	1960	1			
1902	d	728	998	1			
1903	b	1226	1959	1			
1903	m	1226	1960	1			
1903	d	728	1011	1			
1904	b	1226	1959	1			
1904	m	1226	1960	1			
1904	d	728	1022	1			
1905	b	1226	1959	1			
1905	m	1226	1960	1			
1906	b	1226	1959	1			
1906	m	1226	1960	1			
1906	d	728	1041	1			
1907	b	1226	1959	1			
1907	m	1226	1960	1			
1908	b	1226	1959	1			
1908	m	1226	1960	1			
1909	b	1226	1959	1			
1909	m	1226	1960	1			
1910	b	1226	1959	1			
1910	m	1226	1960	1			
1910	d	728	1075	1			
1911	b	1226	1959	1			
1911	m	1226	1960	1			
1912	b	1226	1959	1			
1912	m	1226	1960	1			
1913	b	1226	1959	1			
1913	m	1226	1960	1			
1913	d	1226	1961	1			
1914	b	1226	1959	1			
1914	m	1226	1960	1			
1914	d	1226	1961	1			

Bogaslavas Those items with a Flag code of "7" are in the Vilnius County Register.

Year(s)	Type	Fond	File(s)	Op	A	F	Notes
1816-1818	rs	515	288	25	K	7	Jews
1834	rs	515	298	25	K	7	Jews
1843-1849	rs	515	306	25	K	7	Jews
1849	rs	515	312	25	K	7	Jews
1850-1854	rs	515	273	25	K	7	Jews
1858	rs	515	285	25	K	7	Jews
unknown	rs						
unknown	rs						
unknown	rs	515	299	25	K	7	Jews
unknown	rs	515	320	25	K	7	Jews

Breslauja (Breslav)

Year(s)	Type	Fond	File(s)	Op	A	F	Notes
1795-1831	rs	515	1032	15	K		All Social Classes including Jews
1816-27	rs						Slabada
1816-27	rs						
1871	rs						
1874	rs						

Butrimonys (Butrimantz)

Year(s)	Type	Fond	File(s)	Op	A	F	Notes
1858-1905	rs						
1864	rs	515	125	25			srs, Trakai County
1856	v	728	248	1			
1862	d	728	761	1			

Butrimonys (Butrimantz) continued

Year(s)	Type	Fond	File(s)	Op
1866	b	728	243	3
1866	m	728	244	3
1866	v	728	245	3
1866	d	728	246	3
1867	b	728	247	3
1867	m	728	248	3
1867	v	728	249	3
1868	b	728	250	3
1868	m	728	251	3
1868	v	728	252	3
1868	d	728	253	3
1869	b	728	254	3
1869	v	728	255	3
1869	m	728	256	3
1869	d	728	257	3
1870	b	728	258-259	3
1870	m	728	260-261, 263	3
1870	v	728	262	3
1870	d	728	264	3
1871	b	728	265-266	3
1871	m	728	267	3
1871	v	728	268	3
1871	d	728	269	3
1872	d	728	269, 274	3
1872	b	728	270-271	3
1872	m	728	272	3
1873	b	728	275-276	3
1873	m	728	277	3
1873	v	728	278, 278A	3
1873	d	728	279	3
1874	b	728	280-281	3
1874	m	728	282-283	3
1874	v	728	284	3
1874	d	728	285	3
1875	b	728	286-287	3
1875	m	728	288	3
1875	v	728	289	3
1875	d	728	290	3
1876	d	728	1196	3
1876	b	728	291, 1183, 1184	3
1877	b	728	1184A, 1185	3
1877	m	728	1190	3
1877	d	728	1197	3
1877	v	728	1201	3
1878	b	728	1186	3
1878	m	728	1191	3
1878	d	728	1198	3
1878	v	728	1202-1203	3
1879	b	728	1187, 1187A	3
1879	m	728	1192-1193	3
1879	d	728	1199	3
1879	v	728	1204	3
1880	b	728	1188-1189	3
1880	m	728	1194-1195	3
1880	d	728	1200	3
1881	b	728	292	4
1881	v	728	293	4
1881	d	728	294	4
1882	b	728	292	4
1882	m	728	293	4
1882	v	728	293	4
1882	d	728	294	4
1883	b	728	292	4
1883	m	728	293	4
1883	d	728	294	4
1884	b	728	292	4
1884	m	728	293	4
1884	v	728	293	4
1884	d	728	294	4
1885	m	728	293	4
1885	d	728	294	4
1886	m	728	293	4
1886	d	728	294	4
1887	m	728	293	4
1887	d	728	294	4
1888	b	728	292	4
1888	m	728	293	4
1888	d	728	294	4
1889	b	728	292	4
1889	m	728	293	4
1890	b	728	292	4
1890	m	728	293	4
1890	v	728	293	4
1891	m	728	293	4
1892	m	728	293	4
1892	d	728	294	4
1893	b	728	292	4
1893	m	728	293	4

Butrimonys (Butrimantz) continued

Year(s)	Type	Fond	File(s)	Op	A	F	Notes
1893	d	728	294	4			
1894	b	728	292	4			
1894	m	728	293	4			
1894	v	728	293	4			
1894	d	728	294	4			
1895	b	728	292	4			
1895	m	728	293	4			
1895	v	728	293	4			
1895	d	728	294	4			
1896	b	728	292	4			
1896	m	728	293	4			
1896	v	728	293	4			
1896	d	728	294	4			
1897	b	728	292	4			
1897	m	728	293	4			
1897	v	728	293	4			
1897	d	728	294	4			
1898	m	728	293	4			
1898	d	728	294	4			
1899	b	728	292	4			
1899	m	728	293	4			
1899	v	728	293	4			
1900	b	728	292	4			
1900	m	728	293	4			
1900	d	728	294	4			
1901	b	728	292	4			
1901	m	728	293	4			
1901	d	728	294	4			
1902	b	728	292	4			
1902	v	728	293	4			
1902	d	728	294	4			
1903	b	728	292	4			
1903	d	728	294	4			
1904	b	728	292	4			
1904	m	728	293	4			
1904	d	728	294	4			
1905	b	728	292	4			
1905	m	728	293	4			
1905	d	728	294	4			
1906	b	728	292	4			
1906	m	728	293	4			
1906	d	728	294	4			
1907	b	728	292	4			
1907	m	728	293	4			
1907	d	728	294	4			
1908	b	728	292	4			
1908	v	728	293	4			
1908	d	728	294	4			
1909	b	728	292	4			
1909	d	728	294	4			
1910	b	728	292	4			
1910	m	728	293	4			
1910	d	728	294	4			
1911	b	728	292	4			
1911	m	728	293	4			
1911	d	728	294	4			
1912	b	728	292	4			
1912	m	728	293	4			
1912	d	728	294	4			
1913	m	728	293	4			
1913	d	728	294	4			
1914	b	728	292	4			
1914	m	728	293	4			
1914	d	728	294	4			
1915	d	728	294	4			
1924	v	728	293	4			

Cekiske (Chaikishok)

Year(s)	Type	Fond	File(s)	Op	A	F	Notes
1816	rs						
1874	rs	I-61	1655	1	K		Alphabetic – Jews
1857	b	728	290	1			
1862	b	728	692	1			
1862	m	728	711	1			
1862	d	728	748	1			
1863	b	728	773	1			
1863	m	728	805	1			
1863	v	728	825	1			
1863	d	728	848	1			
1864	b	728	875	1			
1864	m	728	897	1			
1864	v	728	919	1			
1864	d	728	942	1			
1865	b	1226	284	1			
1865	m	1226	285	1			
1865	v	1226	286	1			
1865	d	1226	289	1			
1866	b	1226	290	1			
1866	m	1226	291	1			

Cekiske (Chaikishok) continued

Year(s)	Type	Fond	File(s)	Op	A	F	Notes
1866	v	1226	292	1			
1866	d	1226	293	1			
1867	b	1226	294	1			
1867	m	1226	295	1			
1867	v	1226	296	1			
1867	d	1226	297	1			
1868	b	1226	298	1			
1868	m	1226	299	1			
1868	v	1226	300	1			
1868	d	1226	301	1			
1869	b	1226	302	1			
1869	m	1226	303	1			
1869	v	1226	304	1			
1869	d	1226	305	1			
1870	b	1226	306	1			
1870	m	1226	307	1			
1870	v	1226	308	1			
1870	d	1226	309	1			
1870-1874	k					K	
1871	b	1226	310	1			
1871	m	1226	311	1			
1871	v	1226	312	1			
1871	d	1226	313	1			
1872	b	1226	314	1			
1872	m	1226	315	1			
1872	v	1226	316	1			
1872	d	1226	317	1			
1873	b	1226	318	1			
1873	m	1226	319	1			
1873	v	1226	320	1			
1873	d	1226	321	1			
1874	b	1226	322	1			
1874	m	1226	323	1			
1874	v	1226	324	1			
1874	d	1226	325	1			
1874-1878	k					K	
1875	b	1226	326	1			
1875	m	1226	327	1			
1875	v	1226	328	1			
1875	d	1226	329	1			
1876	b	1226	884	1			
1876	m	1226	889	1			
1876	v	1226	894	1			
1876	d	1226	899	1			
1877	b	1226	885	1			
1877	m	1226	890	1			
1877	v	1226	895	1			
1877	d	1226	900	1			
1878	b	1226	886	1			
1878	m	1226	891	1			
1878	v	1226	896	1			
1878	d	1226	901	1			
1879	b	1226	887	1			
1879	m	1226	892	1			
1879	v	1226	897	1			
1879	d	1226	902	1			
1880	b	1226	888	1			
1880	m	1226	893	1			
1880	v	1226	898	1			
1880	d	1226	903	1			
1881	b	1226	2073	1			
1881	m	1226	2074	1			
1881	v	1226	2075	1			
1881	d	1226	2076	1			
1882	b	1226	2073	1			
1882	m	1226	2074	1			
1882	v	1226	2075	1			
1882	d	1226	2076	1			
1883	b	1226	2073	1			
1883	m	1226	2074	1			
1883	v	1226	2075	1			
1883	d	1226	2076	1			
1884	b	1226	2073	1			
1884	m	1226	2074	1			
1884	v	1226	2075	1			
1884	d	1226	2076	1			
1885	b	1226	2073	1			
1885	m	1226	2074	1			
1885	v	1226	2075	1			
1885	d	1226	2076	1			
1886	b	1226	2073	1			
1886	m	1226	2074	1			
1886	v	1226	2075	1			
1886	d	1226	2076	1			
1887	b	1226	2073	1			
1887	m	1226	2074	1			
1887	v	1226	2075	1			
1887	d	1226	2076	1			

Cekiske (Chaikishok) continued

Year(s)	Type	Fond	File(s)	Op
1888	b	1226	2073	1
1888	m	1226	2074	1
1888	v	1226	2075	1
1888	d	1226	2076	1
1889	b	1226	2073	1
1889	m	1226	2074	1
1889	v	1226	2075	1
1889	d	1226	2076	1
1890	b	1226	2073	1
1890	m	1226	2074	1
1890	v	1226	2075	1
1890	d	1226	2076	1
1891	b	1226	2073	1
1891	m	1226	2074	1
1891	v	1226	2075	1
1891	d	1226	2076	1
1892	b	1226	2073	1
1892	m	1226	2074	1
1892	v	1226	2075	1
1892	d	1226	2076	1
1893	b	1226	2073	1
1893	m	1226	2074	1
1893	v	1226	2075	1
1893	d	1226	2076	1
1894	b	1226	2073	1
1894	m	1226	2074	1
1894	v	1226	2075	1
1894	d	1226	2076	1
1895	b	1226	2073	1
1895	m	1226	2074	1
1895	v	1226	2075	1
1895	d	1226	2076	1
1896	b	1226	2073	1
1896	m	1226	2074	1
1896	v	1226	2075	1
1896	d	1226	2076	1
1897	b	1226	2073	1
1897	m	1226	2074	1
1897	v	1226	2075	1
1897	d	1226	2076	1
1898	b	1226	2073	1
1898	m	1226	2074	1
1898	v	1226	2075	1
1898	d	1226	2076	1
1899	b	1226	2073	1
1899	m	1226	2074	1
1899	v	1226	2075	1
1899	d	1226	2076	1
1900	b	1226	2073	1
1900	m	1226	2074	1
1900	v	1226	2075	1
1900	d	1226	2076	1
1901	b	1226	2073	1
1901	m	1226	2074	1
1901	v	1226	2075	1
1901	d	1226	2076	1
1902	b	1226	2073	1
1902	m	1226	2074	1
1902	v	1226	2075	1
1902	d	1226	2076	1
1903	b	1226	2073	1
1903	m	1226	2074	1
1903	v	1226	2075	1
1903	d	1226	2076	1
1904	b	1226	2073	1
1904	m	1226	2074	1
1904	v	1226	2075	1
1904	d	1226	2076	1
1905	b	1226	2073	1
1905	m	1226	2074	1
1905	v	1226	2075	1
1905	d	1226	2076	1
1906	b	1226	2073	1
1906	m	1226	2074	1
1906	v	1226	2075	1
1906	d	1226	2076	1
1907	b	1226	2073	1
1907	m	1226	2074	1
1907	v	1226	2075	1
1907	d	1226	2076	1
1908	b	1226	2073	1
1908	m	1226	2074	1
1908	v	1226	2075	1
1908	d	1226	2076	1
1909	b	1226	2073	1
1909	m	1226	2074	1
1909	v	1226	2075	1
1909	d	1226	2076	1

Cekiske (Chaikishok) continued

Year(s)	Type	Fond	File(s)	Op	A	F	Notes
1910	b	1226	2073	1			
1910	m	1226	2074	1			
1910	v	1226	2075	1			
1910	d	1226	2076	1			
1911	b	1226	2073	1			
1911	m	1226	2074	1			
1911	v	1226	2075	1			
1911	d	1226	2076	1			
1912	b	1226	2073	1			
1912	m	1226	2074	1			
1912	v	1226	2075	1			
1912	d	1226	2076	1			
1913	b	1226	2073	1			
1913	m	1226	2074	1			
1913	v	1226	2075	1			
1913	d	1226	2076	1			
1914	b	1226	2073	1			
1914	m	1226	2074	1			
1914	v	1226	2075	1			
1914	d	1226	2076	1			

Ciobiskis (Chabishki) Those items with a Flag code of "2" are in the Vilnius County 2nd Okrug Registers. Those with a Flag code of "7" are in the Vilnius County Register.

Year(s)	Type	Fond	File(s)	Op	A	F	Notes
1816-1818	rs	515	288	25	K	7	Jews
1834	rs	515	298	25	K	7	Jews
1843-1849	rs	515	306	25	K	7	Jews
1849	rs	515	312	25	K	7	Jews
1850-1854	rs	515	273	25	K	7	Jews
1858	rs	515	285	25	K	7	Jews
unknown	rs	515	299	25	K	7	Jews
unknown	rs	515	320	25	K	7	Jews
1854	b	728	33-34	1			
1854	m	728	57-58	1			
1855	b	728	135	1			
1855	m	728	158	1			
1856	b	728	217	1			
1856	m	728	239	1			
1857	b	728	288	1			
1857	m	728	307	1			
1858	b	728	358	1			
1859	b	728	437	1			
1860	b	728	506, 525	1			
1861	b	728	607, 609	1			
1862	b	728	679, 688	1			
1862	m	728	713, 721	1			
1863	b	728	787-788	1			
1863	m	728	809-810	1			
1864	b	728	870-871	1			
1865	b	728	960-961	3			
1867	b	728	962-963	3			
1868	b	728	964-965	3			
1868	m	728	966-967	3			
1869	b	728	968-969	3			
1869	m	728	970	3			
1870	b	728	971-972	3			
1871	b	728	973-974	3			
1871	m	728	975-976	3			
1872	b	728	977-978	3			
1872	m	728	979-980	3			
1873	b	728	1030	3		2	
1873	m	728	142, 144	3		2	
1873	d	728	146	3		2	
1874	b	728	148-149	3		2	
1874	m	728	150-151	3		2	
1874	d	728	152, 341	3		2	
1875	b	728	153-154	3		2	
1875	m	728	155-156	3		2	
1875	d	728	157-158	3		2	
1876	b	728	1035	3		2	
1876	m	728	1074	3		2	
1876	d	728	1124	3		2	
1877	b	728	1041	3		2	
1877	m	728	1075-1076	3		2	
1877	d	728	1128	3		2	
1878	b	728	1049	3		2	
1878	m	728	1078	3		2	
1878	d	728	1134	3		2	
1891	b	728	1445	3		2	
1891	m	728	1482	3		2	
1892	b	728	1484	3		2	
1893	b	728	1491	3		2	
1893	m	728	1495	3		2	
1894	b	728	1498	3		2	
1894	b	728	1501	3		2	
1894	m	728	1504	3		2	
1895	m	728	1481	3		2	
1895	b	728	1510	3		2	
1896	m	728	10	4		2	
1896	b	728	9	4		2	

Year(s)	Type	Fond	File(s)	Op	A	F	Notes
Ciobiskis (Chabishki) continued							
1897	b	728	23	4	2		
1897	m	728	23	4	2		
1898	b	728	40	4	2		
1898	m	728	41	4	2		
1898	v	728	42	4	2		
1899	b	728	56	4	2		
1899	m	728	57	4	2		
1900	b	728	68	4	2		
1900	m	728	69	4	2		
1900	d	728	75	4	2		
1901	d	728	75, 83	4	2		
1901	b	728	81-82	4	2		
1902	b	728	96	4	2		
1902	m	728	97	4	2		
1902	d	728	98	4	2		
1903	b	728	109	4	2		
1903	m	728	110	4	2		
1903	d	728	111	4	2		
1904	b	728	122	4	2		
1904	m	728	123	4	2		
1904	d	728	124	4	2		
1905	b	728	135	4	2		
1905	m	728	136	4	2		
1905	v	728	137	4	2		
1905	d	728	75	4	2		
1906	b	728	147	4	2		
1906	m	728	148	4	2		
1906	v	728	149	4	2		
1906	d	728	75	4	2		
1907	b	728	159	4	2		
1907	d	728	75	4	2		
1908	m	728	170	4	2		
1908	d	728	75	4	2		
1909	b	728	181	4	2		
1909	m	728	182	4	2		
1909	v	728	183	4	2		
1909	d	728	75	4	2		
1910	b	728	195	4	2		
1910	m	728	196	4	2		
1911	b	728	209	4	2		
1911	m	728	210	4	2		
1912	m	728	223	4	2		
1913	m	728	236	4	2		
1914	b	728	249	4	2		
1914	m	728	250	4	2		
Darbenai (Darbian)							
1885	b	1226	1319	1			
1886	b	1226	1319	1			
1887	b	1226	1319	1			
1888	b	1226	1319	1			
1889	b	1226	1319	1			
1890	b	1226	1319	1			
unknown	fin	716	130	4			Count Tyshkevich's fonds
Darsuniskis (Darshunishok)							
1858-1905	rs						
1870	b	728	383	3			
1870	m	728	384	3			
1870	v	728	385	3			
1870	d	728	386	3			
1871	b	728	387	3			
1871	m	728	388-389	3			
1871	d	728	391	3			
1872	b	728	392	3			
1872	m	728	393-394	3			
1872	d	728	396	3			
1873	b	728	397	3			
1873	m	728	398-399	3			
1873	d	728	401	3			
1874	b	728	402	3			
1874	m	728	403-404	3			
1874	d	728	406	3			
1875	b	728	407	3			
1875	m	728	408-409	3			
1875	d	728	411	3			
1876	b	728	1223	3			
1876	m	728	1227	3			
1876	d	728	1240	3			
1877	b	728	1224	3			
1877	m	728	1229, 1230A	3			
1877	d	728	1241	3			
1878	b	728	1225	3			
1878	d	728	1242	3			
1879	b	728	1226	3			
1879	m	728	1232-1233	3			
1879	v	728	1238	3			
1879	d	728	1243	3			

Darsuniskis (Darshunishok) continued

Year(s)	Type	Fond	File(s)	Op
1880	d	728	1244	3
1881	b	728	299	4
1881	d	728	300	4
1881	m	728	300	4
1882	b	728	299	4
1882	d	728	300	4
1882	m	728	300	4
1883	b	728	299	4
1883	d	728	300	4
1883	m	728	300	4
1884	m	728	300	4
1886	m	728	300	4
1890	b	728	299	4
1892	m	728	300	4
1894	b	728	299	4
1895	v	728	300	4
1898	b	728	299	4
1898	d	728	300	4
1898	m	728	300	4
1899	b	728	299	4
1899	d	728	300	4
1899	m	728	300	4
1900	b	728	299	4
1900	d	728	300	4
1900	m	728	300	4
1901	b	728	299	4
1901	d	728	300	4
1901	m	728	300	4
1902	b	728	299	4
1902	d	728	300	4
1902	m	728	300	4
1903	b	728	299	4
1903	d	728	300	4
1903	m	728	300	4
1904	b	728	299	4
1904	m	728	300	4
1906	d	728	300	4
1906	m	728	300	4
1907	b	728	299	4
1907	d	728	300	4
1907	m	728	300	4
1908	b	728	299	4
1908	m	728	300	4
1909	b	728	299	4
1909	m	728	300	4
1910	d	728	300	4
1910	m	728	300	4
1911	b	728	299	4
1911	m	728	300	4
1913	b	728	299	4
1913	d	728	300	4
1914	d	728	300	4
1914	m	728	300	4

Daugai (Daug)

Year(s)	Type	Fond	File(s)	Op
1858-1905	rs			
1854	d	728	116	1
1854	b	728	37	1
1854	m	728	54	1
1854	v	728	85	1
1855	b	728	139	1
1855	m	728	160	1
1855	v	728	170	1
1855	d	728	188	1
1856	b	728	208	1
1856	m	728	229	1
1856	v	728	246	1
1858	b	728	348	1
1858	d	728	406	1
1859	b	728	421	1
1859	m	728	440	1
1859	v	728	466	1
1859	d	728	485	1
1860	b	728	505	1
1860	m	728	527	1
1860	d	728	585	1
1861		728	608	1
1861	b	728	608	1
1861	m	728	625	1
1861	v	728	649	1
1861	d	728	671	1
1862		728	687	1
1862	b	728	687	1
1862	m	728	720	1
1862	v	728	730	1
1862	d	728	758	1
1863	m	728	811	1
1864	b	728	869	1

Daugai (Daug) continued

Year(s)	Type	Fond	File(s)	Op	A	F	Notes
1865	b	728	342	3			
1865	m	728	343	3			
1865	v	728	344	3			
1865	d	728	345	3			
1866	m	728	346	3			
1866	v	728	347	3			
1866	d	728	348	3			
1867	m	728	349	3			
1867	v	728	350	3			
1867	d	728	351	3			
1868	b	728	352	3			
1868	m	728	353	3			
1868	d	728	354	3			
1869	b	728	355	3			
1869	m	728	356	3			
1869	v	728	357	3			
1869	d	728	358	3			
1870	b	728	359	3			
1870	m	728	360	3			
1870	d	728	362	3			
1871	b	728	363	3			
1871	m	728	364	3			
1871	d	728	366	3			
1872	b	728	367	3			
1872	m	728	368	3			
1872	v	728	369	3			
1872	d	728	370	3			
1873	b	728	371	3			
1873	m	728	372	3			
1873	v	728	373	3			
1873	d	728	374	3			
1874	b	728	375	3			
1874	m	728	376	3			
1874	v	728	377	3			
1874	d	728	378	3			
1875	b	728	379	3			
1875	m	728	380	3			
1875	d	728	382	3			
1876	b	728	1206	3			
1876	m	728	1211	3			
1876	d	728	1215	3			
1877	b	728	1207	3			
1877	d	728	1216	3			
1878	b	728	1208	3			
1878	m	728	1213	3			
1878	d	728	1217	3			
1879	b	728	1209	3			
1880	b	728	1210	3			
1880	m	728	1214	3			
1880	d	728	1218	3			
1881	b	728	296	4			
1881	m	728	297	4			
1881	v	728	297	4			
1881	d	728	298	4			
1881-1913		728	296	4			
1882	b	728	296	4			
1882	d	728	298	4			
1883	b	728	296	4			
1883	m	728	297	4			
1883	v	728	297	4			
1883	d	728	298	4			
1884	b	728	296	4			
1884	m	728	297	4			
1884	v	728	297	4			
1884	d	728	298	4			
1885	m	728	297	4			
1885	v	728	297	4			
1885	d	728	298	4			
1886	m	728	297	4			
1886	d	728	298	4			
1887	m	728	297	4			
1887	d	728	298	4			
1888	b	728	296	4			
1888	m	728	297	4			
1888	v	728	297	4			
1888	d	728	298	4			
1889	m	728	297	4			
1889	d	728	298	4			
1890	m	728	297	4			
1890	d	728	298	4			
1891	m	728	297	4			
1891	d	728	298	4			
1892	m	728	297	4			
1892	d	728	298	4			
1893	b	728	296	4			
1893	m	728	297	4			
1893	v	728	297	4			
1893	d	728	298	4			

Daugai (Daug) continued

Year(s)	Type	Fond	File(s)	Op	A	F	Notes
1894	b	728	296	4			
1894	d	728	298	4			
1895	b	728	296	4			
1895	m	728	297	4			
1896	b	728	296	4			
1896	m	728	297	4			
1896	d	728	298	4			
1897	b	728	296	4			
1897	m	728	297	4			
1897	d	728	298	4			
1898	b	728	296	4			
1898	m	728	297	4			
1898	d	728	298	4			
1899	b	728	296	4			
1899	m	728	297	4			
1899	d	728	298	4			
1900	b	728	296	4			
1900	m	728	297	4			
1900	d	728	298	4			
1901	b	728	296	4			
1901	m	728	297	4			
1901	d	728	298	4			
1902	b	728	296	4			
1902	m	728	297	4			
1903	b	728	296	4			
1903	m	728	297	4			
1903	d	728	298	4			
1904	b	728	296	4			
1905	b	728	296	4			
1905	m	728	297	4			
1905	d	728	298	4			
1906	b	728	296	4			
1906	m	728	297	4			
1906	d	728	298	4			
1907	b	728	296	4			
1907	m	728	297	4			
1907	d	728	298	4			
1908	b	728	296	4			
1908	m	728	297	4			
1908	v	728	297	4			
1908	d	728	298	4			
1909	b	728	296	4			
1909	m	728	297	4			
1909	d	728	298	4			
1910	b	728	296	4			
1910	m	728	297	4			
1910	d	728	298	4			
1911	b	728	296	4			
1911	m	728	297	4			
1911	d	728	298	4			
1912	b	728	296	4			
1912	m	728	297	4			
1913	b	728	296	4			
1913	m	728	297	4			
1913	d	728	298	4			
1914	d	728	298	4			
1915	m	728	297	4			

Dauglaukis

Year(s)	Type	Fond	File(s)	Op	A	F	Notes
1816	rs						
1839	rs						
1858	rs						
1864	rs						

Daukshe (Dauksiai)

Year(s)	Type	Fond	File(s)	Op	A	F	Notes
1808	m	1236	1	2			
1808	d	1236	2	2			
1808	b	1236	3	32			
1809	m	1236	3	2			
1809	b	1236	3, 4	32			
1809	d	1236	4	2			
1810	b	1236	4	32			
1810	b	1236	5	2			
1810	m	1236	6	2			
1810	d	1236	7	2			
1811	d	1236	10	2			
1811	b	1236	8	2			
1811	m	1236	9	2			
1812	b	1236	11	2			
1812	d	1236	12	2			
1813	b	1236	13	2			
1813	m	1236	14	2			
1814	b	1236	16	2			
1814	m	1236	17	2			
1815	b	1236	18	2			
1815	m	1236	19	2			
1815	d	1236	20	2			
1816	b	1236	21	2			

Daukshe (Dauksiai) continued

Year(s)	Type	Fond	File(s)	Op	A	F	Notes
1816	m	1236	22	2			
1817	b	1236	23	2			
1817	m	1236	24	2			
1818	b	1236	25	2			
1818	m	1236	26	2			
1819	b	1236	27	2			
1819	m	1236	28	2			
1819	d	1236	29	2			
1820	b	1236	30	2			
1820	m	1236	31	2			
1821	b	1236	32	2			
1821	m	1236	33	2			
1822	b	1236	6	32			
1823	d	1236	34	2			
1823	b	1236	60	2			
1824	d	1236	36	2			
1824	b	1236	7	32			
1825	d	1236	38	2			
1825	b	1236	8	32			

Dotnuva (Datnuva)

Year(s)	Type	Fond	File(s)	Op	A	F	Notes
1816	rs						
1834	rs						
1851	rs						
1870	rs				K		
1871	rs				K		
1872	rs				K		
1873	rs				K		
1874	rs	I-61	1647	1	K		Alphabetic - Jews
1875	rs				K		
1876	rs				K		
1877	rs				K		
1878	rs				K		
1836	b	1226	1492	1			
1836	m	1226	1552	1			
1844	b	1226	1493	1			
1854	b	1226	1494-1495	1			
1854	m	1226	1558	1			
1854	d	1226	174, 1745	1			
1855	b	1226	1497	1			
1855	m	1226	1560	1			
1855	d	1226	1749	1			
1856	b	1226	1498	1			
1856	m	1226	1561	1			
1856	d	1226	1750	1			
1857	m	1226	1562	1			
1857	v	1226	1653	1			
1857	d	1226	1752	1			
1858	m	1226	1563	1			
1858	m	1226	1655	1			
1858	v	1226	1655	1			
1858	d	1226	1753	1			
1859	m	1226	1564	1			
1859	v	1226	1657	1			
1859	d	1226	1754	1			
1860	m	1226	1567	1			
1860	v	1226	1658-1659	1			
1860	d	1226	1755	1			
1861	b	1226	1504	1			
1861	m	1226	1569	1			
1861	v	1226	1661	1			
1861	d	1226	1756	1			
1862	b	1226	1505	1			
1862	m	1226	1570	1			
1862	d	1226	1758	1			
1863	m	1226	1571	1			
1863	d	1226	1760	1			
1864	m	1226	1572	1			
1864	v	1226	1665	1			
1864	d	1226	1762	1			
1865	m	1226	1574	1			
1866	m	1226	1575	1			
1866	v	1226	1667	1			
1866	d	1226	1764	1			
1867	m	1226	1577	1			
1867	v	1226	1670	1			
1868	m	1226	1579	1			
1868	v	1226	1672	1			
1868	d	1226	1767	1			
1869	m	1226	1581	1			
1869	v	1226	1674	1			
1870	m	1226	1583	1			
1870	v	1226	1676	1			
1870-74	k				K		
1871	m	1226	1585	1			
1871	v	1226	1678	1			
1872	m	1226	1587	1			
1872	v	1226	1680	1			

Dotnuva (Datnuva) continued

Year(s)	Type	Fond	File(s)	Op	A	F	Notes
1873	m	1226	1590	1			
1873	v	1226	1683	1			
1874	m	1226	1593	1			
1874	v	1226	1686	1			
1874-78	k				K		
1875	m	1226	1596	1			
1875	v	1226	1689	1			
1875	d	1226	1778	1			
1876	m	1226	1599	1			
1876	v	1226	1692	1			
1876	d	1226	1780	1			
1877	m	1226	1602	1			
1877	v	1226	1695	1			
1877	d	1226	1783	1			
1879	b	1226	1522	1			
1880	m	1226	1609	1			
1881	b	1226	1525	1			
1881	m	1226	1612	1			
1881	v	1226	1704	1			
1882	b	1226	1527	1			
1882	m	1226	1615	1			
1882	v	1226	1707	1			
1883	b	1226	1529	1			
1883	m	1226	1618	1			
1883	v	1226	1710	1			
1883	d	1226	1797	1			
1884	b	1226	1531	1			
1884	m	1226	1621	1			
1884	v	1226	1714	1			
1885	b	1226	1533	1			
1885	m	1226	1624	1			
1886	b	1226	1536	1			
1886	m	1226	1627	1			
1887	m	1226	1630	1			
1887	v	1226	1720	1			
1888	b	1226	1538	1			
1888	m	1226	1632	1			
1888	v	1226	1724	1			
1889	b	1226	1540	1			
1889	m	1226	1635	1			
1890	b	1226	1541	1			
1890	m	1226	1637	1			
1891	b	1226	1542	1			
1891	v	1226	1731	1			
1891	d	1226	1815	1			
1892	b	1226	1545	1			
1892	v	1226	1734	1			
1892	d	1226	1818	1			
1893	v	1226	1736	1			
1893	d	1226	1821	1			
1894	d	1226	1824	1			
1895	b	1226	1549	1			
1895	d	1226	1828-1829	1			
1896	b	1226	n/a	2			
1896	d	1226	n/a	2			
1897	b	1226	n/a	2			
1897	d	1226	n/a	2			
1898	b	1226	n/a	2			
1898	d	1226	n/a	2			
1899	b	1226	n/a	2			
1899	d	1226	n/a	2			
1900	b	1226	n/a	2			
1900	d	1226	n/a	2			
1901	b	1226	n/a	2			
1901	d	1226	n/a	2			
1902	b	1226	n/a	2			
1902	d	1226	n/a	2			
1903	b	1226	n/a	2			
1903	d	1226	n/a	2			
1904	b	1226	n/a	2			
1904	d	1226	n/a	2			
1905	b	1226	n/a	2			
1905	d	1226	n/a	2			
1906	b	1226	n/a	2			
1906	d	1226	n/a	2			
1907	b	1226	n/a	2			
1907	d	1226	n/a	2			
1908	b	1226	n/a	2			
1908	d	1226	n/a	2			
1909	b	1226	n/a	2			
1909	d	1226	n/a	2			
1910	b	1226	n/a	2			
1910	d	1226	n/a	2			
1911	b	1226	n/a	2			
1911	d	1226	n/a	2			
1912	b	1226	n/a	2			
1912	d	1226	n/a	2			
1913	b	1226	n/a	2			

Year(s)	Type	Fond	File(s)	Op	A	F	Notes
Dotnuva (Datnuva) continued							
1913	d	1226	n/a	2			
1914	b	1226	n/a	2			
1914	d	1226	n/a	2			
Dubinovo, Bel.							
1816-27	rs						Novo-Aleksandrovsk (Zarasai) County
Dusetos							
1870-71	rs						
1875-1883	rs	1262	58	1			
1883	rs						
Eisiskes (Eishishok)							
1891	b	728	337	4			
1891	m	728	339	4			
1891	d	728	341	4			
1892	b	728	337	4			
1892	m	728	339	4			
1892	d	728	341	4			
1893	b	728	337	4			
1893	m	728	339	4			
1893	d	728	341	4			
1894	b	728	337	4			
1894	m	728	339	4			
1894	d	728	341	4			
1895	m	728	339	4			
1896	b	728	337	4			
1896	m	728	339	4			
1896	d	728	341	4			
1897	b	728	337	4			
1897	m	728	339	4			
1897	d	728	341	4			
1898	b	728	337	4			
1898	m	728	339	4			
1898	d	728	341	4			
1899	b	728	337	4			
1899	m	728	339	4			
1899	d	728	341	4			
1900	b	728	338	4			
1900	m	728	339	4			
1900	d	728	341	4			
1901	b	728	338	4			
1901	m	728	339	4			
1901	d	728	341	4			
1902	b	728	338	4			
1902	m	728	339	4			
1902	d	728	341	4			
1903	b	728	338	4			
1903	m	728	339	4			
1903	v	728	340	4			
1903	d	728	341	4			
1904	fl	227	1	1		K	
1904	b	728	338	4			
1904	d	728	341	4			
1905	b	728	338	4			
1905	d	728	341	4			
1906	b	728	338	4			
1907	b	728	338	4			
1908	b	728	338	4			
1909	v	728	340	4			
1910	v	728	340	4			
1911	v	728	340	4			
1912	v	728	340	4			
1914	v	728	340	4			
Erzvilkas							
1816	rs						
1851	rs						
1870?	rs						
Gargzdai							
1858	rs						srs
1870	rs						
1895	cen		89				Used in 1897 Census.
Garliava (Gudleva)							
1820	m	1014	220	2			
1820	d	1014	221	2			
1914	dl	1-58	42	1			family members listed
1928-1940	bdmv	1226	1345	1			Extracts
1930-1940	bdmv	1226	1346	1			Extracts
Gaure							
1816	rs						
1838	rs						
1864	rs						
1874	rs						

Gelgaudiskis (Gelgudiski)

Year(s)	Type	Fond	File(s)	Op	A	F	Notes
1816	b	1236	62	3			
1816	d	1236	63	3			
1816	m	1236	868	3			
1817	b	1236	62, 64	3			
1817	m	1236	868	3			
1818	b	1236	65	3			
1818	m	1236	66	3			
1818	d	1236	67	3			
1819	b	1236	68	3			
1819	m	1236	69	3			
1819	d	1236	70	3			
1820	b	1236	72	3			
1820	d	1236	73	3			
1820	m	1236	74	3			
1821	d	1236	71	3			
1821	m	1236	75	3			
1822	b	1236	76	3			
1822	m	1236	77	3			
1822	d	1236	78	3			
1823	b	1236	79	3			
1823	m	1236	80	3			
1823	d	1236	81	3			
1824	b	1236	82	3			
1824	m	1236	83	3			
1824	d	1236	84	3			
1825	b	1236	85	3			
1825	m	1236	86	3			
1825	d	1236	87	3			

Gelvonai (Gelvan) Those items with a Flag code of "2" are in the Vilnius County 2nd Okrug Registers. Those with a Flag code of "7" are in the Vilnius County Register.

Year(s)	Type	Fond	File(s)	Op	A	F	Notes
1816-1818	rs	515	288	25	K	7	Jews
1834	rs	515	298	25	K	7	Jews
1843-1849	rs	515	306	25	K	7	Jews
1849	rs	515	312	25	K	7	Jews
1850-1854	rs	515	273	25	K	7	Jews
1858	rs	515	285	25	K	7	Jews
unknown	rs	515	299	25	K	7	Jews
unknown	rs	515	320	25	K	7	Jews
1854	b	728	41-42	1			
1854	m	728	55-56	1			
1854	d	728	95, 100	1			
1855	b	728	131	1			
1855	d	728	192	1			
1856	b	728	205	1			
1856	m	728	225	1			
1856	d	728	267	1			
1857	b	728	277	1			
1857	m	728	278	1			
1857	d	728	329	1			
1858	b	728	349-350	1			
1858	m	728	375-376	1			
1858	d	728	407-408	1			
1859	b	728	426-427	1			
1859	m	728	446-447	1			
1859	d	728	486-487	1			
1860	b	728	507, 520	1			
1860	m	728	540-541	1			
1860	d	728	572-573	1			
1861	b	728	605-606	1			
1861	d	728	658-659	1			
1862	b	728	685-686	1			
1862	m	728	718-719	1			
1862	d	728	756-757	1			
1863	b	728	770, 772	1			
1863	m	728	812-813	1			
1863	d	728	839-840	1			
1864	b	728	867-868	1			
1864	m	728	906-907	1			
1864	d	728	936-937	1			
1865	b	728	292-293	3			
1865	m	728	294-295	3			
1865	d	728	296, 297	3			
1866	b	728	298-299	3			
1866	m	728	300-301	3			
1866	d	728	302-303	3			
1867	b	728	304-305	3			
1867	m	728	306-307	3			
1867	d	728	308-309	3			
1868	b	728	310-311	3			
1868	m	728	312-313	3			
1868	d	728	314-315	3			
1869	b	728	316-317	3			
1869	m	728	318-319	3			
1869	d	728	320-321	3			
1870	d	728	320, 327	3			
1870	b	728	322-323, 328	3			
1870	m	728	324-325	3			
1871	b	728	329	3			

Gelvonai (Gelvan) continued

Year(s)	Type	Fond	File(s)	Op	A	F
1871	m	728	330-331	3		
1871	d	728	333-334	3		
1872	b	728	335-336	3		
1872	m	728	337-338	3		
1872	d	728	339-340	3		
1873	b	728	1030	3	2	
1873	m	728	142	3	2	
1873	m	728	144	3	2	
1873	d	728	146	3	2	
1874	b	728	148-149	3	2	
1874	m	728	150-151	3	2	
1874	d	728	152, 341	3	2	
1875	b	728	153-154	3	2	
1875	m	728	155-156	3	2	
1875	d	728	157-158	3	2	
1876	b	728	1035	3	2	
1876	m	728	1074	3	2	
1876	d	728	1124	3	2	
1877	b	728	1041	3	2	
1877	m	728	1075-1076	3	2	
1877	d	728	1128	3	2	
1878	b	728	1049	3	2	
1878	m	728	1078	3	2	
1878	d	728	1134	3	2	
1891	b	728	1445	3	2	
1891	m	728	1482	3	2	
1892	b	728	1484	3	2	
1893	b	728	1491	3	2	
1893	m	728	1495	3	2	
1894	b	728	1498	3	2	
1894	b	728	1501	3	2	
1894	m	728	1504	3	2	
1895	m	728	1481	3	2	
1895	b	728	1510	3	2	
1896	m	728	10	4	2	
1896	b	728	9	4	2	
1897	b	728	23	4	2	
1897	m	728	23	4	2	
1898	b	728	40	4	2	
1898	m	728	41	4	2	
1898	v	728	42	4	2	
1899	b	728	56	4	2	
1899	m	728	57	4	2	
1900	b	728	68	4	2	
1900	m	728	69	4	2	
1900	d	728	75	4	2	
1901	d	728	75, 83	4	2	
1901	b	728	81-82	4	2	
1902	b	728	96	4	2	
1902	m	728	97	4	2	
1902	d	728	98	4	2	
1903	b	728	109	4	2	
1903	·m	728	110	4	2	
1903	d	728	111	4	2	
1904	b	728	122	4	2	
1904	m	728	123	4	2	
1904	d	728	124	4	2	
1905	b	728	135	4	2	
1905	m	728	136	4	2	
1905	v	728	137	4	2	
1905	d	728	75	4	2	
1906	b	728	147	4	2	
1906	m	728	148	4	2	
1906	v	728	149	4	2	
1906	d	728	75	4	2	
1907	b	728	159	4	2	
1907	d	728	75	4	2	
1908	m	728	170	4	2	
1908	d	728	75	4	2	
1909	b	728	181	4	2	
1909	m	728	182	4	2	
1909	v	728	183	4	2	
1909	d	728	75	4	2	
1910	b	728	195	4	2	
1910	m	728	196	4	2	
1911	b	728	209	4	2	
1911	m	728	210	4	2	
1912	m	728	223	4	2	
1913	m	728	236	4	2	
1914	b	728	249	4	2	
1914	m	728	250	4	2	

Giedraiciai (Gedrovitz) Items for this town are in the Vilnius County 3rd Okrug Registers.

Year(s)	Type	Fond	File(s)	Op	A	F
1892	b	728	1485	3		
1893	b	728	1492	3		
1893	m	728	1493	3		
1894	b	728	1497	3		
1894	m	728	1503	3		

Giedraiciai (Gedrovitz) continued

Year(s)	Type	Fond	File(s)	Op	A	F	Notes
1894	v	728	1515, 1517	3			
1895	b	728	1509	3			
1895	m	728	1512	3			
1896	b	728	11	4			
1896	m	728	12	4			
1897	b	728	25	4			
1897	m	728	26, 428	4			
1897	v	728	27	4			
1897	d	728	32	4			
1898	d	728	32	4			
1898	b	728	43	4			
1898	m	728	43	4			
1899	d	728	32	4			
1899	b	728	58	4			
1899	m	728	59	4			
1900	b	728	70	4			
1900	m	728	71	4			
1900	d	728	75	4			
1901	b	728	364	4			
1901	d	728	75, 85	4			
1901	m	728	84	4			
1902	m	728	100	4			
1902	d	728	101	4			
1902	b	728	99, 364	4			
1903	m	728	112	4			
1903	d	728	113	4			
1903	b	728	429, 364	4			
1904	b	728	125, 364	4			
1904	d	728	126	4			
1905	m	728	133	4			
1905	b	728	431, 364	4			
1905	d	728	75	4			
1906	m	728	150	4			
1906	b	728	432, 364	4			
1906	d	728	75	4			
1907	m	728	160	4			
1907	b	728	433, 364	4			
1907	d	728	75	4			
1908	m	728	171	4			
1908	b	728	434, 364	4			
1908	d	728	75	4			
1909	b	728	184, 364	4			
1909	m	728	185-186	4			
1909	d	728	75	4			
1910	b	728	197, 364	4			
1910	m	728	198, 435	4			
1911	b	728	211, 364	4			
1911	m	728	212, 436	4			
1912	b	728	224, 364	4			
1912	m	728	225	4			
1913	b	728	237, 364	4			
1913	m	728	238	4			
1914	b	728	251, 364	4			
1914	m	728	252	4			
1915	m	728	261	4			

Girkalnis

Year(s)	Type	Fond	File(s)	Op	A	F	Notes
1816	rs						
1851	rs						
1858	rs						
1864	rs						

Grinkiskis (Grinkishok)

Year(s)	Type	Fond	File(s)	Op	A	F	Notes
1816	rs						
1874	rs	I-61	1639	1	K		Alphabetic - Jews
1844	b	728	10	1			
1858	b	1226	1408	1			
1864	d	728	951	1			
1870	jkjc				K		
1873	m	1226	138	1			
1873	v	1226	139, 1896	1			
1873	d	1226	140	1			
1873	b	1226	1409	1			
1874	b	1226	141, 1412	1			
1874	m	1226	142, 1410	1			
1874	v	1226	143, 1897	1			
1874	d	1226	144, 1411	1			
1875	b	1226	145, 1413	1			
1875	m	1226	146, 1415	1			
1875	v	1226	147, 1898	1			
1875	d	1226	148, 1414	1			
1876	b	1226	1130	1			
1876	m	1226	1135	1			
1876	v	1226	1139	1			
1876	d	1226	1144	1			
1877	v	1226	1140	1			
1877	d	1226	1145	1			
1877	b	1226	149, 1131	1			

Grinkiskis (Grinkishok) continued

Year(s)	Type	Fond	File(s)	Op
1878	b	1226	1132, 1416	1
1878	m	1226	1136	1
1878	v	1226	1141	1
1878	d	1226	1146	1
1879	b	1226	1133	1
1879	m	1226	1137	1
1879	v	1226	1142	1
1879	d	1226	1147	1
1880	b	1226	1134, 1418	1
1880	m	1226	1138, 1419	1
1880	v	1226	1143, 1899	1
1880	d	1226	1148, 1417	1
1881	m	1226	1420, 1987	1
1881	d	1226	1421, 1989	1
1881	b	1226	1422, 1986	1
1881	v	1226	1900, 1988	1
1882	m	1226	1421, 1987	1
1882	d	1226	1423, 1989	1
1882	b	1226	1425, 1986	1
1882	v	1226	1901, 1988	1
1883	d	1226	1426, 1989	1
1883	v	1226	1902, 1988	1
1883	b	1226	1986	1
1883	m	1226	1987	1
1884	b	1226	1986	1
1884	m	1226	1987	1
1884	v	1226	1988	1
1884	d	1226	1989	1
1885	b	1226	1986	1
1885	m	1226	1987	1
1885	v	1226	1988	1
1885	d	1226	1989	1
1886	m	1226	1427, 1987	1
1886	d	1226	1428, 1989	1
1886	b	1226	1429, 1986	1
1886	v	1226	1903, 1988	1
1887	d	1226	1430, 1989	1
1887	b	1226	1431, 1986	1
1887	m	1226	1432, 1987	1
1887	v	1226	1904, 1988	1
1888	b	1226	1433, 1986	1
1888	d	1226	1434, 1989	1
1888	m	1226	1435, 1987	1
1888	v	1226	1905, 1988	1
1889	m	1226	1436, 1987	1
1889	d	1226	1437, 1989	1
1889	b	1226	1438, 1986	1
1889	v	1226	1906, 1988	1
1890	d	1226	1439, 1989	1
1890	b	1226	1440, 1986	1
1890	m	1226	1441, 1987	1
1890	v	1226	1907, 1908	1
1891	d	1226	1442, 1989	1
1891	m	1226	1443, 1987	1
1891	b	1226	1444, 1986	1
1891	v	1226	1988	1
1892	b	1226	1986	1
1892	m	1226	1987	1
1892	v	1226	1988	1
1892	d	1226	1989	1
1893	m	1226	1445, 1987	1
1893	b	1226	1446, 1986	1
1893	d	1226	1918, 1989	1
1893	v	1226	1988	1
1894	b	1226	1447, 1986	1
1894	d	1226	1448, 1989	1
1894	v	1226	1908, 1988	1
1894	m	1226	1909, 1987	1
1895	m	1226	1449, 1987	1
1895	d	1226	1450, 1989	1
1895	b	1226	1451, 1986	1
1895	v	1226	1919, 1988	1
1896	d	1226	1452, 1989	1
1896	b	1226	1453, 1986	1
1896	m	1226	1454, 1987	1
1896	v	1226	1988	1
1897	d	1226	1455, 1989	1
1897	m	1226	1456, 1987	1
1897	b	1226	1457, 1986	1
1897	v	1226	1988	1
1898	b	1226	1458, 1986	1
1898	m	1226	1987	1
1898	v	1226	1988	1
1898	d	1226	1989	1
1899	d	1226	1459, 1989	1
1899	m	1226	1460, 1987	1
1899	b	1226	1461, 1986	1
1899	v	1226	1910, 1988	1

Grinkiskis (Grinkishok) continued

Year(s)	Type	Fond	File(s)	Op	A	F	Notes
1900	d	1226	1462, 1989	1			
1900	b	1226	1463, 1986	1			
1900	m	1226	1464, 1987	1			
1900	v	1226	1911, 1988	1			
1901	d	1226	1465, 1989	1			
1901	m	1226	1466, 1987	1			
1901	b	1226	1986	1			
1901	v	1226	1988	1			
1902	m	1226	1467, 1987	1			
1902	b	1226	1986	1			
1902	v	1226	1988	1			
1902	d	1226	1989	1			
1903	b	1226	1986	1			
1903	m	1226	1987	1			
1903	v	1226	1988	1			
1903	d	1226	1989	1			
1904	b	1226	1463, 1986	1			
1904	d	1226	1468, 1989	1			
1904	m	1226	1470, 1987	1			
1904	v	1226	1912, 1988	1			
1905	d	1226	1471, 1989	1			
1905	m	1226	1472, 1987	1			
1905	b	1226	1473, 1986	1			
1905	v	1226	1988	1			
1906	b	1226	1986	1			
1906	m	1226	1987	1			
1906	v	1226	1988	1			
1906	d	1226	1989	1			
1907	d	1226	1427, 1989	1			
1907	b	1226	1475, 1986	1			
1907	v	1226	1913, 1988	1			
1907	m	1226	1987	1			
1908	b	1226	1986	1			
1908	m	1226	1987	1			
1908	v	1226	1988	1			
1908	d	1226	1989	1			
1909	b	1226	1986	1			
1909	m	1226	1987	1			
1909	v	1226	1988	1			
1909	d	1226	1989	1			
1910	d	1226	1476, 1989	1			
1910	m	1226	1477, 1987	1			
1910	b	1226	1478, 1986	1			
1910	v	1226	1914, 1988	1			
1911	d	1226	1479, 1989	1			
1911	b	1226	1480, 1986	1			
1911	v	1226	1915, 1988	1			
1911	m	1226	1987	1			
1912	b	1226	1986	1			
1912	m	1226	1987	1			
1912	v	1226	1988	1			
1912	d	1226	1989	1			
1913	b	1226	1986	1			
1913	m	1226	1987	1			
1913	v	1226	1988	1			
1913	d	1226	1989	1			
1914	b	1226	1986	1			
1914	m	1226	1987	1			
1914	v	1226	1988	1			
1914	d	1226	1989	1			
1915	d	1226	1481	1			
1915	v	1226	1988	1			

Griskablidis (Grishkablid)

Year(s)	Type	Fond	File(s)	Op	A	F	Notes
1815	m	1236	127	3			
1816	m	1236	127	3			
1816	b	1236	128	3			
1816	d	1236	129	3			
1817	b	1236	128, 131	3			
1817	d	1236	129, 132	3			
1818	m	1236	133	3			
1819	m	1236	134	3			
1819	d	1236	135	3			
1820	b	1236	136	3			
1821	b	1236	138	3			
1821	d	1236	139	3			
1822	m	1236	140	3			
1823	b	1236	141	3			
1823	m	1236	143	3			
1823	d	1236	144	3			
1824	d	1236	145	3			
1824	b	1236	146	3			
1825	d	1236	147	3			
1825	m	1236	148	3			

Gruzdziai

Year(s)	Type	Fond	File(s)	Op	A	F	Notes
1912-1916	tpl-r				K		

Gudele (Gudeliai)

Year(s)	Type	Fond	File(s)	Op	A	F	Notes
1815	d	1236	288	4			
1816	d	1236	288	4			
1819	m	1014	200	2			

Iglevo (Igliauka)

Year(s)	Type	Fond	File(s)	Op	A	F	Notes
1823	m	1236	163	3			
1823	d	1236	164	3			
1824	b	1236	165	3			
1824	m	1236	166	3			
1824	d	1236	167	3			
1825	b	1236	168	3			
1825	m	1236	169	3			
1825	d	1236	171	3			

Ilgovo (Ilguva)

Year(s)	Type	Fond	File(s)	Op	A	F	Notes
1814	m	1236	10	11			
1814	d	1236	11	11			
1815	m	1236	10, 12	11			
1815	d	1236	11	11			
1815	d	1236	152	3			
1816	m	1236	12-13	11			
1816	d	1236	14	11			
1816	d	1236	152	3			
1816	b	1236	153	3			
1817	m	1236	13	11			
1817	d	1236	14	11			
1817	b	1236	153	3			
1817	m	1236	154	3			
1817	d	1236	155	3			
1818	m	1236	156	3			
1818	d	1236	157	3			
1819	d	1236	15	11			
1819	m	1236	158	3			
1820	b	1236	159	3			
1820	d	1236	160	3			
1821	d	1236	16	11			
1821	m	1236	161	3			
1821	b	1236	17	11			
1822	m	1236	162	3			
1825	b	1236	1	11			
1825	m	1236	170	3			
1825	d	1236	18	11			

Inturke (Inturik) Items for this town are in the Vilnius County 3rd Okrug Registers.

Year(s)	Type	Fond	File(s)	Op	A	F	Notes
1892	b	728	1485	3			
1893	b	728	1492	3			
1893	m	728	1493	3			
1894	b	728	1497	3			
1894	m	728	1503	3			
1894	v	728	1515, 1517	3			
1895	b	728	1509	3			
1895	m	728	1512	3			

Jasiunai (Yashny) Items for this town are in the Vilnius County 4th Okrug Registers.

Year(s)	Type	Fond	File(s)	Op	A	F	Notes
1885	m	728	353	4			
1886	m	728	353	4			
1887	d	728	1478	3			
1887	m	728	353	4			
1887	b	728	364	4			
1888	d	728	1478	3			
1888	m	728	353	4			
1888	b	728	364	4			
1889	d	728	1478	3			
1889	m	728	353	4			
1889	b	728	364	4			
1890	d	728	1478	3			
1890	b	728	1479	3			
1890	m	728	1480	3			
1890	m	728	353	4			
1890	b	728	364	4			
1891	b	728	1446	3			
1891	d	728	1478	3			
1891	m	728	1483	3			
1891	m	728	353	4			
1891	b	728	364	4			
1892	d	728	1478	3			
1892	b	728	1486, 1553	3			
1892	m	728	1487, 1488, 1554	3			
1892	v	728	1489	3			
1892	m	728	353	4			
1892	b	728	364	4			
1893	d	728	1478	3			
1893	b	728	1490, 1553	3			
1893	m	728	1494, 1554	3			
1893	v	728	1496	3			
1893	m	728	353	4			
1893	b	728	364	4			
1894	b	728	1499, 1553	3			

Jasiunai (Yashny) continued

Year(s)	Type	Fond	File(s)	Op	A	F	Notes
1894	m	728	1505, 1554	3			
1894	v	728	1516	3			
1894	m	728	353	4			
1894	b	728	364	4			
1895	b	728	1508, 1553	3			
1895	m	728	1513, 1556	3			
1895	v	728	1519	3			
1895	v	728	3	4			
1895	m	728	353	4			
1895	b	728	364	4			
1896	b	728	13, 364	4			
1896	m	728	14, 353	4			
1896	b	728	1553	3			
1896	m	728	1556	3			
1897	b	728	28-29, 364	4			
1897	m	728	30, 353, 437	4			
1897	d	728	32	4			
1898	b	728	28, 45, 364	4			
1898	d	728	32	4			
1898	m	728	46, 353, 437	4			
1899	b	728	28, 60, 364	4			
1899	v	728	3	4			
1899	d	728	32	4			
1899	m	728	61, 353, 437	4			
1900	v	728	3	4			
1900	b	728	72, 364	4			
1900	m	728	73-74, 353, 437	4			
1900	d	728	75	4			
1901	v	728	3, 88	4			
1901	d	728	75	4			
1901	b	728	86, 364	4			
1901	m	728	87, 353, 437	4			
1902	m	728	102, 353, 438	4			
1902	d	728	103, 439	4			
1902	b	728	364	4			
1903	b	728	114-115, 364	4			
1903	m	728	116, 353, 438, 444	4			
1903	d	728	117, 439	4			
1904	b	728	127, 364	4			
1904	m	728	128, 353, 438	4			
1904	d	728	129, 439	4			
1905	b	728	139, 364	4			
1905	m	728	140, 353, 438	4			
1905	d	728	75, 141, 439	4			
1906	b	728	151, 364, 441	4			
1906	m	728	152, 353	4			
1906	d	728	75, 153	4			
1907	b	728	161, 364, 441	4			
1907	m	728	162, 353	4			
1907	v	728	3	4			
1907	d	728	75	4			
1908	b	728	172, 364, 441	4			
1908	v	728	3, 173	4			
1908	m	728	353	4			
1908	d	728	75	4			
1909	b	728	187, 364	4			
1909	v	728	3, 188	4			
1909	m	728	353, 442	4			
1909	d	728	75	4			
1910	b	728	199, 364	4			
1910	v	728	3, 200	4			
1910	m	728	353, 443	4			
1911	b	728	213, 364	4			
1911	m	728	214, 353	4			
1911	v	728	215	4			
1912	b	728	226, 364	4			
1912	m	728	227-228, 353	4			
1913	b	728	239, 364	4			
1913	m	728	240, 353	4			
1914	b	728	253, 364	4			
1914	m	728	253-254, 353	4			
1914	v	728	255	4			
1915	m	728	353	4			
1915	b	728	364	4			
1916	b	728	364	4			
1917	b	728	364	4			
1917	b	728	364	4			
1918	b	728	364	4			
1919	b	728	364	4			
1920	b	728	364	4			
1921	b	728	364	4			

Jieznas (Vezna)

Year(s)	Type	Fond	File(s)	Op	A	F	Notes
1858-1905	rs						
1877	b	728	1402	3			
1878	b	728	1403	3			
1879	b	728	1404	3			
1880	b	728	1405	3			

Jieznas (Vezna) continued

Year(s)	Type	Fond	File(s)	Op	A	F	Notes
1881	b	728	303	3			
1882	b	728	303	3			
1882	m	728	303	4			
1883	b	728	303	3			
1884	b	728	303	3			
1885	b	728	303	3			
1885	m	728	303	4			
1886	b	728	303	3			
1886	m	728	303	4			
1887	b	728	303	3			
1887	b	728	303	3			
1887	m	728	303	4			
1888	b	728	303	3			
1889	b	728	303	3			
1890	b	728	303	3			
1890	m	728	303	4			
1891	b	728	303	3			
1892	b	728	303	3			
1892	m	728	303	4			
1893	b	728	303	3			
1894	b	728	303	3			
1894	m	728	303	4			
1895	b	728	303	3			
1895	m	728	303	4			
1896	b	728	303	3			
1896	m	728	303	4			
1897	b	728	303	3			
1897	m	728	303	4			
1898	b	728	303	3			
1898	m	728	303	4			
1900	b	728	303	3			
1900	m	728	303	4			
1901	b	728	303	3			
1902	b	728	303	3			
1902	m	728	303	4			
1903	b	728	303	3			
1904	b	728	303	3			
1904	m	728	303	4			
1905	b	728	303	3			
1907	m	728	303	4			
1909	b	728	303	3			
1909	m	728	303	4			
1910	m	728	303	4			
1911	b	728	303	3			
1911	m	728	303	4			

Jokubonys (Yakubantse) Items for this town are in the Vilnius County 2nd Okrug Registers.

Year(s)	Type	Fond	File(s)	Op	A	F	Notes
1896	m	728	10	4			
1896	b	728	9	4			
1897	b	728	23	4			
1897	m	728	23	4			
1898	b	728	40	4			
1898	m	728	41	4			
1898	v	728	42	4			
1899	b	728	56	4			
1899	m	728	57	4			
1900	b	728	68	4			
1900	m	728	69	4			
1900	d	728	75	4			
1901	d	728	75, 83	4			
1901	b	728	81-82	4			
1902	b	728	96	4			
1902	m	728	97	4			
1902	d	728	98	4			
1903	b	728	109	4			
1903	m	728	110	4			
1903	d	728	111	4			
1904	b	728	122	4			
1904	m	728	123	4			
1904	d	728	124	4			
1905	b	728	135	4			
1905	m	728	136	4			
1905	v	728	137	4			
1905	d	728	75	4			
1906	b	728	147	4			
1906	m	728	148	4			
1906	v	728	149	4			
1906	d	728	75	4			
1907	b	728	159	4			
1907	d	728	75	4			
1908	m	728	170	4			
1908	d	728	75	4			
1909	b	728	181	4			
1909	m	728	182	4			
1909	v	728	183	4			
1909	d	728	75	4			
1910	b	728	195	4			
1910	m	728	196	4			

Jokubonys (Yakubantse) continued

Year(s)	Type	Fond	File(s)	Op	A	F	Notes
1911	b	728	209	4			
1911	m	728	210	4			
1912	m	728	223	4			
1913	m	728	236	4			
1914	b	728	249	4			
1914	m	728	250	4			

Jonava (Yanova)

Year(s)	Type	Fond	File(s)	Op	A	F	Notes
1874	rs				K		Index of Jews
1876	rs						
1851	b				K		
1851	b	I-202	1	1	K		
1852	b				K		
1853	b				K		
1854	b				K		
1854	d	728	119	1			
1854	m	728	79	1			
1854	v	728	93	1			
1854-1860	b	I-202	2-8	1	K		
1855	b				K		
1855	m	728	142	1			
1855	v	728	165	1			
1855	d	728	181	1			
1855	b	I-202	2-8	1	K		
1856	b				K		
1856	m	728	236	1			
1856	v	728	255	1			
1856	d	728	261	1			
1856	b	I-202	2-8	1	K		
1857	b				K		
1857	m	728	310	1			
1857	v	728	322	1			
1857	d	728	334	1			
1857	b	I-202	2-8	1	K		
1858	b				K		
1858	m	728	382	1			
1858	v	728	385	1			
1858	d	728	413	1			
1858	b	I-202	2-8	1	K		
1859	b				K		
1859	m	728	461, 464	1			
1859	d	728	497	1			
1859	b	I-202	2-8	1	K		
1860	b				K		
1860	m	728	545	1			
1860	v	728	566	1			
1860	d	728	590	1			
1860	b	I-202	2-8	1	K		
1861	b				K		
1861	b	728	617	1			
1861	m	728	638	1			
1861	v	728	652	1			
1861	d	728	675	1			
1862	b				K		
1862	m	728	726	1			
1862	v	728	727	1			
1862	d	728	766	1			
1862	b	I-202	9-11	1	K		
1863	b				K		
1863	m	728	814	1			
1863	v	728	831	1			
1863	d	728	856	1			
1863	b	I-202	9-11	1	K		
1864	b				K		
1864	m	728	913	1			
1864	v	728	915	1			
1864	d	728	948	1			
1864	b	I-202	9-11	1	K		
1865	b	1226	330	1			
1865	m	1226	331	1			
1865	v	1226	332	1			
1865	d	1226	333	1			
1866	b	1226	334	1			
1866	m	1226	335	1			
1866	v	1226	336	1			
1866	d	1226	337	1			
1867	b	1226	338	1			
1867	m	1226	339	1			
1867	v	1226	340	1			
1867	d	1226	341	1			
1868	b	1226	342	1			
1868	m	1226	343	1			
1868	v	1226	344	1			
1868	d	1226	345	1			
1869	b	1226	346-347	1			
1869	m	1226	348-349	1			
1869	v	1226	350	1			
1869	d	1226	351	1			

Jonava (Yanova) continued

Year(s)	Type	Fond	File(s)	Op	A	F	Notes
1870	b	1226	352	1			
1870	m	1226	353	1			
1870	v	1226	354	1			
1870	d	1226	355	1			
1870-1874	k				K		
1871	b	1226	356	1			
1871	m	1226	357	1			
1871	v	1226	358	1			
1871	d	1226	359	1			
1872	b	1226	360	1			
1872	m	1226	361	1			
1872	v	1226	362	1			
1872	d	1226	363	1			
1873	b	1226	364	1			
1873	m	1226	365	1			
1873	v	1226	366	1			
1873	d	1226	367	1			
1874	b	1226	368	1			
1874	m	1226	369	1			
1874	v	1226	370	1			
1874	d	1226	371	1			
1874-1878	k				K		
1875	b	1226	372	1			
1875	m	1226	373	1			
1875	v	1226	374	1			
1875	d	1226	375	1			
1876	b	1226	865	1			
1876	m	1226	870	1			
1876	d	1226	875	1			
1877	b	1226	866	1			
1877	m	1226	871	1			
1877	d	1226	876	1			
1877	v	1226	880	1			
1878	b	1226	867	1			
1878	m	1226	872	1			
1878	d	1226	877	1			
1878	v	1226	881	1			
1879	b	1226	868	1			
1879	m	1226	873	1			
1879	d	1226	878	1			
1879	v	1226	882	1			
1880	b	1226	869	1			
1880	m	1226	874	1			
1880	d	1226	879	1			
1880	v	1226	883	1			
1881	b	1226	1308	1			
1881	m	1226	2083	1			
1881	d	1226	2084	1			
1882	b	1226	1308	1			
1882	m	1226	2083	1			
1882	d	1226	2084	1			
1883	b	1226	1308	1			
1883	m	1226	2083	1			
1883	d	1226	2084	1			
1884	b	1226	1308	1			
1884	m	1226	2083	1			
1884	d	1226	2084	1			
1885	b	1226	1308	1			
1885	m	1226	2083	1			
1885	d	1226	2084	1			
1886	b	1226	1308	1			
1886	m	1226	2083	1			
1886	d	1226	2084	1			
1887	b	1226	1308	1			
1887	m	1226	2083	1			
1887	d	1226	2084	1			
1887	fl	202			K		
1887	fl	I-202	12	1	K		
1887	fl	I-202	12	1	K		
1888	b	1226	1308	1			
1888	m	1226	2083	1			
1888	d	1226	2084	1			
1889	b	1226	2080	1			
1889	m	1226	2083	1			
1889	d	1226	2084	1			
1890	b	1226	2080	1			
1890	m	1226	2083	1			
1890	d	1226	2084	1			
1891	b	1226	2080	1			
1891	m	1226	2083	1			
1891	d	1226	2084	1			
1892	b	1226	2080	1			
1892	m	1226	2083	1			
1892	d	1226	2084	1			
1893	b	1226	2080	1			
1893	m	1226	2083	1			
1893	d	1226	2084	1			
1894	b	1226	2080	1			

Year(s)	Type	Fond	File(s)	Op	A	F	Notes
Jonava (Yanova) continued							
1894	m	1226	2083	1			
1894	d	1226	2084	1			
1895	b	1226	2080	1			
1895	m	1226	2083	1			
1895	d	1226	2084	1			
1896	b	1226	2080	1			
1896	m	1226	2083	1			
1897	b	1226	2080	1			
1897	m	1226	2083	1			
1898	b	1226	2081	1			
1899	b	1226	2081	1			
1900	b	1226	2081	1			
1901	b	1226	2082	1			
1902	b	1226	2082	1			
1903	b	1226	2082	1			
1904	b	1226	2082	1			
1905	b	1226	2082	1			
1906	b	1226	2082	1			
1907	b	1226	2082	1			
1908	b	1226	2082	1			
1908	fl	I-202	13-15	1	K		
1909	b	1226	2082	1			
1910	b	1226	2082	1			
1911	b	1226	2082	1			
1912	b	1226	2082	1			
1912-1916	tpl-r				K		
1913	b	1226	2082, 2087-2088	1			
1913	m	1226	2087-2088	1			
1913	v	1226	2087-2088	1			
1913	d	1226	2088	1			
1914	b	1226	2082, 2088	1			
1914	d	1226	2088	1			
1914	m	1226	2088	1			
1914	v	1226	2088	1			
1915	b	1226	2088	1			
1915	d	1226	2088	1			
1915	m	1226	2088	1			
1915	v	1226	2088	1			
unknown	tpl				K		
Joniskelis (Yanishkel)							
1816	rs						
1818	rs						
1834	rs						
1876	rs	213			K		
1883	rs	213			K		
1887	rs	213			K		
1887	b	1226	2077	1			
1887	m	1226	2078	1			
1887	v	1226	2078	1			
1887	d	1226	2079	1			
1888	b	1226	2077	1			
1888	m	1226	2078	1			
1888	v	1226	2078	1			
1888	d	1226	2079	1			
1889	b	1226	2077	1			
1889	m	1226	2078	1			
1889	v	1226	2078	1			
1889	d	1226	2079	1			
1890	b	1226	2077	1			
1890	m	1226	2078	1			
1890	v	1226	2078	1			
1890	d	1226	2079	1			
1891	b	1226	2077	1			
1891	m	1226	2078	1			
1891	v	1226	2078	1			
1891	d	1226	2079	1			
1892	b	1226	2077	1			
1892	m	1226	2078	1			
1892	v	1226	2078	1			
1892	d	1226	2079	1			
1893	b	1226	2077	1			
1893	m	1226	2078	1			
1893	v	1226	2078	1			
1893	d	1226	2079	1			
1894	b	1226	2041, 2077	1			In File 2041, see List 106.
1894	m	1226	2078	1			
1894	v	1226	2078	1			
1894	d	1226	2079	1			
1895	b	1226	2077	1			
1895	m	1226	2078	1			
1895	v	1226	2078	1			
1895	d	1226	2079	1			
1896	b	1226	2077	1			
1896	m	1226	2078	1			
1896	v	1226	2078	1			
1896	d	1226	2079	1			
1897	b	1226	2041, 2077	1			In File 2041, see List 195.

Joniskelis (Yanishkel) continued

Year(s)	Type	Fond	File(s)		Op	A	F	Notes
1897	m	1226	2078		1			
1897	v	1226	2078		1			
1897	d	1226	2079		1			
1898	b	1226	2077		1			
1898	m	1226	2078		1			
1898	v	1226	2078		1			
1898	d	1226	2079		1			
1899	b	1226	2077		1			
1899	m	1226	2078		1			
1899	v	1226	2078		1			
1899	d	1226	2079		1			
1900	b	1226	2077		1			
1900	m	1226	2078		1			
1900	v	1226	2078		1			
1900	d	1226	2079		1			
1901	b	1226	2077		1			
1901	m	1226	2078		1			
1901	v	1226	2078		1			
1901	d	1226	2079		1			
1902	b	1226	2077		1			
1902	m	1226	2078		1			
1902	v	1226	2078		1			
1902	d	1226	2079		1			
1903	b	1226	2077		1			
1903	m	1226	2078		1			
1903	v	1226	2078		1			
1903	d	1226	2079		1			
1903	d	728	1012		1			
1904	b	1226	2077		1			
1904	m	1226	2078		1			
1904	v	1226	2078		1			
1904	d	1226	2079		1			
1905	b	1226	2077		1			
1905	m	1226	2078		1			
1905	v	1226	2078		1			
1905	d	1226	2079		1			
1906	b	1226	2077		1			
1906	m	1226	2078		1			
1906	v	1226	2078		1			
1906	d	1226	2079		1			
1907	b	1226	2077		1			
1907	m	1226	2078		1			
1907	v	1226	2078		1			
1907	d	1226	2079		1			
1908	b	1226	2077		1			
1908	m	1226	2078		1			
1908	v	1226	2078		1			
1908	d	1226	2079		1			
1909	b	1226	2077		1			
1909	m	1226	2078		1			
1909	v	1226	2078		1			
1909	d	1226	2079		1			
1910	b	1226	2077		1			
1910	m	1226	2078		1			
1910	v	1226	2078		1			
1910	d	1226	2079		1			
1911	b	1226	2077		1			
1911	m	1226	2078		1			
1911	v	1226	2078		1			
1911	d	1226	2079		1			
1912	b	1226	2042, 2077		1			In File 2042, see Lists 406 & 446.
1912	m	1226	2078		1			
1912	v	1226	2078		1			
1912	d	1226	2079		1			
1913	b	1226	2042, 2077		1			In File 2042, see Lists 406 & 446.
1913	m	1226	2078		1			
1913	v	1226	2078		1			
1913	d	1226	2079		1			
1914	b	1226	2077		1			
1914	m	1226	2078		1			
1914	v	1226	2078		1			
1914	d	1226	2079		1			

Joniskis

Year(s)	Type	Fond	File(s)		Op	A	F	Notes
1852	rs							
1866	rs							
1877	fl	225					K	
1877	fl	I-225	1		1		K	

Josvainiai (Yosvain)

Year(s)	Type	Fond	File(s)		Op	A	F	Notes
1816	rs							
1834	rs							Kaunas Duma
1874	rs	I-61	1643, 1653		1		K	Index of Jews
1888	rs	I-203	1		1		K	Index of Jews
1836	b	1226	1486		1			
1837	b	1226	1487		1			
1837	d	1226	1742		1			
1838	d	1226	1743		1			

Josvainiai (Yosvain) continued

Year(s)	Type	Fond	File(s)	Op	A	F	Notes
1844	b	1226	1488	1			
1844	m	1226	1554	1			
1844	v	1226	1648	1			
1844	d	1226	1744	1			
1870-1874	k				K		
1873	b	1226	1515	1			
1873	m	1226	1588	1			
1873	v	1226	1682	1			
1873	d	1226	1773	1			
1874	m	1226	1591	1			
1874	v	1226	1685	1			
1874	d	1226	1775	1			
1874	b	1226	1831	1			
1874-1878	k				K		
1875	m	1226	1594	1			
1875	v	1226	1688	1			
1875	d	1226	1777	1			
1875	b	1226	1832	1			
1876	b	1226	1519A	1			
1876	m	1226	1597	1			
1876	v	1226	1691	1			
1876	d	1226	1781	1			
1877	b	1226	1520, 1833	1			
1877	m	1226	1600	1			
1877	v	1226	1694	1			
1877	d	1226	1785	1			
1878	b	1226	1521	1			
1878	m	1226	1604	1			
1878	v	1226	1697	1			
1878	d	1226	1786-1787	1			
1879	m	1226	1606	1			
1879	v	1226	1699	1			
1879	d	1226	1789	1			
1879	b	1226	1834	1			
1880	m	1226	1607	1			
1880	v	1226	1701	1			
1880	d	1226	1791	1			
1880	b	1226	1835	1			
1881	m	1226	1610	1			
1881	v	1226	1703	1			
1881	d	1226	1793	1			
1881	b	1226	1836	1			
1882	m	1226	1613	1			
1882	v	1226	1706	1			
1882	d	1226	1795	1			
1882	b	1226	1837	1			
1883	m	1226	1616	1			
1883	v	1226	1709	1			
1883	d	1226	1799	1			
1883	b	1226	1838	1			
1884	m	1226	1619	1			
1884	v	1226	1712-1713	1			
1884	d	1226	1800-1801	1			
1884	b	1226	1839-1840	1			
1885	m	1226	1623	1			
1885	v	1226	1716	1			
1885	d	1226	1803	1			
1885	b	1226	1841	1			
1886	m	1226	1625	1			
1886	v	1226	1718	1			
1886	d	1226	1805	1			
1886	b	1226	1842	1			
1887	m	1226	1628	1			
1887	v	1226	1721	1			
1887	d	1226	1807	1			
1887	b	1226	1843	1			
1887	fl	203			K		
1888	v	1226	1723	1			
1888	d	1226	1810	1			
1888	b	1226	1844	1			
1889	m	1226	1633	1			
1889	v	1226	1726	1			
1889	d	1226	1812	1			
1889	b	1226	1845	1			
1890	m	1226	1636	1			
1890	v	1226	1728	1			
1890	d	1226	1813	1			
1890	b	1226	1846	1			
1891	m	1226	1639	1			
1891	v	1226	1729	1			
1891	d	1226	1816	1			
1891	b	1226	1847	1			
1892	m	1226	1641	1			
1892	v	1226	1732	1			
1892	d	1226	1819	1			
1892	b	1226	1848	1			
1893	m	1226	1643	1			
1893	v	1226	1737	1			

Josvainiai (Yosvain) continued

Year(s)	Type	Fond	File(s)	Op	A	F	Notes
1893	d	1226	1822	1			
1893	b	1226	1849	1			
1894	m	1226	1645	1			
1894	v	1226	1738	1			
1894	d	1226	1825	1			
1894	b	1226	1850	1			
1895	v	1226	1740	1			
1895	d	1226	1830	1			
1895	b	1226	1851	1			
1896	b	1226	1852	1			
1896	d	1226	n/a	2			
1896	m	1226	n/a	2			
1897	b	1226	1853	1			
1897	d	1226	n/a	2			
1897	m	1226	n/a	2			
1898	b	1226	n/a	2			
1898	d	1226	n/a	2			
1898	m	1226	n/a	2			
1899	b	1226	n/a	2			
1899	d	1226	n/a	2			
1899	m	1226	n/a	2			
1900	b	1226	n/a	2			
1900	d	1226	n/a	2			
1900	m	1226	n/a	2			
1901	b	1226	n/a	2			
1901	d	1226	n/a	2			
1901	m	1226	n/a	2			
1902	b	1226	n/a	2			
1902	d	1226	n/a	2			
1902	m	1226	n/a	2			
1903	b	1226	n/a	2			
1903	d	1226	n/a	2			
1903	m	1226	n/a	2			
1904	b	1226	n/a	2			
1904	d	1226	n/a	2			
1904	m	1226	n/a	2			
1905	b	1226	n/a	2			
1905	d	1226	n/a	2			
1905	m	1226	n/a	2			
1906	b	1226	n/a	2			
1906	d	1226	n/a	2			
1906	m	1226	n/a	2			
1907	b	1226	n/a	2			
1907	d	1226	n/a	2			
1907	m	1226	n/a	2			
1908	b	1226	n/a	2			
1908	d	1226	n/a	2			
1908	m	1226	n/a	2			
1909	b	1226	n/a	2			
1909	d	1226	n/a	2			
1909	m	1226	n/a	2			
1910	b	1226	n/a	2			
1910	d	1226	n/a	2			
1910	m	1226	n/a	2			
1911	b	1226	n/a	2			
1911	d	1226	n/a	2			
1911	m	1226	n/a	2			
1912	b	1226	n/a	2			
1912	d	1226	n/a	2			
1912	m	1226	n/a	2			
1913	b	1226	n/a	2			
1913	d	1226	n/a	2			
1913	m	1226	n/a	2			
1914	b	1226	n/a	2			
1914	d	1226	n/a	2			
1914	m	1226	n/a	2			

Jurbarkas (Yurburg)

Year(s)	Type	Fond	File(s)	Op	A	F	Notes
1816	rs						
1839-1841	rs	515	398	25			
1851	rs	515	1068	15			
1858	rs	1262	76	1			no Jurbarkas records
1863-1878	rs	1262	83	1			
1864	rs	1262	84	1			
1869	rs	1262	127	1			srs
	fin	158	13	1	K		Postal Money Transfers, Bank #31
	p	222	8	1	K		Postal Insurance Notification List
1890	fin	158					Sberegatel'naya kassa
1890	pbr	158	1	1	K		Account Applications, Bank Branch #31
1890-1918	fin	158	7-12	1	K		Postal Bank Account Owner List, Bank #31
1891	pbr	158	1	1	K		Account Applications, Bank Branch #31
1893-1895	prb	222	2	1	K		
1893-1914	prb	222	1	1	K		
1899-1900	prb	222	3	1	K		
1900-1903	prb	222	4	1	K		
1901	pbr	158	2	1	K		Account Applications, Bank Branch #31
1902	pbr	158	2	1	K		Account Applications, Bank Branch #31
1903	pbr	158	2	1	K		Account Applications, Bank Branch #31

Jurbarkas (Yurburg) continued

Year(s)	Type	Fond	File(s)	Op	A	F	Notes
1903-1905	prb	222	5	1	K		
1904	pbr	158	2	1	K		Account Applications, Bank Branch #31
1905	pbr	158	2	1	K		Account Applications, Bank Branch #31
1906	pbr	158	2-3	1	K		Account Applications, Bank Branch #31
1906-1907	prb	222	6	1	K		
1907	pbr	158	3	1	K		Account Applications, Bank Branch #31
1907	p	222	9	1	K		Court Sentence List
1908	pbr	158	3	1	K		Account Applications, Bank Branch #31
1908	prb	222	10	1	K		
1909	pbr	158	3-4	1	K		Account Applications, Bank Branch #31
1910	pbr	158	4	1	K		Account Applications, Bank Branch #31
1911	pbr	158	4	1	K		Account Applications, Bank Branch #31
1911	p	222	12	1	K		Postal Notifications
1912	pbr	158	4-5	1	K		Account Applications, Bank Branch #31
1912	p	222	14	1	K		Postal Notifications
1913	pbr	158	5-6	1	K		Account Applications, Bank Branch #31
1913-1914	prb	222	15	1	K		
1914	pbr	158	6	1	K		Account Applications, Bank Branch #31

Kaimele (Kiduliai)

Year(s)	Type	Fond	File(s)	Op	A	F	Notes
1815	b	1236	240	3			
1815	m	1236	241	3			
1815	d	1236	242	3			
1816	b	1236	240	3			
1816	m	1236	241	3			
1816	d	1236	242	3			
1817	b	1236	243	3			
1817	m	1236	244	3			
1818	b	1236	245	3			
1818	m	1236	246	3			
1819	m	1236	247	3			
1822	b	1236	248	3			
1822	m	1236	249	3			
1823	b	1236	250	3			
1823	m	1236	251	3			
1824	b	1236	252	3			
1824	d	1236	253	3			
1825	d	1236	254	3			
1827	b	1236	693	3			
1827	d	1236	693	3			
1827	m	1236	693	3			
1828	b	1236	694	3			
1828	d	1236	694	3			
1828	m	1236	694	3			
1830	b	1236	695	3			
1830	d	1236	695	3			
1830	m	1236	695	3			
1839	b	1236	696	3			
1839	d	1236	696	3			
1839	m	1236	696	3			
1841	b	1236	697	3			
1841	d	1236	697	3			
1841	m	1236	697	3			
1842	b	1236	698	3			
1842	d	1236	698	3			
1842	m	1236	698	3			
1845	b	1236	699	3			
1845	d	1236	699	3			
1845	m	1236	699	3			

Kalvarija

Year(s)	Type	Fond	File(s)	Op	A	F	Notes
1908	hol						

Kamajai

Year(s)	Type	Fond	File(s)	Op	A	F	Notes
1871	rs						
1875-1883	rs	1262	58	1			

Kapciamiestis (Kopcheva)

Year(s)	Type	Fond	File(s)	Op	A	F	Notes
1812	d	1236	1	30			Fragments
1813	d	1236	1	30			Fragments
1818	d	1236	2	30			Fragments
1823	b	1236	3	30			Fragments

Kaunas (Kovno)

Year(s)	Type	Fond	File(s)	Op	A	F	Notes
1795-1816-1818	rs						Kaunas Duma, Town of Labunava
1811	rs	I-61	65	1	K		
1834	rs	61		1	K		crl
1834	rs	I-61	308	1	K		
1851	rs	I-61	1637	1	K		Alphabetic - Jews
1858-1879	rs	I-196	1	1	K		
1858-1898	rs	I-61	1612-1613	1	K		Jews
1858-1907	rs	I-61	1610-1611	1	K		Jews
1858-1908	rs	I-61	1609	1	K		Jews
1874	rs	I-61	1646	1	K		Alphabetic - Jews
1875-1879	rs	I-196	2	1	K		
1827-1918	fin	715					Property
1836	crl	61		1	K		
1837	prb	61	384	1	K		

Kaunas (Kovno) continued

Year(s)	Type	Fond	File(s)		Op	A	F	Notes
1842	b	1226	150		1			
1843	b	1226	151		1			
1843-1917	p	J-50			1	K		Chancellory of Kaunas Guberniia Civil Governor, "On Issuing Foreign Passports
1843-44	pib	61			1	K		
1845	tcdr	61	555		1	K		Jewish Records
1849	b	1226	152		1			
1850	b	1226	153		1			
1854	b	1226	154		1			
1854-1880	ai	1226	n/a		1			Alphabetic Index, Incomplete
1855	b	1226	155		1			
1858	b	1226	156		1			
1858-1915	fl	I-61	1622, 1626		1	K		Jews
1859	b	1226	157		1			
1860	b	1226	158		1			
1861	b	1226	159-160		1			
1862	b	1226	161		1			
1862	fin	61	2706		2	K		Neviazhsky House Appraisal
1863	b	1226	162		1			
1865	b	1226	163		1			
1866	b	1226	164		1			
1867	b	1226	165		1			
1868	b	1226	166, 1855		1			
1868	dl	61			1	K		Jews
1869	b	1226	167, 1856		1			
1870	de					K		Supervisory Board Members, 47 pages
1870	g					K		See Grinkiskis Community.
1870	hev					K		Owned by Jews
1870	m/r					K		Merchants, New Residents
1870	tpl-a					K		
1870	b	1226	1857		1			
1870-74	k					K		
1871	b	1226	168		1			
1872	b	1226	169		1			
1873	b	1226	170		1			
1873-1915	mer					K		Many Jews, 30 files
1874	dl					K		Jews & Christians, 1150 pages
1874	fl					K		1000 pages
1874	misc					K		Jail and barn installation in the Neviazhsky home
1874	b	1226	171		1			
1874-1892	crl					K		Alphabetic
1874-1899	fl	I-61	1618		1	K		Jews
1874-1907	fl	I-61	1619		1	K		Jews
1874-1908	fl	I-61	1615		1	K		Jews
1874-1908	fl	I-61	1620		1	K		Jews
1874-78	k					K		
1875	b	1226	172		1			
1875-1916	dl							
1876	b	1226	173		1			
1877	b	1226	1003		1			
1878	b	1226	1004		1			
1879	b	1226	1005, 1862		1			
1880	b	1226	1006, 1863		1			
1881	b	1226	174, 1865		1			
1881	m	1226	1866		1			
1882	b	1226	1007, 1867		1			
1882	m	1226	1866		1			
1883	b	1226	1008, 1868		1			
1883	m	1226	1866		1			
1884	b	1226	1009, 1870		1			
1884	m	1226	1869		1			
1885	b	1226	1010, 1872		1			
1885	m	1226	1869		1			
1886	b	1226	1011, 1874		1			
1886	m	1226	1869		1			
1887	b	1226	1012, 1876		1			
1887	m	1226	1869		1			
1887	fl	I-196	4		1	K		
1888	b	1226	1293, 1879		1			
1888	m	1226	1878		1			
1888-1894	ai	1226	1322		1			Alphabetic Index, Incomplete
1889	b	1226	1294, 1880		1			
1889	m	1226	1882		1			
1890	b	1226	1295, 1884		1			
1890	m	1226	1882		1			
1891	b	1226	1296		1			
1891	m	1226	1882		1			
1892	b	1226	1297, 1889		1			
1892	d	1226	1298		1			
1892	m	1226	1888		1			
1893	b	1226	1299, 1890		1			
1893	m	1226	1888		1			
1893	ai	728	361		4			Alphabetic Index, Incomplete
1893-1901	fl	I-61	1614		1	K		Jews
1893-1906	fl	I-61	1616-1617		1	K		Jews
1894	b	1226	1300, 1893, 2086		1			
1894	d	1226	1301		1			

Kaunas (Kovno) continued

Year(s)	Type	Fond	File(s)	Op	A	F	Notes
1894	m	1226	1888	1			
1895	b	1226	1302, 1895, 2086	1			
1895-1902	ai	1226	2086				Alphabetic Index, Incomplete
1896	b	1226	1991, 2086	1			
1896	d	1226	1992	1			
1897	b	1226	1993-1994, 2086	1			
1897	d	1226	1995	1			
1898	b	1226	1996, 2086	1			
1898	d	1226	1997	1			
1899	b	1226	1998, 2086	1			
1899	d	1226	1999	1			
1900	b	1226	2000, 2086	1			
1900	d	1226	2001	1			
1901	b	1226	2002, 2086	1			
1901	d	1226	2003	1			
1901	k	61		1	K		Poor Jews, Recepients
1901-1912	p	1227					People Under Surveillance - Kovna Guberniia Gendarmie Heaquarters
1902	b	1226	2004, 2086	1			
1902	d	1226	2005	1			
1903	b	1226	2006	1			
1903	d	1226	2007	1			
1904	d	1226	2009	1			
1905	d	1226	2010	1			
1906	b	1226	2011	1			
1906	d	1226	2012	1			
1907	b	1226	2013	1			
1907	d	1226	2014	1			
1908	b	1226	2015	1			
1908	d	1226	2016	1			
1908	fl	I-61	1621	1	K		Jews
1909	cr				K		Detailed List of deceased
1909	b	1226	2017	1			
1909	d	1226	2019	1			
1910	b	1226	2020	1			
1910	d	1226	2021	1			
1911	b	1226	2022	1			
1911	d	1226	2023	1			
1912	d	1226	2024	1			
1913	b	1226	2025	1			
1913	m	1226	2026	1			
1913	d	1226	2027	1			
1914	b	1226	2028	1			
1914	m	1226	2029	1			
1914	d	1226	2030	1			
unknown	vl-j				K		2nd Congress of Kaunas Jews

Kaunas County

Year(s)	Type	Fond	File(s)	Op	A	F	Notes
1907	vl				K		6 files, State Duma
unknown	cen				K		20-21 Year old Jews

Kaunas Guberniia

Year(s)	Type	Fond	File(s)	Op	A	F	Notes
1897	rs	768					Population Lists

Kaunas Guberniya

Year(s)	Type	Fond	File(s)	Op	A	F	Notes
1852	dl				K		Full List, Jews
1870	can				K		Paid by Jews only
1870	ml				K		Draftee Documents, 1300 Pages
1870	prb				K		600 pages
1874	ml				K		Draftee Petitions, Jews, 108 Pages
1874	txp				K		Paid by Jews
1901-1914	tpl-l				K		
1915	rc				K		700 files

Kavarskas

Year(s)	Type	Fond	File(s)	Op	A	F	Notes
1858	rs						
1879	rs						

Kedainiai (Keidan)

Those items with a Flag code of "10" are birth records that are collectively convered by files: 54, 68, 70, 73, 79, 81, 84, 87, 90, 93, 96, 98, 99, 102 and 104. Those items with a Flag code of "11" and marriage records that are collectively covered by files 50, 51, 55, 58, 62 and 65. Those items with a Flag code of "12" and divorce records that are collectively covered by files 52, 56, 59, 63, 66, 71, 74, 75, 76, 77, 80, 81, 82, 85, 88, 91, 100, 101 and 103. Those items with a Flag code of "13" and divorce records that are collectively covered by files 53, 57, 60, 64, 67, 69, 72, 78, 83, 86, 89, 92 and 95.

Year(s)	Type	Fond	File(s)	Op	A	F	Notes
1816	rs						
1834	rs						
1822	b	1226	1485	1			
1838	m	1226	1553	1			
1848	b	1226	1489	1			
1849	m	1226	1555	1			
1851	b	1226	1490	1			
1852	b	1226	1491	1			
1854	b	1226	1496	1			
1854	m	1226	1557	1			
1854	v	1226	1649	1			
1855	m	1226	1559	1			
1855	v	1226	1650	1			

Kedainiai (Keidan) continued

Year(s)	Type	Fond	File(s)	Op	A	F	Notes
1855	d	1226	1748	1			
1856	b	1226	1499	1			
1856	v	1226	1651	1			
1856	d	1226	1751	1			
1857	b	1226	1500	1			
1857	v	1226	1652	1			
1858	b	1226	1501	1			
1858	v	1226	1654	1			
1858	d	1226	1747	1			
1859	b	1226	1502	1			
1859	m	1226	1565	1			
1859	v	1226	1656	1			
1860	b	1226	1503	1			
1860	m	1226	1566	1			
1861	m	1226	1568	1			
1861	v	1226	1660	1			
1861	d	1226	1757	1			
1862	b	1226	1506	1			
1862	v	1226	1662	1			
1862	d	1226	1759	1			
1863	b	1226	1507	1			
1863	v	1226	1663	1			
1863	d	1226	1761	1			
1864	v	1226	1664	1			
1864	d	1226	1763	1			
1865	b	1226	1508	1			
1865	m	1226	1573	1			
1865	v	1226	1666	1			
1866	b	1226	1509	1			
1866	v	1226	1668	1			
1866	d	1226	1765	1			
1867	b	1226	1510	1			
1867	m	1226	1576	1			
1867	v	1226	1669	1			
1867	d	1226	1766	1			
1868	b	1226	1511	1			
1868	m	1226	1578	1			
1868	v	1226	1671	1			
1868	d	1226	1768	1			
1868	dl	61		1	K		
1869	b	1226	1512	1			
1869	m	1226	1580	1			
1869	v	1226	1673	1			
1869	d	1226	1769	1			
1870	b	1226	1513	1			
1870	m	1226	1582	1			
1870	v	1226	1675	1			
1870	d	1226	1770	1			
1870-74	k				K		
1871	dl				K		
1871	b	1226	1514	1			
1871	m	1226	1584	1			
1871	v	1226	1677	1			
1871	d	1226	1771	1			
1872	dl				K		
1872	m	1226	1586	1			
1872	v	1226	1679	1			
1872	d	1226	1772	1			
1873	b	1226	1516	1			
1873	m	1226	1589	1			
1873	v	1226	1681	1			
1873	d	1226	1774	1			
1874	fl				K		
1874	b	1226	1517	1			
1874	m	1226	1592	1			
1874	v	1226	1684	1			
1874	d	1226	1776	1			
1874	fl	I-61	1626A-1626B, 1642	1	K		Index of Jews
1874-78	k				K		
1875	b	1226	1518	1			
1875	m	1226	1595	1			
1875	v	1226	1687	1			
1875	d	1226	1779	1			
1876	b	1226	1519	1			
1876	m	1226	1598	1			
1876	v	1226	1690	1			
1876	d	1226	1782	1			
1877	b	1226	1520	1			
1877	m	1226	1601	1			
1877	v	1226	1693	1			
1877	d	1226	1784	1			
1878	b	1226	1521	1			
1878	m	1226	1603	1			
1878	v	1226	1696	1			
1878	d	1226	1788	1			
1879	b	1226	1523	1			
1879	m	1226	1605	1			
1879	m	1226	1605	1			

Kedainiai (Keidan) continued

Year(s)	Type	Fond	File(s)	Op	A	F	Notes
1879	v	1226	1698	1			
1879	v	1226	1698	1			
1879	d	1226	1790	1			
1879	d	1226	1790	1			
1880	b	1226	1524	1			
1880	b	1226	1524	1			
1880	m	1226	1608	1			
1880	m	1226	1608	1			
1880	v	1226	1700	1			
1880	v	1226	1700	1			
1880	d	1226	1792	1			
1880	d	1226	1792	1			
1881	b	1226	1526	1			
1881	b	1226	1526	1			
1881	m	1226	1611	1			
1881	m	1226	1611	1			
1881	v	1226	1702	1			
1881	v	1226	1702	1			
1881	d	1226	1794	1			
1881	d	1226	1794	1			
1882	b	1226	1528	1			
1882	b	1226	1528	1			
1882	m	1226	1614	1			
1882	m	1226	1614	1			
1882	v	1226	1705	1			
1882	v	1226	1705	1			
1882	d	1226	1796	1			
1883	b	1226	1530	1			
1883	m	1226	1617	1			
1883	v	1226	1708	1			
1883	d	1226	1798	1			
1884	b	1226	1532	1			
1884	m	1226	1620	1			
1884	v	1226	1711	1			
1884	d	1226	1802	1			
1885	b	1226	1534	1			
1885	m	1226	1622	1			
1885	v	1226	1715	1			
1885	d	1226	1804	1			
1886	b	1226	1535	1			
1886	m	1226	1626	1			
1886	v	1226	1717	1			
1886	d	1226	1806	1			
1887	b	1226	1537	1			
1887	m	1226	1629	1			
1887	v	1226	1719	1			
1887	d	1226	1808-1809	1			
1887	hol	I-203	1	1	K		
1888	b	1226	1539	1			
1888	m	1226	1631	1			
1888	v	1226	1722	1			
1888	d	1226	1811	1			
1889	m	1226	1634	1			
1889	v	1226	1725	1			
1890	m	1226	1638	1			
1890	v	1226	1727	1			
1890	d	1226	1814	1			
1891	m	1226	1640	1			
1891	v	1226	1730	1			
1891	d	1226	1817	1			
1892	b	1226	1546	1			
1892	m	1226	1642	1			
1892	v	1226	1733	1			
1892	d	1226	1820	1			
1893	m	1226	1644	1			
1893	v	1226	1735	1			
1893	d	1226	1823	1			
1894	m	1226	1646	1			
1894	v	1226	1739	1			
1894	d	1226	1826	1			
1895	b	1226	1550	1			
1895	m	1226	1647	1			
1895	v	1226	1741	1			
1895	d	1226	1827	1			
1896	d	1226		2		13	
1896	m	1226		2		11	
1896	v	1226		2		12	
1897	b	1226		2		10	
1897	d	1226		2		13	
1897	m	1226		2		11	
1897	v	1226		2		12	
1898	d	1226		2		13	
1898	m	1226		2		11	
1898	v	1226		2		12	
1899	b	1226		2		10	
1899	d	1226		2		13	
1899	m	1226		2		11	
1899	v	1226		2		12	

Kedainiai (Keidan) continued

Year(s)	Type	Fond	File(s)		Op	A	F	Notes
1900	d	1226			2		13	
1900	m	1226			2		11	
1900	v	1226			2		12	
1901	b	1226			2		10	
1901	d	1226			2		13	
1901	v	1226			2		12	
1902	b	1226			2		10	
1902	d	1226			2		13	
1902	v	1226			2		12	
1903	b	1226			2		10	
1903	d	1226			2		13	
1903	m	1226			2		11	
1903	v	1226			2		12	
1904	b	1226			2		10	
1904	d	1226			2		13	
1904	v	1226			2		12	
1905	b	1226			2		10	
1905	d	1226			2		13	
1905	v	1226			2		12	
1906	b	1226			2		10	
1906	d	1226			2		13	
1906	v	1226			2		12	
1907	b	1226			2		10	
1907	d	1226			2		13	
1907	v	1226			2		12	
1908	b	1226			2		10	
1908	d	1226			2		13	
1908	v	1226			2		12	
1909	b	1226			2		10	
1909	d	1226			2		13	
1909	v	1226			2		12	
1910	b	1226			2		10	
1910	d	1226			2		13	
1910	v	1226			2		12	
1911	b	1226			2		10	
1911	d	1226			2		13	
1911	v	1226			2		12	
1912	b	1226			2		10	
1912	d	1226			2		13	
1912	v	1226			2		12	
1913	b	1226			2		10	
1913	d	1226			2		13	
1913	v	1226			2		12	
1914	b	1226			2		10	
1914	d	1226			2		13	
1914	v	1226			2		12	
unknown	fl					K		

Kelme (Kelem)

Year(s)	Type	Fond	File(s)		Op	A	F	Notes
1806	rs	91	441			A		
1811	rs							Town Property Inventory - Probably Estates Only
1834	rs							srs of Kelme Estate
1837	rs							
1843	rs							srs of Kelme Estate
1851	rs	515	1086		15			
1863-1878	rs	1262	83		1			
1873	rs							
1795-1799	resl							Nationality unlisted
1832		91	449			A		Town Property Inventory - Probably Estates Only
1843								Alphabetic List of Kelme Estate Residents; no Jews!
1891	tpl	91	387			A		
1895	cen							

Kelme & region (Kelem)

Year(s)	Type	Fond	File(s)		Op	A	F	Notes
1816	rs							Estate Resident List

Kernave (Kernave)

Year(s)	Type	Fond	File(s)		Op	A	F	Notes
1870	b	728	139		3			
1873	b	728	1030		3		2	
1873	m	728	142, 144		3		2	
1873	d	728	146		3		2	
1874	b	728	148-149		3		2	
1874	m	728	150-151		3		2	
1874	d	728	152, 341		3		2	
1875	b	728	153-154		3		2	
1875	m	728	155-156		3		2	
1875	d	728	157-158		3		2	
1876	b	728	1035		3		2	
1876	m	728	1074		3		2	
1876	d	728	1124		3		2	
1877	b	728	1041		3		2	
1877	m	728	1075-1076		3		2	
1877	d	728	1128		3		2	
1878	b	728	1049		3		2	
1878	m	728	1078		3		2	

Kernave (Kernave) continued

Year(s)	Type	Fond	File(s)	Op	A	F	Notes
1878	d	728	1134	3		2	
1891	b	728	1445	3		2	
1891	m	728	1482	3		2	
1892	b	728	1484	3		2	
1893	b	728	1491	3		2	
1893	m	728	1495	3		2	
1894	b	728	1498	3		2	
1894	b	728	1501	3		2	
1894	m	728	1504	3		2	
1895	m	728	1481	3		2	
1895	b	728	1510	3		2	
1896	m	728	10	4		2	
1896	b	728	9	4		2	
1897	b	728	23	4		2	
1897	m	728	23	4		2	
1898	b	728	40	4		2	
1898	m	728	41	4		2	
1898	v	728	42	4		2	
1899	b	728	56	4		2	
1899	m	728	57	4		2	
1900	b	728	68	4		2	
1900	m	728	69	4		2	
1900	d	728	75	4		2	
1901	d	728	75, 83	4		2	
1901	b	728	81-82	4		2	
1902	b	728	96	4		2	
1902	m	728	97	4		2	
1902	d	728	98	4		2	
1903	b	728	109	4		2	
1903	m	728	110	4		2	
1903	d	728	111	4		2	
1904	b	728	122	4		2	
1904	m	728	123	4		2	
1904	d	728	124	4		2	
1905	b	728	135	4		2	
1905	m	728	136	4		2	
1905	v	728	137	4		2	
1905	d	728	75	4		2	
1906	b	728	147	4		2	
1906	m	728	148	4		2	
1906	v	728	149	4		2	
1906	d	728	75	4		2	
1907	b	728	159	4		2	
1907	d	728	75	4		2	
1908	m	728	170	4		2	
1908	d	728	75	4		2	
1909	b	728	181	4		2	
1909	m	728	182	4		2	
1909	v	728	183	4		2	
1909	d	728	75	4		2	
1910	b	728	195	4		2	
1910	m	728	196	4		2	
1911	b	728	209	4		2	
1911	m	728	210	4		2	
1912	m	728	223	4		2	
1913	m	728	236	4		2	
1914	b	728	249	4		2	
1914	m	728	250	4		2	

Klykoliai

Year(s)	Type	Fond	File(s)	Op	A	F	Notes
1858	rs						
1866-69	rs						
1864	ml	1250	836	1			Jewish Residents, Military Commander of Siauliai County
1912-1916	tpl-r				K		

Knyszyn, Poland (Knysinas)

Year(s)	Type	Fond	File(s)	Op	A	F	Notes
1871	m	728	1124	1			

Krakes

Year(s)	Type	Fond	File(s)	Op	A	F	Notes
1816	rs						
1874	rs	I-61	1651	1	K		Alphabetic - Jews
1870-74	k				K		
1874-78	k				K		
1877	fl	J-199	1	1	K		
1889	fl	199			K		

Krakiai (Krok)

Year(s)	Type	Fond	File(s)	Op	A	F	Notes
1844	b	728	12	1			
1844	m	728	14	1			
1844	d	728	21	1			
1854	d	728	117	1			
1854	b	728	35	1			
1854	m	728	80	1			
1854	v	728	94	1			
1855	b	728	137	1			
1855	m	728	153	1			
1855	v	728	174	1			

			Page(s)	Op
				1
				1
				1
				1
				1
				1
				1
				1
				1
			, 416	1
				1
				1
			, 500	1
				1
				1
				1
				1
				1
				1
				1
				1
				1
				1
				1
m				1
984	d	728		1
1865	v	1226	175	1
1865	d	1226	176	1
1866	d	1226	170	1
1866	m	1226	177	1
1866	v	1226	178, 181	1
1867	m	1226	180	1
1867	d	1226	182	1
1868	m	1226	183	1
1868	v	1226	184	1
1868	d	1226	185	1
1869	m	1226	186	1
1869	v	1226	187	1
1869	d	1226	188	1
1870	m	1226	189	1
1870	v	1226	190	1
1870	d	1226	191	1
1871	m	1226	192	1
1871	v	1226	193	1
1871	d	1226	194	1
1872	m	1226	195	1
1872	v	1226	196	1
1872	d	1226	197	1
1873	m	1226	198	1
1873	v	1226	199	1
1873	d	1226	200	1
1874	m	1226	201	1
1874	v	1226	202	1
1874	d	1226	203	1
1875	m	1226	204	1
1875	v	1226	205	1
1875	d	1226	206	1
1876	m	1226	1013	1
1876	d	1226	1018	1
1876	v	1226	1022	1
1877	m	1226	1014	1
1877	d	1226	1019	1
1877	v	1226	207	1
1878	m	1226	1015	1
1878	v	1226	1023	1
1879	m	1226	1016	1
1879	d	1226	1020	1
1879	v	1226	1024	1
1880	m	1226	1017	1
1880	d	1226	1021	1
1880	v	1226	1025	1
1881	b	1226	2031	1
1882	b	1226	2031	1
1883	b	1226	2031	1
1884	b	1226	2031	1
1885	b	1226	2031	1
1886	b	1226	2031	1
1887	b	1226	2031	1
1888	b	1226	2031	1
1889	b	1226	2031	1
1890	b	1226	2031	1
1891	b	1226	1543, 2031	1
1892	b	1226	1544, 2031	1

Krakiai (Krok) continued
1893	b	1226	1547, 2031	1
1894	b	1226	1548, 2031	1
1895	b	1226	1551, 2031	1
1896	b	1226	2031	1
1896	b	1226	n/a	2
1897	b	1226	2031	1
1897	b	1226	n/a	2
1898	b	1226	2031	1
1898	b	1226	n/a	2
1899	b	1226	2031	1
1899	b	1226	n/a	2
1900	b	1226	2031	1
1900	b	1226	n/a	2
1901	b	1226	2031	1
1901	b	1226	n/a	2
1902	b	1226	2031	1
1902	b	1226	n/a	2
1903	b	1226	2031	1
1903	b	1226	n/a	2
1904	b	1226	2031	1
1904	b	1226	n/a	2
1905	b	1226	2031	1
1905	b	1226	n/a	2
1906	b	1226	2031	1
1906	b	1226	n/a	2
1907	b	1226	2031	1
1907	b	1226	n/a	2
1908	b	1226	2031	1
1908	b	1226	n/a	2
1909	b	1226	2031	1
1909	b	1226	n/a	2
1910	b	1226	2031	1
1910	b	1226	n/a	2
1911	b	1226	2031	1
1911	b	1226	n/a	2
1912	b	1226	2031	1
1912	b	1226	n/a	2
1913	b	1226	2031	1
1913	d	1226	n/a	2
1913	m	1226	n/a	2
1914	b	1226	2031	1
1914	d	1226	n/a	2
1914	m	1226	n/a	2

Krasna (Krosna)
1812	m	1014	194	2
1812	b	1236	49	2
1813	b	1236	50	2
1815	m	1014	195	2
1816	b	1236	51	2
1817	b	1014	196	2
1818	b	1236	52	2
1820	b	1236	53	2
1821	m	1236	54	2
1825	b	1236	55	2

Kraziai (Kruzh)
1816	rs				
1840	rs				
1851	rs				
1864	rs				
1873	rs				
1887	pib	219			K

Krekenava (Krakinova)
1816	rs				
1818	rs				
1834	rs				
1874	rs				K	Index of Jews

Kretinga (Kretinga)
| 1859 | rs | | | | |
| 1870 | rs | | | | |

Kudirkos Naumiestis (Vladislavov)
1812	b	1236	446	3
1812	d	1236	447	3
1813	b	1236	446, 448	3
1813	d	1236	447, 450	3
1813	m	1236	449	3
1814	b	1236	448, 451	3
1814	m	1236	449, 452	3
1814	d	1236	450, 453-454	3
1815	b	1236	451, 456	3
1815	m	1236	452, 457, 459	3
1815	d	1236	453-454, 458, 460	3
1816	b	1236	456, 462	3
1816	m	1236	457, 459, 465	3

Kudirkos Naumiestis (Vladislavov) continued

Year(s)	Type	Fond	File(s)	Op	A	F	Notes
1816	d	1236	458, 460, 464	3			
1817	b	1236	462, 466-467	3			
1817	d	1236	464, 470-471	3			
1817	m	1236	465, 468-469	3			
1818	b	1236	472-473	3			
1818	d	1236	474	3			
1819	d	1014	219	2			
1819	b	1236	475, 478	3			
1819	m	1236	476-477	3			
1819	d	1236	88	4			
1820	b	1236	480-481	3			
1820	m	1236	482-483	3			
1820	d	1236	484-485	3			
1821	b	1236	90	4			
1821	m	1236	92-93	4			
1821	d	1236	94	4			
1822	d	1236	101	4			
1822	b	1236	95-96	4			
1822	m	1236	98-99	4			
1823	b	1236	102-103	4			
1823	m	1236	104-105	4			
1823	d	1236	107	4			
1824	b	1236	108-109	4			
1824	d	1236	112	4			
1825	b	1236	113	4			
1825	m	1236	114-115	4			For File 114, with Catholic records.
1825	d	1236	118	4			
1827	b	1236	120	4			
1827	d	1236	120	4			
1827	m	1236	120	4			
1828	b	1236	122	4			
1828	d	1236	122	4			
1828	m	1236	122	4			
1830	b	1236	124	4			
1830	d	1236	124	4			
1830	m	1236	124	4			
1832	b	1236	127	4			
1832	d	1236	127	4			
1832	m	1236	127	4			
1833	b	1014	182	2			
1833	d	1014	182	2			
1833	m	1014	182	2			
1834	b	1236	128	4			
1834	d	1236	128	4			
1835	b	1236	128	4			
1835	d	1236	128	4			
1836	b	1236	130	4			
1836	d	1236	130	4			
1837	b	1236	132	4			
1837	d	1236	132	4			
1837	m	1236	132	4			
1844	b	1236	139	4			
1844	d	1236	139	4			
1844	m	1236	139	4			
1845	b	1236	142	4			
1845	d	1236	142	4			
1845	m	1236	142	4			
1846	b	1236	143	4			
1846	d	1236	143	4			
1846	m	1236	143	4			
1848	b	1236	149	4			
1848	d	1236	149	4			
1848	m	1236	149	4			
1850	b	1236	151	4			
1850	d	1236	151	4			
1850	m	1236	151	4			
1851	b	1108	2	1			
1851	d	1108	2	1			
1851	m	1108	2	1			
1852	b	1236	153	4			
1852	d	1236	153	4			
1852	m	1236	153	4			
1853	d	1236	155	4			
1853	m	1236	155	4			
1854	b	1236	57	1			
1854	d	1236	57	1			
1854	m	1236	57	1			
1856	b	1236	162	4			
1856	d	1236	162	4			
1856	m	1236	162	4			
1857	b	1236	163	4			
1857	d	1236	163	4			
1857	m	1236	163	4			
1860	b	1236	167	4			
1860	d	1236	167	4			
1860	m	1236	167	4			
1861	b	1236	168	4			
1861	d	1236	168	4			

Kudirkos Naumiestis (Vladislavov) continued

Year(s)	Type	Fond	File(s)	Op	A	F	Notes
1861	m	1236	168	4			
1862	b	1236	170	4			
1862	d	1236	170	4			
1862	m	1236	170	4			
1864	b	1236	171	4			
1864	d	1236	171	4			
1864	m	1236	171	4			
1865	b	1236	173	4			
1865	d	1236	173	4			
1865	m	1236	173	4			
1866	b	1236	175	4			
1866	d	1236	175	4			
1866	m	1236	175	4			
1869	b	1236	179	4			
1869	d	1236	179	4			
1869	m	1236	179	4			
1870	b	1014	184	2			From May through Dec.
1870	d	1014	184	2			
1870	m	1014	184	2			
1874	b	1236	182	4			
1874	d	1236	182	4			
1874	m	1236	182	4			

Kupiskis (Kupishok)

Year(s)	Type	Fond	File(s)	Op	A	F	Notes
1851	rs						
1858	rs	1262	16-17	1			
1874	rs	1262	21	1			
1879	rs						
1870	m	1226	1353	1			
1871	m	1226	1354	1			
1871	d	1226	1355	1			
1872	d	1226	1356	1			
1873	d	1226	1357	1			
1874	m	1226	1358	1			
1874	d	1226	1359	1			
1875	d	1226	1360	1			
1875	m	1226	1361	1			
1877	m	1226	1362	1			
1877	d	1226	1363-1364	1			
1878	m	1226	1365	1			
1878	d	1226	1366	1			
1879	m	1226	1367	1			
1879	d	1226	1368	1			
1880	m	1226	1369	1			
1880	d	1226	1370	1			
1881	m	1226	1371	1			
1881	d	1226	1372	1			
1882	m	1226	1373	1			
1883	m	1226	1374	1			
1883	d	1226	1375	1			
1884	m	1226	1376	1			
1884	d	1226	1377	1			
1885	m	1226	1378	1			
1886	d	1226	1288	1			
1886	m	1226	1379	1			
1887	m	1226	1380	1			
1888	m	1226	1381	1			
1888	d	1226	1382	1			
1889	m	1226	1383	1			
1889	d	1226	1384	1			
1890	m	1226	1385	1			
1890	d	1226	1386	1			
1891	m	1226	1387	1			
1891	d	1226	2094	1			
1892	m	1226	1388	1			
1892	d	1226	1389	1			
1893	m	1226	1390	1			
1894	m	1226	1391	1			
1894	d	1226	1392	1			
1895	m	1226	1393	1			
1895	d	1226	2094	1			
1896	m	1226	1394	1			
1897	m	1226	1395	1			
1897	v	1226	1396	1			
1897	d	1226	1397	1			
1898	m	1226	1398	1			
1898	d	1226	1399	1			
1898	v	1226	2095	1			
1899	m	1226	1400	1			
1899	d	1226	2094	1			
1899	v	1226	2095	1			
1900	v	1226	2095	1			
1900	b	1226	2096	1			
1900	m	1226	2097	1			
1900	d	1226	2098	1			
1901	v	1226	2095	1			
1901	m	1226	2097	1			
1902	m	1226	2097	1			

Kupiskis (Kupishok) continued

Year(s)	Type	Fond	File(s)	Op	A	F	Notes
1903	m	1226	2097	1			
1905	b	1226	2096	1			
1905	m	1226	2097	1			
1906	b	1226	2096	1			
1906	m	1226	2097	1			
1906	d	1226	2098	1			
1907	b	1226	2096	1			
1907	m	1226	2097	1			
1907	d	1226	2098	1			
1908	d	1226	2098	1			
1908	b	1226	2099	1			
1908	m	1226	2100	1			
1909	d	1226	2098	1			
1909	b	1226	2099	1			
1909	m	1226	2100	1			
1910	d	1226	2098	1			
1910	b	1226	2099	1			
1910	m	1226	2100	1			
1911	d	1226	2098	1			
1911	b	1226	2099	1			
1911	m	1226	2100	1			
1912	m	1226	2100	1			
1912	b	1226	2101	1			
1912	d	1226	2102	1			
1913	m	1226	2100	1			
1913	b	1226	2101	1			
1913	d	1226	2102	1			
1914	m	1226	2100	1			
1914	b	1226	2101	1			
1914	d	1226	2102	1			

Kurenets

Year(s)	Type	Fond	File(s)	Op	A	F	Notes
1851	rs	515	946	15			srs
1858	rs	515	1053	15			Alphabetical - Jews

Kursenai

Year(s)	Type	Fond	File(s)	Op	A	F	Notes
1852	rs						
1858	rs						
1866-69	rs						
unknown	resl	223				K	

Kvedarna

Year(s)	Type	Fond	File(s)	Op	A	F	Notes
1816	rs						
1842	rs						
1851	rs						
1870?	rs						

Laibiskis (Leibishok) Items for this town are in the Vilnius County 4th Okrug Registers.

Year(s)	Type	Fond	File(s)	Op	A	F	Notes
1885	m	728	353	4			
1886	m	728	353	4			
1887	m	728	353	4			
1887	b	728	364	4			
1888	m	728	353	4			
1888	b	728	364	4			
1889	m	728	353	4			
1889	b	728	364	4			
1890	m	728	353	4			
1890	b	728	364	4			
1891	m	728	353	4			
1891	b	728	364	4			
1892	m	728	353	4			
1892	b	728	364	4			
1893	m	728	353	4			
1893	b	728	364	4			
1894	m	728	353	4			
1894	b	728	364	4			
1895	v	728	3	4			
1895	m	728	353	4			
1895	b	728	364	4			
1896	b	728	13, 364	4			
1896	m	728	14, 353	4			
1897	b	728	28-29, 364	4			
1897	m	728	30, 353, 437	4			
1897	d	728	32	4			
1898	b	728	28, 45, 364	4			
1898	d	728	32	4			
1898	m	728	46, 353, 437	4			
1899	b	728	28, 60, 364	4			
1899	v	728	3	4			
1899	d	728	32	4			
1899	m	728	61, 353, 437	4			
1900	v	728	3	4			
1900	b	728	72, 364	4			
1900	m	728	73-74, 353, 437	4			
1900	d	728	75	4			
1901	v	728	3, 88	4			
1901	d	728	75	4			
1901	b	728	86, 364	4			

Laibiskis (Leibishok) continued
1901	m	728	87, 353, 437	4			
1902	m	728	102, 353, 438	4			
1902	d	728	103, 439	4			
1902	b	728	364	4			
1903	b	728	114-115, 364	4			
1903	m	728	116, 353, 438, 444	4			
1903	d	728	117, 439	4			
1904	b	728	127, 364	4			
1904	m	728	128, 353, 438	4			
1904	d	728	129, 439	4			
1905	b	728	139, 364	4			
1905	m	728	140, 353, 438	4			
1905	d	728	75, 141, 439	4			
1906	b	728	151, 364, 441	4			
1906	m	728	152, 353	4			
1906	d	728	75, 153	4			
1907	b	728	161, 364, 441	4			
1907	m	728	162, 353	4			
1907	v	728	3	4			
1907	d	728	75	4			
1908	b	728	172, 364, 441	4			
1908	v	728	3, 173	4			
1908	m	728	353	4			
1908	d	728	75	4			
1909	b	728	187, 364	4			
1909	v	728	3, 188	4			
1909	m	728	353, 442	4			
1909	d	728	75	4			
1910	b	728	199, 364	4			
1910	v	728	3, 200	4			
1910	m	728	353, 443	4			
1911	b	728	213, 364	4			
1911	m	728	214, 353	4			
1911	v	728	215	4			
1912	b	728	226, 364	4			
1912	m	728	227-228, 353	4			
1913	b	728	239, 364	4			
1913	m	728	240, 353	4			
1914	b	728	253, 364	4			
1914	m	728	253-254, 353	4			
1914	v	728	255	4			
1915	m	728	353	4			
1915	b	728	364	4			
1916	b	728	364	4			
1917	b	728	364	4			
1917	b	728	364	4			
1918	b	728	364	4			
1919	b	728	364	4			
1920	b	728	364	4			
1921	b	728	364	4			

Laizuva
| 1858 | rs | | | | | | |

Leckava
1858	rs						
1866	rs						
1912-1916	tpl-r				K		

Leipalingis (Laipun)
1808	m	1236	1	29			
1809	m	1236	1-2	29			
1809	d	1236	3	29			
1810	m	1236	2, 4	29			
1810	d	1236	3, 12	29			
1811	d	1236	12	29			
1811	m	1236	4	29			
1812	d	1236	13	29			
1812	m	1236	5	29			
1813	m	1236	6	29			
1814	m	1236	7	29			
1814	d	1236	8	29			
1815	d	1236	10	29			
1815	m	1236	9	29			
1816	d	1236	11	29			
1819	d	1236	14	29			

Liatzkava
| 1858 | rs | | | | | | |
| 1866 | rs | | | | | | |

Linkuva (Linkova)
1816	rs						
1818	rs	515	425	25			
1834-35	rs	515	427, 431	25			
1858-71	rs	I-214	1	1	K		Jews
1857-71	ta						
1859	b	728	420	1			

Linkuva (Linkova) continued

Year(s)	Type	Fond	File(s)		Op	A	F	Notes
1862	b	728	693		1			
1864	m	728	898		1			
1865	b	1226	473		1			
1865	m	1226	474		1			
1865	v	1226	475		1			
1865	d	1226	476		1			
1866	b	1226	477		1			
1866	m	1226	478		1			
1866	v	1226	479		1			
1866	d	1226	480		1			
1867	b	1226	481		1			
1867	v	1226	482		1			
1867	d	1226	483		1			
1868	b	1226	484		1			
1868	v	1226	485		1			
1868	d	1226	486		1			
1869	b	1226	487		1			
1869	m	1226	488		1			
1869	v	1226	489		1			
1869	d	1226	490		1			
1870	b	1226	491		1			
1870	m	1226	492		1			
1870	v	1226	493		1			
1870	d	1226	494		1			
1871	b	1226	495		1			
1871	m	1226	496		1			
1871	v	1226	497		1			
1871	d	1226	498		1			
1872	b	1226	499		1			
1872	m	1226	500		1			
1872	v	1226	501		1			
1872	d	1226	502		1			
1873	b	1226	503		1			
1873	m	1226	504		1			
1873	v	1226	505		1			
1873	d	1226	506		1			
1874	b	1226	507		1			
1874	m	1226	508		1			
1874	v	1226	509		1			
1874	d	1226	510		1			
1875	b	1226	511		1			
1875	m	1226	512		1			
1875	v	1226	513		1			
1875	d	1226	514		1			
1876	b	1226	1058		1			
1876	m	1226	1063		1			
1876	v	1226	1068		1			
1876	d	1226	1074		1			
1877	b	1226	1059		1			
1877	m	1226	1064		1			
1877	v	1226	1069		1			
1877	d	1226	1075		1			
1878	b	1226	1060		1			
1878	m	1226	1065		1			
1878	v	1226	1070		1			
1878	d	1226	1076		1			
1879	b	1226	1061		1			
1879	m	1226	1066		1			
1879	v	1226	1071		1			
1879	d	1226	1077		1			
1880	b	1226	1062		1			
1880	m	1226	1067		1			
1880	v	1226	1072		1			
1880	d	1226	1078		1			
1883	fl					K		
1883	fl	I-214	4		1	K		Jews
1905-1913	dl					K		
1908	fl					K		
1908	fl	I-214	8		1	K		Alphabetic - Jews
1908	fl	I-214	9		1	K		

Lioliai

Year(s)	Type	Fond	File(s)		Op	A	F	Notes
1816	rs							
1839	rs							

Liskiava (Lishkova)

Year(s)	Type	Fond	File(s)		Op	A	F	Notes
1808	b	1236	3		24			
1808	d	1236	4		24			
1809	b	1236	3		24			
1809	d	1236	4		24			
1810	b	1236	5		24			
1810	m	1236	7		24			
1810	d	1236	8		24			
1811	b	1236	5, 10		24			
1811	m	1236	7, 11		24			
1811	d	1236	8, 12		24			
1812	b	1236	10		24			
1812	m	1236	11		24			

Liskiava (Lishkova) continued

Year(s)	Type	Fond	File(s)	Op
1812	d	1236	12	24
1815	b	1236	13	24
1815	m	1236	14	24
1815	d	1236	15	24
1816	b	1236	13	24
1816	m	1236	14	24
1816	d	1236	15	24
1817	b	1236	16	24
1817	m	1236	17	24
1817	d	1236	18	24
1818	b	1236	19	24
1818	m	1236	20	24
1818	d	1236	21	24
1819	b	1236	22	24
1819	m	1236	23	24
1819	d	1236	24	24
1820	d	1236	25	24
1820	m	1236	26	24
1820	b	1236	27	24
1821	b	1236	28	24
1821	m	1236	29	24
1822	b	1236	30	24
1822	m	1236	31	24
1822	d	1236	32	24
1823	b	1236	33	24
1823	m	1236	34	24
1823	d	1236	35	24
1824	b	1236	36	24
1824	m	1236	37	24
1824	d	1236	38	24
1825	b	1236	39	24
1825	m	1236	40	24

Liudvinavas

Year(s)	Type
unknown	rs

Luksiai (Lukshi)

Year(s)	Type	Fond	File(s)	Op
1814	m	1236	267	3
1814	d	1236	268	3
1815	m	1236	267	3
1815	b	1236	269	3
1815	d	1236	271	3
1816	b	1236	269	3
1816	m	1236	270	3
1816	d	1236	273	3
1817	b	1236	272	3
1817	m	1236	274	3
1817	d	1236	275	3
1818	b	1236	277	3
1818	m	1236	278	3
1818	d	1236	279	3
1819	b	1236	280	3
1820	m	1236	283	3
1820	d	1236	284	3
1820	b	1236	285	3
1821	b	1236	287	3
1823	b	1236	289	3
1823	m	1236	290	3
1824	m	1236	293	3
1824	d	1236	294	3
1825	b	1236	295	3
1825	m	1236	296	3
1825	d	1236	298	3

Luoke

Year(s)	Type
1858	rs
1866	rs

Lyduvenai

Year(s)	Type
1851	rs

Lygumai

Year(s)	Type
1816	rs
1818	rs
1858	rs
1866	rs

Lygumos

Year(s)	Type	Fond	File(s)	Op	A	F	Notes
1908	fl	224				K	

Maisogola (Maishigola) Items for this town are in the Vilnius County 2nd Okrug Registers.

Year(s)	Type	Fond	File(s)	Op
1873	b	728	1030	3
1873	m	728	142, 144	3
1873	d	728	146	3
1874	b	728	148-149	3
1874	m	728	150-151	3
1874	d	728	152, 341	3
1875	b	728	153-154	3

Maisogola (Maishigola) continued

Year(s)	Type	Fond	File(s)	Op
1875	m	728	155-156	3
1875	d	728	157-158	3
1876	b	728	1035	3
1876	m	728	1074	3
1876	d	728	1124	3
1877	b	728	1041	3
1877	m	728	1075-1076	3
1877	d	728	1128	3
1878	b	728	1049	3
1878	m	728	1078	3
1878	d	728	1134	3
1891	b	728	1445	3
1891	m	728	1482	3
1892	b	728	1484	3
1893	b	728	1491	3
1893	m	728	1495	3
1894	b	728	1498	3
1894	b	728	1501	3
1894	m	728	1504	3
1895	m	728	1481	3
1895	b	728	1510	3
1896	m	728	10	4
1896	b	728	9	4
1897	b	728	23	4
1897	m	728	23	4
1898	b	728	40	4
1898	m	728	41	4
1898	v	728	42	4
1899	b	728	56	4
1899	m	728	57	4
1900	b	728	68	4
1900	m	728	69	4
1900	d	728	75	4
1901	d	728	75, 83	4
1901	b	728	81-82	4
1902	b	728	96	4
1902	m	728	97	4
1902	d	728	98	4
1903	b	728	109	4
1903	m	728	110	4
1903	d	728	111	4
1904	b	728	122	4
1904	m	728	123	4
1904	d	728	124	4
1905	b	728	135	4
1905	m	728	136	4
1905	v	728	137	4
1905	d	728	75	4
1906	b	728	147	4
1906	m	728	148	4
1906	v	728	149	4
1906	d	728	75	4
1907	b	728	159	4
1907	d	728	75	4
1908	m	728	170	4
1908	d	728	75	4
1909	b	728	181	4
1909	m	728	182	4
1909	v	728	183	4
1909	d	728	75	4
1910	b	728	195	4
1910	m	728	196	4
1911	b	728	209	4
1911	m	728	210	4
1912	m	728	223	4
1913	m	728	236	4
1914	b	728	249	4
1914	m	728	250	4

Marijampole (Mariampole)

Year(s)	Type	Fond	File(s)	Op
1808	d	1236	331	3
1809	d	1236	331	3
1810	d	1236	331, 333	3
1810	m	1236	332	3
1811	m	1236	332	3
1811	d	1236	333	3
1811	b	1236	334	3
1812	b	1236	334-335	3
1812	m	1236	336	3
1812	d	1236	337-338	3
1813	d	1236	338, 341	3
1813	b	1236	339	3
1813	m	1236	340	3
1814	b	1236	339, 342	3
1814	d	1236	341, 345	3
1814	m	1236	343-344	3
1815	b	1236	342, 346	3
1815	m	1236	344, 347	3

Marijampole (Mariampole) continued

Year(s)	Type	Fond	File(s)	Op
1815	d	1236	345, 348	3
1816	b	1236	346, 352	3
1816	d	1236	348, 351	3
1816	m	1236	349-350	3
1817	m	1236	350, 355-356	3
1817	d	1236	351, 357	3
1817	b	1236	353-354	3
1818	b	1236	358-359	3
1818	m	1236	360	3
1818	d	1236	361	3
1819	b	1236	362	3
1819	m	1236	363	3
1819	d	1236	365	3
1820	b	1236	366	3
1820	m	1236	367	3
1820	d	1236	368	3
1821	b	1236	369	3
1821	m	1236	370	3
1822	b	1236	371	3
1822	m	1236	372	3
1822	d	1236	373	3
1823	d	1014	212	2
1823	b	1108	3	1
1823	b	1236	374	3
1823	m	1236	375	3
1824	b	1236	377	3
1824	m	1236	378	3
1824	d	1236	379	3
1825	b	1236	380	3
1825	m	1236	381	3
1825	d	1236	382	3
1826	b	1236	383	3
1826	d	1236	383	3
1826	m	1236	383	3
1827	b	1236	386	3
1827	d	1236	386	3
1827	m	1236	386	3
1828	b	1236	387	3
1828	d	1236	387	3
1828	m	1236	387	3
1829	b	1236	388	3
1829	d	1236	388	3
1829	m	1236	388	3
1830	b	1236	389	3
1830	d	1236	389	3
1830	m	1236	389	3
1831	b	1236	390	3
1831	d	1236	390	3
1831	m	1236	390	3
1832	b	1236	391	3
1832	d	1236	391	3
1832	m	1236	391	3
1834	b	1236	392	3
1834	d	1236	392	3
1834	m	1236	392	3
1835	b	1236	396	3
1835	d	1236	396	3
1835	m	1236	396	3
1836	b	1236	397	3
1836	d	1236	397	3
1836	m	1236	397	3
1837	b	1236	398	3
1837	d	1236	398	3
1837	m	1236	398	3
1838	b	1236	400	3
1838	d	1236	400	3
1838	m	1236	400	3
1839	b	1236	401	3
1839	d	1236	401	3
1839	m	1236	401	3
1840	b	1236	402	3
1840	d	1236	402	3
1840	m	1236	402	3
1841	b	1236	403	3
1841	d	1236	403	3
1841	m	1236	403	3
1842	b	1236	404	3
1842	d	1236	404	3
1842	m	1236	404	3
1843	b	1236	408	3
1843	d	1236	408	3
1843	m	1236	408	3
1844	b	1236	406	3
1844	d	1236	406	3
1844	m	1236	406	3
1846	b	1236	409	3
1846	d	1236	409	3
1846	m	1236	409	3

Marijampole (Mariampole) continued

Year(s)	Type	Fond	File(s)		Op	A	F	Notes
1847	b	1236	411		3			
1847	d	1236	411		3			
1847	m	1236	411		3			
1848	b	1236	412		3			
1848	d	1236	412		3			
1848	m	1236	412		3			
1849	b	1236	415		3			
1849	d	1236	415		3			
1849	m	1236	415		3			
1850	b	1236	416		3			
1850	d	1236	416		3			
1850	m	1236	416		3			
1851	b	1236	417		3			
1851	d	1236	417		3			
1851	m	1236	417		3			
1852	b	1236	418		3			
1852	d	1236	418		3			
1852	m	1236	418		3			
1853	b	1236	419		3			
1853	d	1236	419		3			
1853	m	1236	419		3			
1854	b	1236	420		3			
1854	d	1236	420		3			
1854	m	1236	420		3			
1859	b	1236	423		3			
1859	d	1236	423		3			
1859	m	1236	423		3			
1860	b	1236	425		3			
1860	d	1236	425		3			
1860	m	1236	425		3			
1863	b	1236	430		3			
1863	d	1236	430		3			
1863	m	1236	430		3			
1864	b	1236	431		3			
1864	d	1236	431		3			
1864	m	1236	431		3			
1865	b	1236	433		3			
1865	d	1236	433		3			
1865	m	1236	433		3			
1866	b	1236	434		3			
1866	d	1236	434		3			
1866	m	1236	434		3			
1867	b	1236	435		3			
1867	d	1236	435		3			
1867	m	1236	435		3			
1869	b	1236	437		3			
1869	d	1236	437		3			
1869	m	1236	437		3			
1870	b	1236	439		3			
1870	d	1236	439		3			
1870	m	1236	439		3			
1871	b	1236	441		3			
1871	d	1236	441		3			
1871	m	1236	441		3			
1872	b	1236	442		3			
1872	d	1236	442		3			
1872	m	1236	442		3			
1873	b	1236	443		3			
1873	d	1236	443		3			
1873	m	1236	443		3			
1874	b	1236	444		3			
1874	d	1236	444		3			
1874	m	1236	444		3			
1875	b	1236	445		3			
1875	d	1236	445		3			
1875	m	1236	445		3			
1876	b	1108	4		1			
1876	d	1108	4		1			
1876	m	1108	4		1			
1878	b	1108	5		1			
1878	d	1108	5		1			
1878	m	1108	5		1			
1885	b	1108	6		1			
1885	d	1108	6		1			
1885	m	1108	6		1			
1893	b	1014	217		2			
1893	d	1014	217		2			
1893	m	1014	217		2			
1899	b	1108	7		1			
1899	d	1108	7		1			
1899	m	1108	7		1			

Merkine (Merech)

Year(s)	Type	Fond	File(s)		Op	A	F	Notes
1858	rs	515	110-122		25			srs, Trakai County
1858-1905	rs							srs, Trakai County
1859	rs	515	123		25			srs, Trakai County
1860	rs	515	124		25			srs, Trakai County
1861	rs	515	124		25			srs, Trakai County

Merkine (Merech) continued

Year(s)	Type	Fond	File(s)	Op	A	F	Notes
1862	rs	515	124	25			srs, Trakai County
1863	rs	515	124	25			srs, Trakai County
1864	rs	515	125-126	25			srs, Trakai County
1865	rs	515	127	25			srs, Trakai County
1867	rs	515	128	25			srs, Trakai County
1868	rs	515	128-129	25			srs, Trakai County
1869	rs	515	129-130	25			srs, Trakai County
1870	rs	515	130-131	25			srs, Trakai County
1871	rs	515	132	25			srs, Trakai County
1872	rs	515	133	25			srs, Trakai County
1873	rs	515	133	25			srs, Trakai County
1874	rs	515	133	25			srs, Trakai County
1905	rs	515	144	25			srs, Trakai County
1906	rs	515	144	25			srs, Trakai County
1907	rs	515	144	25			srs, Trakai County
1908	rs	515	144	25			srs, Trakai County
1854	m	728	71	1			
1855	d	728	185	1			
1856	b	728	84	1			
1860	b	728	514	1			
1860	d	728	576	1			
1861	m	728	622	1			
1861	d	728	666	1			
1863	b	728	781	1			
1863	m	728	797	1			
1864	b	728	866	1			
1864	m	728	905	1			
1864	v	728	918	1			
1864	d	728	935	1			
1865	b	728	455	3			
1865	m	728	456	3			
1865	v	728	457	3			
1865	d	728	458	3			
1866	b	728	459-460	3			
1867	b	728	460	3			
1867	d	728	461	3			
1868	m	728	462	3			
1869	b	728	463	3			
1870	d	728	464	3			
1871	d	728	465	3			
1872	d	728	46, 467	3			
1872	b	728	466	3			
1873	b	728	469	3			
1873	d	728	47, 472	3			
1873	m	728	470	3			
1873	v	728	471	3			
1874	b	728	474	3			
1874	m	728	475	3			
1874	d	728	477	3			
1875	b	728	478	3			
1875	v	728	479	3			
1875	d	728	95, 480	3			
1877	b	728	1338	3			
1877	m	728	1339	3			
1877	d	728	314	4			
1881	m	728	313	4			
1883	d	728	314	4			
1884	m	728	313	4			
1884	d	728	314	4			
1885	m	728	313	4			
1885	d	728	314	4			
1886	m	728	313	4			
1886	d	728	314	4			
1887	m	728	313	4			
1887	d	728	314	4			
1888	m	728	313	4			
1888	m	728	313	4			
1889	b	728	312	4			
1889	d	728	314	4			
1890	b	728	312	4			
1890	m	728	313	4			
1890	d	728	314	4			
1891	b	728	312	4			
1891	d	728	314	4			
1892	b	728	312	4			
1892	m	728	313	4			
1892	d	728	314	4			
1893	b	728	312	4			
1893	m	728	313	4			
1893	d	728	314	4			
1894	m	728	313	4			
1894	d	728	314	4			
1895	b	728	312	4			
1895	m	728	313	4			
1896	b	728	312	4			
1896	m	728	313	4			
1896	d	728	314	4			
1897	b	728	312	4			

Merkine (Merech) continued

Year(s)	Type	Fond	File(s)	Op	A	F	Notes
1897	m	728	313	4			
1898	b	728	312	4			
1898	m	728	313	4			
1898	d	728	314	4			
1899	b	728	312	4			
1899	m	728	313	4			
1900	b	728	312	4			
1900	m	728	313	4			
1900	d	728	314	4			
1901	b	728	312	4			
1901	m	728	313	4			
1902	b	728	312	4			
1902	m	728	313	4			
1903	b	728	312	4			
1903	m	728	313	4			
1903	d	728	314	4			
1904	b	728	312	4			
1904	m	728	313	4			
1904	d	728	314	4			
1905	b	728	312	4			
1905	m	728	313	4			
1905	d	728	314	4			
1906	b	728	312	4			
1906	m	728	313	4			
1907	b	728	312	4			
1907	m	728	313	4			
1908	b	728	312	4			
1908	m	728	313	4			
1908	d	728	314	4			
1909	b	728	312	4			
1909	m	728	313	4			
1910	b	728	312	4			
1910	m	728	313	4			
1910	d	728	314	4			
1911	b	728	312	4			
1911	m	728	313	4			
1911	d	728	314	4			
1912	b	728	312	4			
1912	m	728	313	4			
1912	d	728	314	4			
1913	b	728	312	4			
1913	m	728	313	4			
1914	b	728	312	4			
1914	m	728	313	4			
1914	d	728	314	4			
1938	d	728	342	4			

Meskuiciai

Year(s)	Type	Fond	File(s)	Op	A	F	Notes
1912-1916	tpl-r				K		

Michailiskes (Mikhalishok) Those items with a Flag code of "2" are in the Vilnius County 2nd Okrug Registers. Those with a Flag code of "4" are in the Vilnius County 4th Okrug Registers. Those with a Flag code of "7" are in the Vilnius County Register.

Year(s)	Type	Fond	File(s)	Op	A	F	Notes
1816-1818	rs	515	288	25	K	7	Jews
1834	rs	515	298	25	K	7	Jews
1843-1849	rs	515	306	25	K	7	Jews
1849	rs	515	312	25	K	7	Jews
1850-1854	rs	515	273	25	K	7	Jews
1858	rs	515	285	25	K	7	Jews
unknown	rs	515	299	25	K	7	Jews
unknown	rs	515	320	25	K	7	Jews
1854	d	728	102	1			
1854	b	728	46	1			
1854	b	728	49	2			
1854	m	728	50	2			
1854	d	728	51	2			
1854	m	728	67	1			
1855	b	728	134	1			
1855	m	728	151	1			
1855	d	728	197	1			
1856	b	728	212	1			
1856	m	728	235	1			
1856	v	728	250	1			
1856	d	728	274	1			
1857	b	728	279	1			
1857	m	728	309	1			
1857	d	728	328	1			
1858	b	728	196	2			
1858	m	728	197	2			
1858	d	728	198	2			
1858	b	728	353	1			
1858	m	728	378	1			
1859	b	728	238	2			
1859	m	728	239	2			
1859	d	728	240	2			
1859	b	728	430	1			
1859	m	728	449	1			
1859	d	728	490, 495	1			
1860	b	728	280	2			

Michailiskes (Mikhalishok) continued

Year(s)	Type	Fond	File(s)	Op	A	F	Notes
1860	m	728	281	2			
1860	d	728	282	2			
1860	b	728	516	1			
1860	m	728	537	1			
1860	d	728	577	1			
1861	b	728	308	2			
1861	m	728	309	2			
1861	d	728	310	2			
1861	b	728	602	1			
1861	m	728	623	1			
1861	d	728	662	1			
1862	b	728	338	2			
1862	m	728	339	2			
1862	d	728	340	2			
1862	b	728	684	1			
1862	m	728	705	1			
1862	d	728	755	1			
1863	b	728	775, 779	1			
1863	m	728	803-804	1			
1863	d	728	842-843	1			
1863	v	728	845	1			
1864	m	728	386	2			
1864	b	728	387	2			
1864	d	728	388	2			
1864	b	728	863	1			
1864	m	728	910	1			
1864	d	728	932	1			
1865	b	728	481-482	3			
1865	m	728	483-484	3			
1865	d	728	485-486	3			
1866	b	728	487-488	3			
1866	m	728	489-490	3			
1866	d	728	491-492	3			
1867	b	728	493-494	3			
1867	m	728	495-496	3			
1867	d	728	497-498	3			
1868	b	728	499-500	3			
1868	m	728	501-502	3			
1868	d	728	503-504	3			
1869	b	728	505, 508	3			
1869	m	728	506-507	3			
1869	d	728	509-510	3			
1870	b	728	511-512	3			
1870	m	728	513-514	3			
1870	d	728	515-516	3			
1871	b	728	517-518	3			
1871	m	728	519-520, 522	3			
1871	d	728	521	3			
1872	b	728	523-524	3			
1872	m	728	525	3			
1872	d	728	526, 1401	3			
1873	b	728	1030	3		2	
1873	m	728	142	3		2	
1873	m	728	144	3		2	
1873	d	728	146	3		2	
1873	d	728	146	3		2	
1874	b	728	148-149	3		2	
1874	m	728	150-151	3		2	
1874	d	728	152, 341	3		2	
1874	d	728	152, 341	3		2	
1874	m	728	527	3			
1875	b	728	153-154	3		2	
1875	m	728	155-156	3		2	
1875	d	728	157-158	3		2	
1875	d	728	157-158	3		2	
1876	b	728	1035	3		2	
1876	m	728	1074	3		2	
1876	d	728	1124	3		2	
1876	d	728	1124	3		2	
1877	b	728	1041	3		2	
1877	m	728	1075-1076	3		2	
1877	d	728	1128	3		2	
1877	d	728	1128	3		2	
1878	b	728	1049	3		2	
1878	m	728	1078	3		2	
1878	m	728	1078	3		2	
1878	d	728	1134	3		2	
1878	d	728	1134	3		2	
1879	d	728	1521	3			
1884	b	728	1522	3			
1885	d	728	1521	3			
1885	b	728	1522	3			
1885	m	728	1522	3			
1885	m	728	353	4		4	
1886	d	728	1521	3			
1886	d	728	1521	3			
1886	b	728	1522	3			
1886	m	728	353	4		4	
1886	m	728	528	3			

Michailiskes (Mikhalishok) continued

Year(s)	Type	Fond	File(s)	Op	A	F	Notes
1887	d	728	1478	3		4	
1887	b	728	1522	3			
1887	m	728	353	4		4	
1887	b	728	364	4		4	
1888	d	728	1478	3		4	
1888	m	728	353	4		4	
1888	b	728	364	4		4	
1889	d	728	1478	3		4	
1889	m	728	353	4		4	
1889	b	728	364	4		4	
1890	d	728	1478	3		4	
1890	b	728	1479	3		4	
1890	m	728	1480	3		4	
1890	m	728	353	4		4	
1890	b	728	364	4		4	
1891	b	728	1445	3		2	
1891	b	728	1446	3		4	
1891	d	728	1478	3		4	
1891	m	728	1482	3		2	
1891	m	728	1482	3		2	
1891	m	728	1483	3		4	
1891	m	728	353	4		4	
1891	b	728	364	4		4	
1892	d	728	1478	3		4	
1892	b	728	1484	3		2	
1892	b	728	1486, 1553	3		4	
1892	m	728	1487, 1488, 1554	3		4	
1892	v	728	1489	3		4	
1892	m	728	353	4		4	
1892	b	728	364	4		4	
1893	d	728	1478	3		4	
1893	b	728	1490, 1553	3		4	
1893	b	728	1491	3		2	
1893	m	728	1494, 1554	3		4	
1893	m	728	1495	3		2	
1893	m	728	1495	3		2	
1893	v	728	1496	3		4	
1893	m	728	353	4		4	
1893	b	728	364	4		4	
1894	b	728	1498, 1501	3		2	
1894	b	728	1499, 1553	3		4	
1894	m	728	1504	3		2	
1894	m	728	1505, 1554	3		4	
1894	v	728	1516	3		4	
1894	m	728	353	4		4	
1894	b	728	364	4		4	
1895	m	728	1481	3		2	
1895	b	728	1508, 1553	3		4	
1895	b	728	1510	3		2	
1895	m	728	1513, 1556	3		4	
1895	v	728	1519	3		4	
1895	v	728	3	4		4	
1895	m	728	353	4		4	
1895	b	728	364	4		4	
1896	b	728	13, 364	4		4	
1896	m	728	14, 353	4		4	
1896	b	728	1553	3		4	
1896	m	728	1556	3		4	
1897	b	728	28-29, 364	4		4	
1897	m	728	30, 353, 437	4		4	
1897	d	728	32	4		4	
1898	b	728	28, 45, 364	4		4	
1898	d	728	32	4		4	
1898	m	728	46, 353, 437	4		4	
1899	b	728	28, 60, 364	4		4	
1899	v	728	3	4		4	
1899	d	728	32	4		4	
1899	m	728	61, 353, 437	4		4	
1900	v	728	3	4		4	
1900	b	728	72, 364	4		4	
1900	m	728	73-74, 353, 437	4		4	
1900	d	728	75	4		4	
1901	v	728	3, 88	4		4	
1901	d	728	75	4		4	
1901	b	728	86, 364	4		4	
1901	m	728	87, 353, 437	4		4	
1902	m	728	102, 353, 438	4		4	
1902	d	728	103, 439	4		4	
1902	b	728	364	4		4	
1903	b	728	114-115, 364	4		4	
1903	m	728	116, 353, 438, 444	4		4	
1903	d	728	117, 439	4		4	
1904	b	728	127, 364	4		4	
1904	m	728	128, 353, 438	4		4	
1904	d	728	129, 439	4		4	
1905	b	728	139, 364	4		4	
1905	m	728	140, 353, 438	4		4	
1905	d	728	75, 141, 439	4		4	

Michailiskes (Mikhalishok) continued

Year(s)	Type	Fond	File(s)	Op	A	F	Notes
1906	b	728	151, 364, 441	4		4	
1906	m	728	152, 353	4		4	
1906	d	728	75, 153	4		4	
1907	b	728	161, 364, 441	4		4	
1907	m	728	162, 353	4		4	
1907	v	728	3	4		4	
1907	d	728	75	4		4	
1908	d	728	1521	3			
1908	b	728	172, 364, 441	4		4	
1908	v	728	3, 173	4		4	
1908	m	728	353	4		4	
1908	d	728	75	4		4	
1909	b	728	187, 364	4		4	
1909	v	728	3, 188	4		4	
1909	m	728	353, 442	4		4	
1909	d	728	75	4		4	
1910	b	728	199, 364	4		4	
1910	v	728	3, 200	4		4	
1910	m	728	353, 443	4		4	
1911	b	728	213, 364	4		4	
1911	m	728	214, 353	4		4	
1911	v	728	215	4		4	
1912	b	728	226, 364	4		4	
1912	m	728	227-228, 353	4		4	
1913	b	728	239, 364	4		4	
1913	m	728	240, 353	4		4	
1914	b	728	253, 364	4		4	
1914	m	728	253-254, 353	4		4	
1914	v	728	255	4		4	
1915	m	728	353	4		4	
1915	b	728	364	4		4	
1916	b	728	364	4		4	
1917	b	728	364	4		4	
1917	b	728	364	4		4	
1918	b	728	364	4		4	
1919	b	728	364	4		4	
1920	b	728	364	4		4	
1921	b	728	364	4		4	
1923	d	728	1521	3			
1923	b	728	1522	3			
1923	m	728	1522	3			
1924	d	728	1521	3			
1924	b	728	1522	3			
1924	m	728	1522	3			
1925	d	728	1521	3			
1925	b	728	1522	3			
1925	m	728	1522	3			
1926	d	728	1521	3			
1926	b	728	1522	3			
1926	m	728	1522	3			
1927	d	728	1521	3			
1927	b	728	1522	3			
1927	m	728	1522	3			
1928	d	728	1521	3			
1928	b	728	1522	3			
1928	m	728	1522	3			
1929	d	728	1521	3			
1929	b	728	1522	3			
1929	m	728	1522	3			
1930	d	728	1521	3			
1930	b	728	1522	3			
1930	m	728	1522	3			
1931	d	728	1521	3			
1931	b	728	1522	3			
1931	m	728	1522	3			
1932	d	728	1521	3			
1932	b	728	1522	3			
1932	m	728	1522	3			
1933	d	728	1521	3			
1933	b	728	1522	3			
1933	m	728	1522	3			
1934	d	728	1521	3			
1934	b	728	1522	3			
1934	m	728	1522	3			
1935	d	728	1521	3			
1935	b	728	1522	3			
1935	m	728	1522	3			
1936	d	728	1521	3			
1936	b	728	1522	3			
1936	m	728	1522	3			
1937	d	728	1521	3			
1937	b	728	1522	3			
1937	m	728	1522	3			
1938	d	728	1521	3			
1938	b	728	1522	3			
1938	m	728	1522	3			
1939	d	728	1521	3			
1939	b	728	1522	3			

Michailiskes (Mikhalishok) continued

Year(s)	Type	Fond	File(s)	Op	A	F	Notes
1939	m	728	1522	3			

Moletai (Maliat) Those items with a Flag code of "3" are in the Vilnius County 3rd Okrug Registers. Those with a Flag code of "7" are in the Vilnius County Register.

Year(s)	Type	Fond	File(s)	Op	A	F	Notes
1816–1818	rs	515	288	25	K	7	Jews
1834	rs	515	298	25	K	7	Jews
1843–1849	rs	515	306	25	K	7	Jews
1849	rs	515	312	25	K	7	Jews
1850–1854	rs	515	273	25	K	7	Jews
1858	rs	515	285	25	K	7	Jews
unknown	rs	515	299	25	K	7	Jews
unknown	rs	515	320	25	K	7	Jews
1854	d	728	112–113	1			
1854	b	728	39, 40	1			
1854	m	728	61–62	1			
1855	b	728	133	1			
1855	m	728	159	1			
1855	v	728	173	1			
1855	d	728	195	1			
1856	b	728	207	1			
1856	m	728	227	1			
1856	v	728	243	1			
1856	d	728	269	1			
1857	b	728	280	1			
1857	m	728	302	1			
1857	d	728	327	1			
1858	b	728	354–355	1			
1858	m	728	366–367	1			
1858	d	728	401–402	1			
1859	b	728	431–432	1			
1859	m	728	450–451	1			
1859	v	728	468–469	1			
1859	d	728	491, 494	1			
1860	b	728	517–518	1			
1860	m	728	538–539	1			
1860	d	728	574–575	1			
1861	b	728	596–597	1			
1861	m	728	620, 624	1			
1861	d	728	660–661	1			
1862	b	728	682–683	1			
1862	m	728	716–717	1			
1862	v	728	729	1			
1862	d	728	753–754	1			
1863	b	728	778, 786	1			
1863	m	728	801–802	1			
1863	v	728	822–823	1			
1863	d	728	844, 851	1			
1864	b	728	864–865	1			
1864	m	728	911–912	1			
1864	v	728	916–917	1			
1864	d	728	933–934	1			
1865	b	728	529–530	3			
1865	m	728	531–532	3			
1865	v	728	533–534	3			
1865	d	728	535–536	3			
1866	b	728	537–538	3			
1866	m	728	539–540	3			
1866	v	728	541–542	3			
1866	d	728	543–544	3			
1867	b	728	545–546	3			
1867	m	728	547–548	3			
1867	v	728	549–550	3			
1867	d	728	551–552	3			
1868	b	728	553–554	3			
1868	m	728	555–556	3			
1868	v	728	557–558	3			
1868	d	728	559–560	3			
1869	b	728	561–562	3			
1869	m	728	563	3			
1869	d	728	564–565	3			
1870	b	728	566–567	3			
1870	m	728	568–569	3			
1870	d	728	570–571	3			
1871	b	728	572–573	3			
1871	m	728	574–575	3			
1871	v	728	576–577	3			
1871	d	728	578–579	3			
1872	b	728	580–581	3			
1872	d	728	582–583	3			
1892	b	728	1485	3		3	
1893	b	728	1492	3		3	
1893	m	728	1493	3		3	
1894	b	728	1497	3		3	
1894	m	728	1503	3		3	
1894	v	728	1515, 1517	3		3	
1895	b	728	1509	3		3	
1895	m	728	1512	3		3	
1898	d	728	315	4			
1900	d	728	315	4			

Moletai (Maliat) continued

Year(s)	Type	Fond	File(s)	Op	A	F	Notes
1901	d	728	315	4			
1902	d	728	315	4			
1905	d	728	315	4			
1906	d	728	315	4			
1907	d	728	315	4			
1908	d	728	315	4			
1909	d	728	315	4			
1910	d	728	315	4			
1911	d	728	315	4			
1912	d	728	315	4			
1913	d	728	315	4			
1914	d	728	315	4			
1915	d	728	315	4			

Musninkai (Musnik) Those items with a Flag code of "2" are in the Vilnius County 2nd Okrug Registers. Those with a Flag code of "7" are in the Vilnius County Register.

Year(s)	Type	Fond	File(s)	Op	A	F	Notes
1816-1818	rs	515	288	25	K	7	Jews
1834	rs	515	298	25	K	7	Jews
1843-1849	rs	515	306	25	K	7	Jews
1849	rs	515	312	25	K	7	Jews
1850-1854	rs	515	273	25	K	7	Jews
1858	rs	515	285	25	K	7	Jews
unknown	rs	515	299	25	K	7	Jews
unknown	rs	515	320	25	K	7	Jews
1854	d	728	114-115	1			
1854	b	728	44-45	1			
1854	m	728	65-66	1			
1855	b	728	132	1			
1855	m	728	150	1			
1855	d	728	194	1			
1856	b	728	202	1			
1856	m	728	223	1			
1856	d	728	266	1			
1857	b	728	283	1			
1857	m	728	298	1			
1857	d	728	324	1			
1858	b	728	351-352	1			
1858	d	728	409, 411	1			
1859	b	728	428-429	1			
1859	d	728	488-489	1			
1860	b	728	513, 515	1			
1860	m	728	535-536	1			
1860	d	728	578-579	1			
1861	b	728	599-600	1			
1861	m	728	630-631	1			
1861	d	728	665	1			
1862	b	728	680-681	1			
1862	m	728	714-715	1			
1862	d	728	751-752	1			
1863	b	728	776-777	1			
1863	d	728	846-847	1			
1864	b	728	861-862	1			
1864	m	728	908-909	1			
1864	d	728	930-931	1			
1865	b	728	584-585	3			
1865	d	728	586-587	3			
1866	b	728	588-589	3			
1866	m	728	590-591	3			
1866	d	728	592-593	3			
1867	b	728	594-595	3			
1867	m	728	596-597	3			
1867	d	728	598-599	3			
1868	b	728	600-601	3			
1868	m	728	602-603	3			
1868	d	728	604-606	3			
1869	b	728	607-608	3			
1869	m	728	609-610	3			
1869	d	728	611-612	3			
1870	b	728	613	3			
1870	m	728	614	3			
1870	d	728	615	3			
1871	b	728	616-617	3			
1871	m	728	618-619	3			
1871	d	728	620-621	3			
1872	b	728	622-623	3			
1872	m	728	624-625	3			
1872	d	728	626-627	3			
1873	b	728	1030	3		2	
1873	m	728	142, 144	3		2	
1873	d	728	146	3		2	
1874	b	728	148-149	3		2	
1874	m	728	150-151	3		2	
1874	d	728	152, 341	3		2	
1875	b	728	153-154	3		2	
1875	m	728	155-156	3		2	
1875	d	728	157-158	3		2	
1876	b	728	1035	3		2	
1876	m	728	1074	3		2	
1876	d	728	1124	3		2	

Year(s)	Type	Fond	File(s)	Op	A	F	Notes	Page 66

Musninkai (Musnik) continued

Year(s)	Type	Fond	File(s)	Op	A	F
1877	b	728	1041	3	2	
1877	m	728	1075-1076	3	2	
1877	d	728	1128	3	2	
1878	b	728	1049	3	2	
1878	m	728	1078	3	2	
1878	d	728	1134	3	2	
1891	b	728	1445	3	2	
1891	m	728	1482	3	2	
1892	b	728	1484	3	2	
1893	b	728	1491	3	2	
1893	m	728	1495	3	2	
1894	b	728	1498	3	2	
1894	b	728	1501	3	2	
1894	m	728	1504	3	2	
1895	m	728	1481	3	2	
1895	b	728	1510	3	2	
1896	m	728	10	4	2	
1896	b	728	9	4	2	
1897	b	728	23	4	2	
1897	m	728	23	4	2	
1898	b	728	40	4	2	
1898	m	728	41	4	2	
1898	v	728	42	4	2	
1899	b	728	56	4	2	
1899	m	728	57	4	2	
1900	b	728	68	4	2	
1900	m	728	69	4	2	
1900	d	728	75	4	2	
1901	d	728	75, 83	4	2	
1901	b	728	81-82	4	2	
1902	b	728	96	4	2	
1902	m	728	97	4	2	
1902	d	728	98	4	2	
1903	b	728	109	4	2	
1903	m	728	110	4	2	
1903	d	728	111	4	2	
1904	b	728	122	4	2	
1904	m	728	123	4	2	
1904	d	728	124	4	2	
1905	b	728	135	4	2	
1905	m	728	136	4	2	
1905	v	728	137	4	2	
1905	d	728	75	4	2	
1906	b	728	147	4	2	
1906	m	728	148	4	2	
1906	v	728	149	4	2	
1906	d	728	75	4	2	
1907	b	728	159	4	2	
1907	d	728	75	4	2	
1908	m	728	170	4	2	
1908	d	728	75	4	2	
1909	b	728	181	4	2	
1909	m	728	182	4	2	
1909	v	728	183	4	2	
1909	d	728	75	4	2	
1910	b	728	195	4	2	
1910	m	728	196	4	2	
1911	b	728	209	4	2	
1911	m	728	210	4	2	
1912	m	728	223	4	2	
1913	m	728	236	4	2	
1914	b	728	249	4	2	
1914	m	728	250	4	2	

Namajunai

Year(s)	Type	Fond	File(s)	Op	Notes
various	bdm	728	303	4	See Jieznas Record Book.

Naujadvaris (Novodvor)

Year(s)	Type	Fond	File(s)	Op
1897	d	728	1052	1
1898	d	728	967	1
1899	d	728	973	1
1900	d	728	1123	1
1900	m	728	980	1
1901	m	728	988	1
1901	d	728	991	1
1902	d	728	1002	1
1902	m	728	997	1
1903	m	728	1008	1
1903	d	728	1010	1
1904	m	728	1021	1
1905	m	728	1030	1
1906	m	728	1036	1
1908	m	728	1059	1
1909	m	728	1066	1
1910	m	728	1072	1
1911	m	728	1079	1
1912	m	728	1086	1
1913	m	728	1091	1

Naujadvaris (Novodvor) continued

Year(s)	Type	Fond	File(s)	Op	A	F	Notes
1914	m	728	1097	1			

Naujamiestis (Novigorod) Was a suburb of Vilnius. Those items with a Flag code of "7" are in the Vilnius County Register.

Year(s)	Type	Fond	File(s)	Op	A	F	Notes
1816	rs	728					
1816–1818	rs	515	288	25	K	7	Jews
1818	rs	728					
1834	rs	515	298	25	K	7	Jews
1834	rs	728					
1843–1849	rs	515	306	25	K	7	Jews
1848	rs	728					
1849	rs	515	312	25	K	7	Jews
1850–1854	rs	515	273	25	K	7	Jews
1858	rs	515	285	25	K	7	Jews
unknown	rs	515	299	25	K	7	Jews
unknown	rs	515	320	25	K	7	Jews
1854	m	728	55	2			
1854	d	728	56–57	2			
1854	b	728	672–673	3			
1855	b	728	87–88	2			
1855	m	728	89–90	2			
1855	v	728	91	2			
1855	d	728	92–93	2			
1856	b,m,d	728	120	1			
1856	b	728	120–121	2			
1856	m	728	122–123	2			
1856	v	728	124	2			
1856	d	728	125–126	2			
1857	b	728	158–159	2			
1857	m	728	160–161	2			
1857	v	728	162	2			
1857	d	728	163–164	2			
1858	b	728	199–200	2			
1858	m	728	201, 203	2			
1858	d	728	204–205	2			
1859	b	728	241–242	2			
1859	m	728	243–244	2			
1859	d	728	245	2			
1860	m	728	262, 284	2			
1860	b	728	283	2			
1860	d	728	285–286	2			
1860	b	728	674	3			
1861	b	728	320	2			
1861	m	728	321	2			
1861	d	728	322	2			
1861	b	728	674	3			
1862	b	728	341–342	2			
1862	m	728	343	2			
1862	d	728	344	2			
1862	b	728	674	3			
1863	b	728	366	2			
1863	m	728	367–368	2			
1863	b	728	674	3			
1864	m	728	202	2			
1864	b	728	389	2			
1864	b	728	674	3			
1864	m	728	675	3			
1865	b	728	674, 676	3			
1865	m	728	677	3			
1866	b	728	678, 1031	3			
1866	m	728	679–680	3			
1867	b	728	681, 1031	3			
1867	m	728	682–683	3			
1868	b	728	684, 1031	3			
1868	m	728	685	3			
1869	b	728	686, 1031	3			
1869	m	728	687–688	3			
1870	b	728	689–690	3			
1870	m	728	691–692	3			
1871	b	728	693	3			
1871	m	728	695–696	3			
1872	b	728	193, 1032	3			
1872	b	728	697	3			
1872	m	728	698–699	3			
1873	b	728	189	3			
1874	b	728	190–191	3			
1874	b	728	362, 365	4			
1875	b	728	192	3			
1875	b	728	362, 365	4			
1876	b	728	1034	3			
1876	d	728	1072–1073	3			
1876	b	728	362, 365	4			
1877	b	728	1042	3			
1877	d	728	1077–1077A	3			
1877	b	728	362, 365	4			
1878	b	728	1048	3			
1878	d	728	1083	3			
1878	b	728	362, 365	4			

Naujamiestis (Novigorod) continued

Year(s)	Type	Fond	File(s)	Op	A	F	Notes
1879	b	728	1051, 1117	3			
1879	b	728	362, 365	4			
1880	b	728	1104, 1117	3			
1880	b	728	362, 365	4			
1881	b	728	1106, 1117	3			
1881	b	728	362, 365	4			
1882	b	728	1064, 1112, 1117	3			
1882	b	728	362, 365	4			
1883	b	728	1068	3			
1883	b	728	362, 365	4			
1884	b	728	1165	3			
1884	b	728	362, 365	4			
1885	b	728	1068, 1168	3			
1885	b	728	362, 365	4			
1886	b	728	1122, 1171	3			
1886	b	728	362, 365	4			
1887	b	728	1175, 1421	3			
1887	b	728	362, 365	4			
1888	b	728	1421, 1424	3			
1888	b	728	362, 365	4			
1889	b	728	1421, 1429	3			
1889	b	728	362, 365	4			
1890	b	728	1437, 1439	3			
1890	b	728	362, 365	4			
1891	b	728	1447	3			
1891	b	728	362, 365	4			
1892	b	728	1453	3			
1892	b	728	362, 365	4			
1893	b	728	1459	3			
1893	b	728	362, 365	4			
1894	b	728	1466, 1500	3			
1894	m	728	1506	3			
1894	b	728	362, 365, 421	4			
1894	m	728	427	4			
1895	b	728	1507	3			
1895	v	728	1518	3			
1895	m	728	427	4			
1896	m	728	427	4			
1896	b	728	7, 362, 365	4			
1897	b	728	21, 362, 365	4			
1897	m	728	22, 427	4			
1898	b	728	36-37, 39, 362, 365	4			
1898	m	728	427	4			
1899	b	728	37, 53, 362, 365	4			
1899	m	728	54, 427	4			
1899	v	728	55	4			
1900	b	728	37, 66, 362, 365	4			
1900	m	728	67, 427	4			
1900	d	728	75	4			
1901	d	728	75	4			
1901	b	728	94, 362, 365, 426	4			
1902	b	728	94, 362, 365	4			
1903	b	728	108, 362, 365	4			
1904	b	728	108, 362, 365	4			
1905	b	728	133-134, 362, 365	4			
1905	d	728	75	4			
1906	b	728	146, 362, 365	4			
1906	d	728	75	4			
1907	b	728	158, 362, 365	4			
1907	d	728	75	4			
1908	b	728	167-169, 362, 364-365	4			
1908	d	728	75	4			
1909	b	728	168, 180, 364	4			
1909	d	728	75	4			
1910	b	728	168, 364	4			
1911	b	728	207	4			
1912	b	728	221-222	4			
1913	b	728	235	4			
1914	b	728	246	4			

Naujoji Vilna (Novo-Vileisk) Those items with a Flag code of "4" are in the Vilnius County 4th Okrug Registers.

Year(s)	Type	Fond	File(s)	Op	A	F	Notes
1885	m	728	353	4		4	
1886	m	728	353	4		4	
1887	d	728	1478	3		4	
1887	m	728	353	4		4	
1887	b	728	364	4		4	
1888	d	728	1478	3		4	
1888	m	728	353	4		4	
1888	b	728	364	4		4	
1889	d	728	1478	3		4	
1889	m	728	353	4		4	
1889	b	728	364	4		4	
1890	d	728	1478	3		4	
1890	b	728	1479	3		4	
1890	m	728	1480	3		4	
1890	m	728	353	4		4	
1890	b	728	364	4		4	
1891	b	728	1446	3		4	

Naujoji Vilna (Novo-Vileisk) continued

Year(s)	Type	Fond	File(s)	Op	A	F	Notes
1891	d	728	1478	3		4	
1891	m	728	1483	3		4	
1891	m	728	353	4		4	
1891	b	728	364	4		4	
1892	d	728	1478	3		4	
1892	b	728	1486, 1553	3		4	
1892	m	728	1487, 1488, 1554	3		4	
1892	v	728	1489	3		4	
1892	m	728	353	4		4	
1892	b	728	364	4		4	
1893	d	728	1478	3		4	
1893	b	728	1490, 1553	3		4	
1893	m	728	1494, 1554	3		4	
1893	v	728	1496	3		4	
1893	m	728	353	4		4	
1893	b	728	364	4		4	
1894	b	728	1499, 1553	3		4	
1894	m	728	1505, 1554	3		4	
1894	v	728	1516	3		4	
1894	m	728	353	4		4	
1894	b	728	364	4		4	
1895	b	728	1508, 1553	3		4	
1895	m	728	1513, 1556	3		4	
1895	v	728	1519	3		4	
1895	v	728	3	4		4	
1895	m	728	353	4		4	
1895	b	728	364	4		4	
1896	b	728	13, 364	4		4	
1896	m	728	14, 353	4		4	
1896	b	728	1553	3		4	
1896	m	728	1556	3		4	
1897	b	728	28-29, 364	4		4	
1897	m	728	30, 353, 437	4		4	
1897	d	728	32	4		4	
1898	b	728	28, 45, 364	4		4	
1898	d	728	32	4		4	
1898	m	728	46, 353, 437	4		4	
1899	b	728	28, 60, 364	4		4	
1899	v	728	3	4		4	
1899	d	728	32	4		4	
1899	m	728	61, 353, 437	4		4	
1900	v	728	3	4		4	
1900	b	728	72, 364	4		4	
1900	m	728	73-74, 353, 437	4		4	
1900	d	728	75	4		4	
1901	v	728	3, 88	4		4	
1901	d	728	75	4		4	
1901	b	728	86, 364	4		4	
1901	m	728	87, 353, 437	4		4	
1902	m	728	102, 353, 438	4		4	
1902	d	728	103, 439	4		4	
1902	b	728	364	4		4	
1903	b	728	114-115, 364	4		4	
1903	m	728	116, 353, 438, 444	4		4	
1903	d	728	117, 439	4		4	
1904	b	728	127, 364	4		4	
1904	m	728	128, 353, 438	4		4	
1904	d	728	129, 439	4		4	
1905	b	728	139, 364	4		4	
1905	m	728	140, 353, 438	4		4	
1905	d	728	75, 141, 439	4		4	
1906	b	728	151, 364, 441	4		4	
1906	m	728	152, 353	4		4	
1906	d	728	75, 153	4		4	
1907	b	728	161, 364, 441	4		4	
1907	m	728	162, 353	4		4	
1907	v	728	3	4		4	
1907	d	728	75	4		4	
1908	b	728	172, 364, 441	4		4	
1908	v	728	3, 173	4		4	
1908	m	728	353	4		4	
1908	d	728	75	4		4	
1909	b	728	187, 364	4		4	
1909	v	728	3, 188	4		4	
1909	m	728	353, 442	4		4	
1909	d	728	75	4		4	
1910	b	728	199, 364	4		4	
1910	v	728	3, 200	4		4	
1910	m	728	353, 443	4		4	
1911	b	728	213, 364	4		4	
1911	m	728	214, 353	4		4	
1911	v	728	215	4		4	
1912	b	728	226, 364	4		4	
1912	m	728	227-228, 353	4		4	
1913	b	728	239, 364	4		4	
1913	m	728	240, 353	4		4	
1914	b	728	253, 364	4		4	
1914	m	728	253-254, 353	4		4	

Year(s)	Type	Fond	File(s)	Op	A	F	Notes

Naujoji Vilna (Novo-Vileisk) continued

Year(s)	Type	Fond	File(s)	Op	A	F	Notes
1914	v	728	255	4		4	
1915	m	728	353	4		4	
1915	b	728	364	4		4	
1916	b	728	364	4		4	
1917	b	728	364	4		4	
1917	b	728	364	4		4	
1918	b	728	364	4		4	
1919	b	728	364	4		4	
1920	b	728	364	4		4	
1921	b	728	364	4		4	

Naujoji Zagare

Year(s)	Type	Fond	File(s)	Op	A	F	Notes
1895	cen						

Nemaksciai

Year(s)	Type	Fond	File(s)	Op	A	F	Notes
1816	rs						
1839	rs						
1851	rs						
1874	rs						

Nemencine (Nemenchin) Those items with a Flag code of "3" are in the Vilnius County 3rd Okrug Registers. Those with a Flag code of "7" are in the Vilnius County Register.

Year(s)	Type	Fond	File(s)	Op	A	F	Notes
1816-1818	rs	515	288	25	K	7	Jews
1834	rs	515	298	25	K	7	Jews
1843-1849	rs	515	306	25	K	7	Jews
1849	rs	515	312	25	K	7	Jews
1850-1854	rs	515	273	25	K	7	Jews
1858	rs	515	285	25	K	7	Jews
unknown	rs	515	299	25	K	7	Jews
unknown	rs	515	320	25	K	7	Jews
1854	d	728	101	1			
1854	b	728	43	1			
1854	b	728	52	2			
1854	d	728	52	2			
1854	m	728	53	2			
1854	m	728	63	1			
1855	b	728	138	1			
1855	m	728	157	1			
1855	d	728	193	1			
1856	b	728	203	1			
1856	d	728	204	1			
1856	m	728	224	1			
1892	b	728	1485	3		3	
1893	b	728	1492	3		3	
1893	m	728	1493	3		3	
1894	b	728	1497	3		3	
1894	m	728	1503	3		3	
1894	v	728	1515, 1517	3		3	
1895	b	728	1509	3		3	
1895	m	728	1512	3		3	
1896	b	728	11	4		3	
1896	m	728	12	4		3	
1897	b	728	25	4		3	
1897	v	728	27	4		3	
1897	d	728	32	4		3	
1897	m	728	428	4		3	
1898	d	728	32	4		3	
1898	b	728	43	4		3	
1898	m	728	43	4		3	
1899	d	728	32	4		3	
1899	b	728	58	4		3	
1899	m	728	59	4		3	
1900	b	728	70, 364	4		3	
1900	m	728	71	4		3	
1900	d	728	75	4		3	
1901	b	728	364	4		3	
1901	d	728	75, 85	4		3	
1901	m	728	84	4		3	
1902	m	728	100	4		3	
1902	d	728	101	4		3	
1902	b	728	99, 364	4		3	
1903	m	728	112	4		3	
1903	d	728	113	4		3	
1903	b	728	429, 364	4		3	
1904	b	728	125, 364	4		3	
1904	d	728	126	4		3	
1905	m	728	133	4		3	
1905	b	728	431, 364	4		3	
1905	d	728	75	4		3	
1906	m	728	150	4		3	
1906	b	728	432, 364	4		3	
1906	d	728	75	4		3	
1907	m	728	160	4		3	
1907	b	728	433, 364	4		3	
1907	d	728	75	4		3	
1908	m	728	171	4		3	
1908	b	728	434, 364	4		3	
1908	d	728	75	4		3	
1909	b	728	184, 364	4		3	

Nemencine (Nemenchin) continued

Year(s)	Type	Fond	File(s)	Op	A	F
1909	m	728	185-186	4		3
1909	d	728	75	4		3
1910	b	728	197, 364	4		3
1910	m	728	198, 435	4		3
1911	b	728	211, 364	4		3
1911	m	728	212, 436	4		3
1912	b	728	224, 364	4		3
1912	m	728	225	4		3
1913	b	728	237, 364	4		3
1913	m	728	238	4		3
1914	b	728	251, 364	4		3
1914	m	728	252	4		3
1915	m	728	261	4		3

Nemunaitis (Nemunaitz)

Year(s)	Type	Fond	File(s)	Op	A	F
1858-1905	rs					
1854	m	728	74	1		
1854	v	728	87	1		
1855	b	728	124	1		
1855	m	728	162	1		
1856	b	728	211	1		
1856	m	728	234	1		
1856	v	728	249	1		
1857	m	728	299	1		
1858	v	728	391	1		
1861	m	728	632	1		
1863	d	728	852	1		
1864	b	728	628	3		
1865	b	728	630A	3		
1865	m	728	631	3		
1866	m	728	633	3		
1866	d	728	634	3		
1867	m	728	635	3		
1867	d	728	636	3		
1869	m	728	637	3		
1870	b	728	638-639	3		
1870	m	728	640	3		
1870	v	728	641	3		
1870	d	728	642	3		
1871	b	728	643-644	3		
1871	m	728	645	3		
1871	v	728	646	3		
1871	d	728	647	3		
1872	b	728	648-649	3		
1872	m	728	650	3		
1872	d	728	651-652	3		
1873	b	728	653-654	3		
1873	m	728	655	3		
1873	d	728	657-658, 941A	3		
1874	b	728	659-661	3		
1874	m	728	662	3		
1874	d	728	664-665	3		
1875	b	728	666-667	3		
1875	m	728	668	3		
1875	d	728	670	3		
1876	b	728	1393-1393A	3		
1876	d	728	1398	3		
1876	m	728	671	3		
1877	b	728	1394-1395	3		
1877	d	728	1399	3		
1877	m	728	317	4		
1878	b	728	1396	3		
1879	b	728	1396A	3		
1880	b	728	1397	3		
1881	b	728	316	4		
1882	b	728	316	4		
1883	b	728	316	4		
1883	m	728	317	4		
1884	b	728	316	4		
1884	m	728	317	4		
1885	b	728	316	4		
1885	m	728	317	4		
1886	b	728	316	4		
1886	m	728	317	4		
1887	b	728	316	4		
1887	m	728	317	4		
1887	v	728	317	4		
1888	b	728	316	4		
1888	m	728	317	4		
1889	b	728	316	4		
1889	m	728	317	4		
1889	v	728	317	4		
1889	d	728	318	4		
1890	b	728	316	4		
1890	v	728	317	4		
1890	d	728	318	4		
1891	b	728	316	4		
1891	m	728	317	4		

Nemunaitis (Nemunaitz) continued

Year(s)	Type	Fond	File(s)	Op	Notes
1891	v	728	317	4	
1891	d	728	318	4	
1892	b	728	316	4	
1892	m	728	317	4	
1892	v	728	317	4	
1892	d	728	318	4	
1893	b	728	316	4	
1893	m	728	317	4	
1894	b	728	316	4	
1894	m	728	317	4	
1894	d	728	318	4	
1895	b	728	316	4	
1896	m	728	317	4	
1896	d	728	318	4	
1897	b	728	316	4	
1897	m	728	317	4	
1897	d	728	318	4	
1898	b	728	316	4	
1898	m	728	317	4	
1898	d	728	318	4	
1899	b	728	316	4	
1899	m	728	317	4	
1899	d	728	318	4	
1900	m	728	317	4	
1900	d	728	318	4	
1901	b	728	316	4	
1901	m	728	317	4	
1901	d	728	318	4	
1902	b	728	316	4	
1902	m	728	317	4	
1902	d	728	318	4	
1903	b	728	316	4	
1903	m	728	317	4	
1903	v	728	317	4	
1903	d	728	318	4	
1904	b	728	316	4	
1904	m	728	317	4	
1904	v	728	317	4	
1904	d	728	318	4	
1905	d	728	318	4	
1906	b	728	316	4	
1906	m	728	317	4	
1906	v	728	317	4	
1906	d	728	318	4	
1907	b	728	316	4	
1907	v	728	317	4	
1907	d	728	318	4	
1908	d	728	318	4	
1909	b	728	316	4	
1909	m	728	317	4	
1909	v	728	317	4	
1909	d	728	318	4	
1910	d	728	318	4	
1911	d	728	318	4	
1912	b	728	316	4	
1912	m	728	317	4	
1913	b	728	316	4	
1913	m	728	317	4	
1913	d	728	318	4	

Novyy Dvor, Belarus (Naujadvaris)

Year(s)	Type	Fond	File(s)	Op	Notes
1896	b	728	319	4	Lida County
1897	b	728	319	4	Lida County
1897	m	728	320	4	Lida County
1898	b	728	319	4	Lida County
1898	m	728	320	4	Lida County
1899	b	728	319	4	Lida County
1899	m	728	320	4	Lida County
1900	b	728	319	4	Lida County
1901	b	728	319	4	Lida County
1902	b	728	319	4	Lida County
1903	b	728	444	4	Lida County
1904	b	728	445	4	Lida County
1905	b	728	319	4	Lida County
1906	b	728	319	4	Lida County
1906	d	728	320	4	Lida County
1907	b	728	319	4	Lida County
1907	d	728	320	4	Lida County
1908	b	728	319	4	Lida County
1908	d	728	320	4	Lida County
1909	b	728	319	4	Lida County
1909	d	728	320	4	Lida County
1910	b	728	319	4	Lida County
1910	d	728	320	4	Lida County
1911	b	728	319	4	Lida County
1911	d	728	320	4	Lida County
1912	b	728	319	4	Lida County
1912	d	728	320	4	Lida County

Novyy Dvor, Belarus (Naujadvaris) continued

Year(s)	Type	Fond	File(s)	Op	A	F	Notes
1913	b	728	319	4			Lida County
1913	d	728	320	4			Lida County
1914	b	728	319	4			Lida County
1914	d	728	320	4			Lida County
unknown	fl	228			K		Lida County

Orlya, Belarus (Orly)

Year(s)	Type	Fond	File(s)	Op	A	F	Notes
1896	b	728	1044	1			Lida County
1897	b	728	1043	1			Lida County
1897	m	728	1053	1			Lida County
1898	b	728	962	1			Lida County
1898	m	728	965	1			Lida County
1899	b	728	969	1			Lida County
1900	b	728	976	1			Lida County
1901	b	728	984	1			Lida County
1902	b	728	993	1			Lida County
1904	b	728	1017	1			Lida County
1905	b	728	1026	1			Lida County
1906	b	728	1033	1			Lida County
1907	b	728	1042, 1054	1			Lida County
1909	b	728	1061	1			Lida County
1910	b	728	1069	1			Lida County
1911	b	728	1078	1			Lida County
1912	b	728	1084	1			Lida County
1913	b	728	1088	1			Lida County
1914	b	728	1095	1			Lida County

Paberze (Podberezhe) Those items with a Flag code of "2" are in the Vilnius County 2nd Okrug Registers. Those with a Flag code of "3" are in the Vilnius County 3rd Okrug Registers. Those with a Flag code of "7" are in the Vilnius County Register.

Year(s)	Type	Fond	File(s)	Op	A	F	Notes
1816-1818	rs	515	288	25	K	7	Jews
1834	rs	515	298	25	K	7	Jews
1843-1849	rs	515	306	25	K	7	Jews
1849	rs	515	312	25	K	7	Jews
1850-1854	rs	515	273	25	K	7	Jews
1858	rs	515	285	25	K	7	Jews
unknown	rs	515	299	25	K	7	Jews
unknown	rs	515	320	25	K	7	Jews
1838	b	728	2	1			
1838	m	728	3	1			
1838	d	728	4	1			
1839	b	728	2	1			
1840	b	728	2	1			
1841	b	728	2	1			
1842	b	728	2	1			
1843	b	728	2	1			
1844	b	728	2	1			
1845	b	728	2	1			
1846	b	728	2	1			
1847	b	728	2	1			
1848	b	728	2	1			
1849	b	728	2	1			
1850	b	728	2	1			
1851	b	728	2	1			
1852	b	728	2	1			
1853	b	728	2	1			
1854	d	728	103	1			
1854	b	728	47	1			
1854	b	728	58	2			
1854	m	728	59	2			
1854	d	728	60	2			
1854	m	728	68	1			
1855	b	728	127	1			
1855	m	728	146	1			
1855	v	728	169	1			
1855	d	728	187	1			
1856	b	728	209	1			
1856	m	728	230	1			
1856	v	728	244	1			
1856	d	728	270	1			
1857	b	728	289	1			
1857	m	728	305	1			
1857	v	728	318	1			
1857	d	728	332	1			
1858	b	728	206	2			
1858	m	728	207	2			
1858	d	728	208	2			
1858	b	728	343	1			
1858	m	728	363	1			
1858	d	728	398	1			
1859	b	728	247	2			
1859	m	728	248	2			
1859	d	728	249	2			
1859	b	728	435	1			
1859	d	728	481	1			
1859	m	728	493	1			
1860	b	728	287	2			
1860	m	728	288	2			
1860	b	728	510	1			

Paberze (Podberezhe) continued

Year(s)	Type	Fond	File(s)	Op	A	F	Notes
1860	m	728	532	1			
1860	d	728	582-583	1			
1861	b	728	311	2			
1861	m	728	312	2			
1861	d	728	313	2			
1861	b	728	601	1			
1861	m	728	621	1			
1861	d	728	664	1			
1862	b	728	697	1			
1862	m	728	708	1			
1862	d	728	745	1			
1863	b	728	369	2			
1863	m	728	370	2			
1863	d	728	371	2			
1863	b	728	784	1			
1863	m	728	800	1			
1863	d	728	855	1			
1864	b	728	390	2			
1864	m	728	391	2			
1864	d	728	392	2			
1864	b	728	793	3			
1864	m	728	794	3			
1864	d	728	795	3			
1865	b	728	796-797	3			
1865	m	728	798-799	3			
1865	d	728	801-802	3			
1866	b	728	803-805	3			
1866	m	728	806-807	3			
1866	d	728	809-810	3			
1867	b	728	811-812	3			
1867	m	728	813-814	3			
1867	d	728	816-817	3			
1868	b	728	818-819	3			
1868	m	728	820-821	3			
1868	d	728	823-824	3			
1869	b	728	825	3			
1869	d	728	826	3			
1873	b	728	1030	3		2	
1873	m	728	142	3		2	
1873	m	728	144	3		2	
1873	d	728	146	3		2	
1874	b	728	148-149	3		2	
1874	m	728	150-151	3		2	
1874	d	728	152, 341	3		2	
1875	b	728	153-154	3		2	
1875	m	728	155-156	3		2	
1875	d	728	157-158	3		2	
1876	b	728	1035	3		2	
1876	m	728	1074	3		2	
1876	d	728	1124	3		2	
1877	b	728	1041	3		2	
1877	m	728	1075-1076	3		2	
1877	d	728	1128	3		2	
1878	b	728	1049	3		2	
1878	m	728	1078	3		2	
1878	d	728	1134	3		2	
1891	b	728	1445	3		2	
1891	m	728	1482	3		2	
1892	b	728	1484	3		2	
1893	b	728	1491	3		2	
1893	m	728	1495	3		2	
1894	b	728	1498	3		2	
1894	b	728	1501	3		2	
1894	m	728	1504	3		2	
1895	m	728	1481	3		2	
1895	b	728	1510	3		2	
1896	b	728	11	4		3	
1896	m	728	12	4		3	
1897	b	728	25	4		3	
1897	v	728	27	4		3	
1897	d	728	32	4		3	
1897	m	728	428	4		3	
1898	d	728	32	4		3	
1898	b	728	43	4		3	
1898	m	728	43	4		3	
1899	d	728	32	4		3	
1899	b	728	58	4		3	
1899	m	728	59	4		3	
1900	b	728	70, 364	4		3	
1900	m	728	71	4		3	
1900	d	728	75	4		3	
1901	b	728	364	4		3	
1901	d	728	75, 85	4		3	
1901	m	728	84	4		3	
1902	m	728	100	4		3	
1902	d	728	101	4		3	
1902	b	728	99, 364	4		3	
1903	m	728	112	4		3	
1903	d	728	113	4	A	3	

Paberze (Podberezhe) continued

Year(s)	Type	Fond	File(s)	Op	A	F
1903	b	728	429, 364	4	3	
1904	b	728	125, 364	4	3	
1904	d	728	126	4	3	
1905	m	728	133	4	3	
1905	b	728	431, 364	4	3	
1905	d	728	75	4	3	
1906	m	728	150	4	3	
1906	b	728	432, 364	4	3	
1906	d	728	75	4	3	
1907	m	728	160	4	3	
1907	b	728	433, 364	4	3	
1907	d	728	75	4	3	
1908	m	728	171	4	3	
1908	b	728	434, 364	4	3	
1908	d	728	75	4	3	
1909	b	728	184, 364	4	3	
1909	m	728	185-186	4	3	
1909	d	728	75	4	3	
1910	b	728	197, 364	4	3	
1910	m	728	198, 435	4	3	
1911	b	728	211, 364	4	3	
1911	m	728	212, 436	4	3	
1912	b	728	224, 364	4	3	
1912	m	728	225	4	3	
1913	b	728	237, 364	4	3	
1913	m	728	238	4	3	
1914	b	728	251, 364	4	3	
1914	m	728	252	4	3	
1915	m	728	261	4	3	

Pabrade

no vital records

Pajurys

Year(s)	Type
1816	rs
1858	rs
1874	rs

Pakruojis (Pokroi)

Year(s)	Type	Fond	File(s)	Op
1816	rs			
1818	rs			
1834	rs			
1865	b	1226	515	1
1865	m	1226	516	1
1865	v	1226	517	1
1865	d	1226	518	1
1866	b	1226	519	1
1866	m	1226	520	1
1866	v	1226	521	1
1866	d	1226	522	1
1867	b	1226	523	1
1867	m	1226	524	1
1867	v	1226	525	1
1867	d	1226	526	1
1868	b	1226	527	1
1868	m	1226	528	1
1868	v	1226	529	1
1868	d	1226	530	1
1869	b	1226	531	1
1869	m	1226	532	1
1869	v	1226	533	1
1869	d	1226	534	1
1870	b	1226	535	1
1870	m	1226	536	1
1870	v	1226	537	1
1870	d	1226	538	1
1871	b	1226	539	1
1871	m	1226	540	1
1871	v	1226	541	1
1871	d	1226	542	1
1872	b	1226	543	1
1872	m	1226	544	1
1872	v	1226	545	1
1872	d	1226	546	1
1873	b	1226	547	1
1873	m	1226	548	1
1873	v	1226	549	1
1873	d	1226	550	1
1874	b	1226	551	1
1874	m	1226	552	1
1874	v	1226	553	1
1874	d	1226	554	1
1875	b	1226	555	1
1875	m	1226	556	1
1875	v	1226	557	1
1875	d	1226	558	1
1876	b	1226	1079	1
1876	m	1226	1084	1

Year(s)	Type	Fond	File(s)	Op	A	F	Notes
Pakruojis (Pokroi) continued							
1876	v	1226	1089	1			
1876	d	1226	1094	1			
1877	b	1226	1080	1			
1877	m	1226	1085	1			
1877	v	1226	1090	1			
1877	d	1226	1095	1			
1878	b	1226	1081	1			
1878	m	1226	1086	1			
1878	v	1226	1091	1			
1878	d	1226	1096	1			
1879	b	1226	1082	1			
1879	m	1226	1087	1			
1879	v	1226	1092	1			
1879	d	1226	1097	1			
1880	b	1226	1083	1			
1880	m	1226	1083	1			
1880	v	1226	1093	1			
1880	d	1226	1098	1			
1881	b	1226	2037	1			
1881	m	1226	2038	1			
1881	v	1226	2039	1			
1881	d	1226	2040	1			
1882	b	1226	2037	1			
1882	m	1226	2038	1			
1882	v	1226	2039	1			
1882	d	1226	2040	1			
1883	b	1226	2037	1			
1883	m	1226	2038	1			
1883	v	1226	2039	1			
1883	d	1226	2040	1			
1884	b	1226	2037	1			
1884	m	1226	2038	1			
1884	v	1226	2039	1			
1884	d	1226	2040	1			
1885	b	1226	2037	1			
1885	m	1226	2038	1			
1885	v	1226	2039	1			
1885	d	1226	2040	1			
1886	b	1226	2037	1			
1886	m	1226	2038	1			
1886	v	1226	2039	1			
1886	d	1226	2040	1			
1887	b	1226	2037	1			
1887	m	1226	2038	1			
1887	v	1226	2039	1			
1887	d	1226	2040	1			
1888	b	1226	2037	1			
1888	m	1226	2038	1			
1888	v	1226	2039	1			
1888	d	1226	2040	1			
1889	b	1226	2037	1			
1889	m	1226	2038	1			
1889	v	1226	2039	1			
1889	d	1226	2040	1			
1890	b	1226	2037	1			
1890	m	1226	2038	1			
1890	v	1226	2039	1			
1890	d	1226	2040	1			
1891	b	1226	2037	1			
1891	m	1226	2038	1			
1891	v	1226	2039	1			
1891	d	1226	2040	1			
1892	b	1226	2037	1			
1892	m	1226	2038	1			
1892	v	1226	2039	1			
1892	d	1226	2040	1			
1893	b	1226	2037	1			
1893	m	1226	2038	1			
1893	v	1226	2039	1			
1893	d	1226	2040	1			
1894	b	1226	2037	1			
1894	m	1226	2038	1			
1894	v	1226	2039	1			
1894	d	1226	2040	1			
1895	b	1226	2037	1			
1895	m	1226	2038	1			
1895	v	1226	2039	1			
1895	d	1226	2040	1			
1896	b	1226	2037	1			
1896	m	1226	2038	1			
1896	v	1226	2039	1			
1896	d	1226	2040	1			
1897	b	1226	2037	1			
1897	m	1226	2038	1			
1897	v	1226	2039	1			
1897	d	1226	2040	1			
1898	b	1226	2037	1			
1898	m	1226	2038	1			

Pakruojis (Pokroi) continued

Year(s)	Type	Fond	File(s)	Op	A	F	Notes
1898	v	1226	2039	1			
1898	d	1226	2040	1			
1899	b	1226	2037	1			
1899	m	1226	2038	1			
1899	v	1226	2039	1			
1899	d	1226	2040	1			
1900	b	1226	2037	1			
1900	m	1226	2038	1			
1900	v	1226	2039	1			
1900	d	1226	2040	1			
1900	d	728	983	1			
1901	b	1226	2037	1			
1901	m	1226	2038	1			
1901	v	1226	2039	1			
1901	d	1226	2040	1			
1901	d	728	990	1			
1902	b	1226	2037	1			
1902	m	1226	2038	1			
1902	v	1226	2039	1			
1902	d	1226	2040	1			
1902	d	728	999	1			
1903	b	1226	2037	1			
1903	m	1226	2038	1			
1903	v	1226	2039	1			
1903	d	1226	2040	1			
1904	b	1226	2037	1			
1904	m	1226	2038	1			
1904	v	1226	2039	1			
1904	d	1226	2040	1			
1905	b	1226	2037	1			
1905	m	1226	2038	1			
1905	v	1226	2039	1			
1905	d	1226	2040	1			
1906	b	1226	2037	1			
1906	m	1226	2038	1			
1906	v	1226	2039	1			
1906	d	1226	2040	1			
1907	b	1226	2037	1			
1907	m	1226	2038	1			
1907	v	1226	2039	1			
1907	d	1226	2040	1			
1907	d	728	1051	1			
1908	b	1226	2037	1			
1908	m	1226	2038	1			
1908	v	1226	2039	1			
1908	d	1226	2040	1			
1909	b	1226	2037	1			
1909	m	1226	2038	1			
1909	v	1226	2039	1			
1909	d	1226	2040	1			
1909	d	728	1068	1			
1910	b	1226	2037	1			
1910	m	1226	2038	1			
1910	v	1226	2039	1			
1910	d	1226	2040	1			
1911	b	1226	2037	1			
1911	m	1226	2038	1			
1911	v	1226	2039	1			
1911	d	1226	2040	1			
1912	b	1226	2037	1			
1912	m	1226	2038	1			
1912	v	1226	2039	1			
1912	d	1226	2040	1			
1913	b	1226	2037	1			
1913	m	1226	2038	1			
1913	v	1226	2039	1			
1913	d	1226	2040	1			
1914	b	1226	2037	1			
1914	m	1226	2038	1			
1914	v	1226	2039	1			
1914	d	1226	2040	1			

Pampenai (Pumpian)

Year(s)	Type	Fond	File(s)	Op	A	F	Notes
1816	rs						
1818	rs						
1834	rs						
1874	fl	215			K		

Pandelys

Year(s)	Type	Fond	File(s)	Op	A	F	Notes
1871	rs						

Panemune (Ponemun-Fergissa)

Year(s)	Type	Fond	File(s)	Op	A	F	Notes
1815	b	1236	1	1		K	
1815	m	1236	2	1		K	
1816	b	1236	1	1		K	
1816	m	1236	2, 4	1		K	
1816	d	1236	5	1		K	
1817	m	1236	4, 7	1		K	

Panemune (Ponemun-Fergissa) continued

Year(s)	Type	Fond	File(s)	Op	A	F	Notes
1817	d	1236	5, 8	1		K	
1817	b	1236	6	1		K	
1818	m	1236	10	1		K	
1818	d	1236	12	1		K	
1818	b	1236	9	1		K	
1819	b	1236	13	1		K	
1819	m	1236	14	1		K	
1820	m	1236	15	1		K	
1821	m	1236	17	1		K	
1821	d	1236	19	1		K	
1822	d	1236	20	1		K	
1823	b	1236	21	1		K	
1824	b	1236	22	1		K	
1824	m	1236	23	1		K	
1824	d	1236	25	1		K	
1825	b	1236	26	1		K	
1825	m	1236	28	1		K	
1825	d	1236	29	1		K	
1826	d	1108	8	1		K	
1827	d	1108	8	1		K	
1828	d	1108	8	1		K	
1829	d	1108	8	1		K	
1830	d	1108	8	1		K	
1831	d	1108	8	1		K	
1832	d	1108	8	1		K	
1833	d	1108	8	1		K	
1834	d	1108	8	1		K	
1835	d	1108	8	1		K	
1836	d	1108	8	1		K	
1866	tpl	1073	538	1			

Panemunelis

no vital records

Panevezys (Ponevezh)

Year(s)	Type	Fond	File(s)	Op	A	F	Notes
1816	rs						
1818	rs						
1834-35	rs						
1853	rs						
1844	b	1226	602	1			
1854	b	1226	603	1			
1857	b	1226	604	1			
1858	b	1226	605-606	1			
1859	b	1226	607	1			
1860	b	1226	608	1			
1861	b	1226	609	1			
1862	b	1226	610	1			
1867	b	1226	611	1			
1872	m	1226	612	1			
1872	v	1226	613	1			
1872	d	1226	614	1			
1873	b	1226	615-616	1			
1873	m	1226	617	1			
1873	d	1226	618-619	1			
1874	b	1226	620-621	1			
1874	m	1226	622	1			
1874	v	1226	623	1			
1874	d	1226	624	1			
1875	b	1226	625-626	1			
1875	m	1226	627	1			
1875	v	1226	628	1			
1875	d	1226	629, 1073	1			
1876	b	1226	1112	1			
1876	v	1226	1120	1			
1876	d	1226	1125	1			
1876	m	1226	2043	1			
1877	b	1226	1113	1			
1877	v	1226	1121	1			
1877	d	1226	1126	1			
1877	m	1226	2043	1			
1878	b	1226	1114	1			
1878	m	1226	1117, 2043	1			
1878	v	1226	1122	1			
1878	d	1226	1127	1			
1879	b	1226	1115	1			
1879	v	1226	1123	1			
1879	d	1226	1128	1			
1879	m	1226	2043	1			
1880	b	1226	1116	1			
1880	m	1226	1119, 2043	1			
1880	v	1226	1124	1			
1880	d	1226	1129	1			
1881	b	1226	1309	1			
1881	d	1226	1310	1			
1881	m	1226	1402, 2043	1			
1882	b	1226	1309	1			
1882	d	1226	1310	1			
1882	m	1226	1402, 2043	1			

Panevezys (Ponevezh) continued

Year(s)	Type	Fond	File(s)			Op	A	F	Notes
1883	b	1226	1309			1			
1883	b	1226	1309			1			
1883	d	1226	1310			1			
1883	m	1226	1402,	1407,	2043	1			
1884	b	1226	1309			1			
1884	d	1226	1310			1			
1884	m	1226	1402,	2043		1			
1885	b	1226	1309			1			
1885	d	1226	1310			1			
1885	m	1226	1402,	2043		1			
1886	b	1226	1309			1			
1886	d	1226	1310,	1403		1			
1886	m	1226	1402,	2043		1			
1887	b	1226	1309			1			
1887	d	1226	1310,	1403		1			
1887	m	1226	1402,	2043		1			
1888	b	1226	1309			1			
1888	d	1226	1310,	1403		1			
1888	m	1226	1402,	2043		1			
1889	d	1226	1310,	1403		1			
1889	m	1226	1402,	2043		1			
1890	d	1226	1310,	1403		1			
1890	m	1226	1402,	2043		1			
1891	m	1226	1402,	2043		1			
1891	d	1226	1403,	2045		1			
1892	m	1226	1402,	2043		1			
1892	d	1226	1403,	2045		1			
1892	b	1226	2032			1			In File 2032, see List 187.
1893	m	1226	1402,	2043		1			
1893	d	1226	1403,	2045		1			
1893	b	1226	2041			1			
1894	m	1226	1402,	2043		1			
1894	d	1226	1403,	2045		1			
1894	b	1226	2041			1			
1895	m	1226	1402,	2043		1			
1895	d	1226	1403,	2045		1			
1895	b	1226	1406,	2041		1			
1896	m	1226	1402,	2043		1			
1896	d	1226	1403,	2045		1			
1896	b	1226	2041			1			
1897	m	1226	1402,	2043		1			
1897	d	1226	1403,	2045		1			
1897	b	1226	2041			1			
1898	m	1226	1402,	2044		1			
1898	d	1226	1403,	2045		1			
1898	b	1226	2041			1			
1899	m	1226	1402,	2044		1			
1899	b	1226	2041			1			
1899	d	1226	2045			1			
1900	b	1226	2042			1			
1900	m	1226	2044			1			
1900	d	1226	2045			1			
1901	b	1226	2042			1			
1901	m	1226	2044			1			
1901	d	1226	2045			1			
1902	b	1226	2042			1			
1902	m	1226	2044			1			
1902	d	1226	2046			1			
1903	b	1226	2042			1			
1903	m	1226	2044			1			
1903	d	1226	2046			1			
1904	b	1226	2042			1			
1904	m	1226	2044			1			
1904	d	1226	2046			1			
1905	b	1226	2042			1			
1905	m	1226	2044			1			
1905	d	1226	2046			1			
1905	b	1226	n/a			2			
1906	b	1226	2042			1			
1906	m	1226	2044			1			
1906	d	1226	2046			1			
1907	b	1226	2042			1			
1907	m	1226	2044			1			
1907	d	1226	2046			1			
1908	b	1226	2042			1			
1908	m	1226	2044			1			
1908	d	1226	2046			1			
1909	b	1226	2042			1			
1909	m	1226	2044			1			
1909	d	1226	2046			1			
1910	b	1226	2042			1			
1910	m	1226	2044			1			
1910	d	1226	2046			1			
1911	b	1226	2042			1			
1911	m	1226	2044			1			
1911	d	1226	2046			1			
1912	b	1226	2042			1			
1912	m	1226	2044			1			

Year(s)	Type	Fond	File(s)	Op	A	F	Notes	Page 80

Panevezys (Ponevezh) continued

Year(s)	Type	Fond	File(s)	Op	A	F	Notes
1912	d	1226	2046	1			
1913	b	1226	2042	1			
1913	m	1226	2044	1			
1913	d	1226	2046	1			
1914	b	1226	2042	1			
1914	m	1226	2044	1			
1914	d	1226	2046	1			
1915	b	1226	2042	1			
1915	m	1226	2044	1			
1915	d	1226	2046	1			

Panevezys County

Year(s)	Type	Fond	File(s)	Op	A	F	Notes
1898	rs	26	2	1	K		List of Jews residing outside the towns of Panevezys County.
1873	tpl				K		

Papile

Year(s)	Type	Fond	File(s)	Op	A	F	Notes
1858	rs						
1866	rs						

Pasvalys (Posvol)

Year(s)	Type	Fond	File(s)	Op	A	F	Notes
1816	rs						
1818	rs						
1834	rs						
1853	rs						
1858	rs						
1859	rs						
1864	rs						
1868	rs						
1872-75	rs						
1854	d	728	105	1			
1854	b	728	49	1			
1854	m	728	77	1			
1855	b	728	121	1			
1855	m	728	154	1			
1855	d	728	182	1			
1856	b	728	201	1			
1856	m	728	231	1			
1856	v	728	245	1			
1856	d	728	271	1			
1857	b	728	286	1			
1857	m	728	304	1			
1857	v	728	316	1			
1857	d	728	330	1			
1858	b	728	339	1			
1858	m	728	371	1			
1858	d	728	403	1			
1859	m	728	443	1			
1860	b	728	519	1			
1860	m	728	543	1			
1860	v	728	563	1			
1860	d	728	571	1			
1861	m	728	619	1			
1861	d	728	667	1			
1864	d	728	941	1			
1866	b	1226	630	1			
1866	m	1226	631	1			
1866	v	1226	632	1			
1866	d	1226	633	1			
1867	b	1226	634	1			
1867	m	1226	635	1			
1867	v	1226	636	1			
1867	d	1226	637	1			
1868	b	1226	638	1			
1868	m	1226	639	1			
1868	v	1226	640	1			
1868	d	1226	641	1			
1869	b	1226	642	1			
1869	m	1226	643	1			
1869	v	1226	644	1			
1869	d	1226	645	1			
1870	b	1226	646	1			
1870	m	1226	647	1			
1870	v	1226	648	1			
1870	d	1226	649	1			
1871	b	1226	650	1			
1871	m	1226	651	1			
1871	v	1226	652	1			
1871	d	1226	653	1			
1872	b	1226	654	1			
1872	m	1226	655	1			
1872	v	1226	656	1			
1872	d	1226	657	1			
1873	b	1226	658	1			
1873	m	1226	659	1			
1873	v	1226	660	1			
1873	d	1226	661	1			
1874	b	1226	662	1			

Year(s)	Type	Fond	File(s)		Op	A	F	Notes
Pasvalys (Posvol) continued								
1874	m	1226	663		1			
1874	v	1226	664		1			
1874	d	1226	665		1			
1882	b	1226	1311		1			
1882	d	1226	1312		1			
1882	m	1226	2049		1			
1883	b	1226	1309, 1311		1			In File 1309, see List 119.
1883	d	1226	1312		1			
1883	m	1226	2049, 2103		1			
1884	b	1226	1311		1			
1884	d	1226	1312		1			
1884	m	1226	2049, 2103		1			
1884	v	1226	2104		1			
1885	b	1226	1309, 1311		1			In File 1309, see List 205.
1885	d	1226	1312–1313		1			
1885	m	1226	2049, 2103		1			
1885–87	fl	216				K		
1886	b	1226	1311		1			
1886	d	1226	1312–1313		1			
1886	m	1226	2049, 2103		1			
1886	v	1226	2104		1			
1887	b	1226	1311		1			
1887	d	1226	1312–1313		1			
1887	m	1226	2049, 2103		1			
1887	v	1226	2104		1			
1887	fl	I–216	44		1			
1888	b	1226	1311		1			
1888	d	1226	1312–1313		1			
1888	m	1226	2049, 2103		1			
1888	v	1226	2104		1			
1889	b	1226	1311		1			
1889	d	1226	1312–1313		1			
1889	m	1226	2049, 2103		1			
1890	d	1226	1312–1313		1			
1890	m	1226	2049, 2103		1			
1890	v	1226	2104		1			
1891	d	1226	1312–1313		1			
1891	m	1226	2049, 2103		1			
1892	d	1226	1312		1			
1892	m	1226	2049, 2103		1			
1893	b	1226	1311		1			
1893	d	1226	1312		1			
1893	m	1226	2049, 2103		1			
1894	b	1226	1311, 2047		1			
1894	d	1226	1312		1			
1894	m	1226	2049, 2103		1			
1895	b	1226	2047		1			
1895	m	1226	2049, 2103		1			
1895	d	1226	2050		1			
1896	b	1226	2047		1			
1896	m	1226	2049, 2103		1			
1896	d	1226	2050		1			
1897	b	1226	2047		1			
1897	m	1226	2049, 2103		1			
1897	d	1226	2050		1			
1898	b	1226	2047		1			
1898	m	1226	2049, 2103		1			
1898	d	1226	2050		1			
1899	b	1226	2047		1			
1899	m	1226	2049, 2103		1			
1899	d	1226	2050		1			
1900	b	1226	2047		1			
1900	m	1226	2049, 2104		1			
1900	d	1226	2050		1			
1900	v	1226	2104		1			
1901	b	1226	2048		1			
1901	d	1226	2050		1			
1901	m	1226	2104		1			
1901	v	1226	2104		1			
1902	b	1226	2048		1			
1902	d	1226	2050		1			
1902	m	1226	2104		1			
1902	v	1226	2104		1			
1903	b	1226	2048		1			
1903	d	1226	2050		1			
1903	v	1226	2104		1			
1904	b	1226	2042, 2048		1			In File 2042, see List 178.
1904	d	1226	2050		1			
1904	m	1226	2104		1			
1905	b	1226	2048		1			
1905	d	1226	2050		1			
1905	m	1226	2104		1			
1906	b	1226	2048		1			
1906	d	1226	2050		1			
1906	m	1226	2104		1			
1907	b	1226	2042, 2048		1			In File 2042, see List 232.
1907	d	1226	2050		1			
1907	m	1226	2104		1			

Pasvalys (Posvol) continued

Year(s)	Type	Fond	File(s)	Op	A	F	Notes
1908	fl				K		
1908	b	1226	2048	1			
1908	d	1226	2050	1			
1908	m	1226	2104	1			
1908	fl	I-216	47	1			
1909	b	1226	2048	1			
1909	d	1226	2050	1			
1909	m	1226	2104	1			
1909	v	1226	2104	1			
1910	b	1226	2048	1			
1910	d	1226	2050	1			
1910	m	1226	2104	1			
1911	b	1226	2048	1			
1911	d	1226	2050	1			
1911	m	1226	2104	1			
1912	b	1226	2048	1			
1912	d	1226	2050	1			
1912	m	1226	2104	1			
1913	b	1226	2048	1			
1913	d	1226	2050	1			
1913	m	1226	2104	1			
1914	b	1226	2048	1			
1914	d	1226	2050	1			
1914	m	1226	2104	1			
1915	dl				K		
1915	d	1226	2050	1			

Pikeliai

Year(s)	Type	Fond	File(s)	Op	A	F	Notes
1871	rs						

Ploksciai (Blagoslavenstvo)

Year(s)	Type	Fond	File(s)	Op	A	F	Notes
1812	b	1236	1	3			
1812	m	1236	2	3			
1812	d	1236	3	3			
1813	m	1236	2	3			
1813	d	1236	4	3			
1814	d	1236	4, 6	3			
1814	b	1236	5	3			
1815	b	1236	5, 8	3			
1815	d	1236	6, 10	3			
1815	m	1236	9	3			
1816	d	1236	10	3			
1816	b	1236	8	3			
1816	m	1236	9, 11	3			
1817	m	1236	11	3			
1817	b	1236	12	3			
1817	d	1236	13	3			
1818	m	1236	14	3			
1819	m	1236	15	3			
1819	d	1236	17	3			
1820	m	1236	18	3			
1821	m	1236	19	3			
1821	d	1236	20	3			
1822	m	1236	22	3			
1822	d	1236	23	3			
1823	m	1236	25	3			
1823	d	1236	26	3			
1824	b	1236	27	3			
1824	m	1236	28	3			
1824	d	1236	29	3			
1825	d	1236	32	3			
1825	b	1236	33	3			

Plunge (Plungian)

Year(s)	Type	Fond	File(s)	Op	A	F	Notes
1851	rs	1262	89	1			
1859	rs	1262	93	1			
1868	rs	1262	95	1			
1837	b	1226	1920	1			
1838	b	1226	1921	1			
1839	b	1226	1922-1923	1			
1839	v	1226	1924	1			
1840	b	1226	1925	1			
1841	b	1226	1926	1			
1842	b	1226	1927	1			
1842	d	1226	1928	1			
1844	b	1226	1929	1			
1844	d	1226	1930	1			
1844	v	1226	1931	1			
1845	v	1226	1932	1			
1846	b	1226	1933	1			
1846	m	1226	1934	1			
1846	v	1226	1935	1			
1847	b	1226	1936	1			
1848	b	1226	1937	1			
1848	m	1226	1938	1			
1849	b	1226	1939	1			
1854	d	728	106	1			
1854	b	728	48	1			

Plunge (Plungian) continued

Year(s)	Type	Fond	File(s)	Op	A	F	Notes
1854	m	728	75	1			
1854	v	728	82	1			
1855	b	728	122	1			
1855	m	728	152	1			
1855	v	728	166	1			
1855	d	728	180	1			
1856	b	728	198	1			
1856	m	728	232	1			
1856	v	728	241	1			
1856	d	728	263	1			
1857	b	728	285, 296	1			
1857	v	728	315	1			
1857	d	728	323	1			
1858	b	728	359	1			
1858	m	728	368	1			
1858	v	728	387	1			
1858	d	728	395	1			
1859	m	575	1	1	K		
1859	b	728	419	1			
1859	v	728	465	1			
1859	d	728	476	1			
1859	m	I-575	1	1	K		
1860	m	575	2	1	K		
1860	b	728	502	1			
1860	v	728	565	1			
1860	d	728	589	1			
1860	m	I-575	2	1	K		
1861	m	728	642	1			
1861	d	728	656	1			
1862	v	728	738	1			
1862	d	728	763	1			
1863	m	575	3	1	K		
1863	b	728	768	1			
1863	v	728	830	1			
1863	d	728	835	1			
1863	m	I-575	3	1	K		
1864	b	1226	1940	1			
1864	m	1226	1941	1			
1864	d	1226	1942	1			
1864	v	1226	1943	1			
1864	m	575	4	1	K		
1864	b	728	876	1			
1864	v	728	926	1			
1864	d	728	944	1			
1864	m	I-575	4	1	K		
1865	b	1226	708, 1944	1			
1865	m	1226	709, 1945	1			
1865	v	1226	710, 1947	1			
1865	d	1226	711, 1946	1			
1866	b	1226	712, 1948	1			
1866	m	1226	713, 1949	1			
1866	v	1226	714, 1951	1			
1866	d	1226	715, 1950	1			
1867	b	1226	716	1			
1867	m	1226	717	1			
1867	v	1226	718	1			
1867	d	1226	719	1			
1868	b	1226	720, 1952	1			
1868	m	1226	721, 1953	1			
1868	v	1226	722, 1955	1			
1868	d	1226	723, 1954	1			
1869	m	1226	1956	1			
1869	b	1226	724	1			
1869	v	1226	725	1			
1869	d	1226	726, 1957	1			
1870	b	1226	727, 1244	1			
1870	m	1226	728	1			
1870	v	1226	729	1			
1870	d	1226	730	1			
1871	b	1226	731	1			
1871	m	1226	732, 1245	1			
1871	v	1226	733	1			
1871	d	1226	734, 1246	1			
1872	b	1226	735	1			
1872	m	1226	736, 1247	1			
1872	v	1226	738	1			
1872	d	1226	739-740	1			
1873	b	1226	741	1			
1873	m	1226	742, 1248	1			
1873	v	1226	743	1			
1873	d	1226	744	1			
1874	b	1226	745	1			
1874	m	1226	746, 1249	1			
1874	v	1226	747, 1958	1			
1874	d	1226	748-749	1			
1875	b	1226	750	1			
1875	m	1226	751, 1250	1			
1875	v	1226	752, 1212	1			

Plunge (Plungian) continued

Year(s)	Type	Fond	File(s)	Op	A	F	Notes
1875	d	1226	753, 1251	1			
1876	b	1226	1200	1			
1876	m	1226	1205, 1252	1			
1876	d	1226	1207, 1253	1			
1876	v	1226	1213–1214	1			
1877	b	1226	1201, 1254	1			
1877	d	1226	1208, 1256	1			
1877	v	1226	1215–1216	1			
1877	m	1226	1255	1			
1878	b	1226	1202, 1257	1			
1878	d	1226	1209, 1259	1			
1878	v	1226	1217–1218	1			
1878	m	1226	1258	1			
1879	b	1226	1203	1			
1879	d	1226	1210, 1261	1			
1879	v	1226	1219–1220	1			
1879	m	1226	1260	1			
1880	b	1226	1204, 1262	1			
1880	m	1226	1206, 1263	1			
1880	d	1226	1211, 1264	1			
1880	v	1226	1221–1223	1			
1881	b	1226	1265	1			
1881	m	1226	1266, 2034	1			
1881	v	1226	1267	1			
1881	d	1226	1268, 2035	1			
1882	b	1226	1269	1			
1882	m	1226	1270, 2034	1			
1882	v	1226	1271	1			
1882	d	1226	2035	1			
1883	m	1226	1272, 2034	1			
1883	v	1226	1273	1			
1883	d	1226	1274, 2035	1			
1884	m	1226	1275, 2034	1			
1884	v	1226	1276	1			
1884	d	1226	2035	1			
1885	v	1226	1277	1			
1885	d	1226	1278, 2035	1			
1885	m	1226	2034	1			
1886	m	1226	1279, 2034	1			
1886	v	1226	1280	1			
1886	d	1226	2035	1			
1887	m	1226	1281, 2034	1			
1887	v	1226	1282	1			
1887	b	1226	2032	1			
1887	d	1226	2035	1			
1888	b	1226	2032	1			
1888	m	1226	2034	1			
1888	d	1226	2035	1			
1889	b	1226	2032	1			
1889	m	1226	2034	1			
1889	d	1226	2035	1			
1890	b	1226	2032	1			
1890	m	1226	2034	1			
1890	d	1226	2035	1			
1891	b	1226	2032	1			
1891	m	1226	2034	1			
1891	d	1226	2035	1			
1892	b	1226	2032	1			
1892	m	1226	2034	1			
1892	d	1226	2035	1			
1893	b	1226	2032	1			
1893	m	1226	2034	1			
1893	d	1226	2035	1			
1894	b	1226	2032	1			
1894	m	1226	2034	1			
1894	d	1226	2036	1			
1895	b	1226	2032	1			
1895	m	1226	2034	1			
1895	d	1226	2036	1			
1896	b	1226	2032	1			
1896	m	1226	2034	1			
1896	d	1226	2036	1			
1897	b	1226	2032	1			
1897	m	1226	2034	1			
1897	d	1226	2036	1			
1898	b	1226	2032	1			
1898	m	1226	2034	1			
1898	d	1226	2036	1			
1899	b	1226	2033	1			
1899	m	1226	2034	1			
1899	d	1226	2036	1			
1900	b	1226	2033	1			
1900	m	1226	2034	1			
1900	d	1226	2036	1			
1901	b	1226	2033	1			
1901	m	1226	2034	1			
1901	d	1226	2036	1			
1902	b	1226	2033	1			

Plunge (Plungian) continued

Year(s)	Type	Fond	File(s)	Op
1902	m	1226	2034	1
1902	d	1226	2036	1
1903	b	1226	2033	1
1903	m	1226	2034	1
1903	d	1226	2036	1
1904	b	1226	2033	1
1904	m	1226	2034	1
1904	d	1226	2036	1
1905	b	1226	2033	1
1905	m	1226	2034	1
1905	d	1226	2036	1
1906	b	1226	2033	1
1906	m	1226	2034	1
1906	d	1226	2036	1
1907	b	1226	2033	1
1907	m	1226	2034	1
1907	d	1226	2036	1
1908	b	1226	2033	1
1908	m	1226	2034	1
1908	d	1226	2036	1
1909	b	1226	2033	1
1909	m	1226	2034	1
1909	d	1226	2036	1
1910	b	1226	2033	1
1910	m	1226	2034	1
1910	d	1226	2036	1
1911	b	1226	2033	1
1911	m	1226	2034	1
1911	d	1226	2036	1
1912	b	1226	2033	1
1912	m	1226	2034	1
1912	d	1226	2036	1
1913	b	1226	2033	1
1913	m	1226	2034	1
1913	d	1226	2036	1
1914	d	1226	2036	1

Prienai (Pren)

Year(s)	Type	Fond	File(s)	Op
1808	b	1236	495	3
1809	b	1236	495	3
1810	d	1236	497	3
1810	b	1236	498	3
1810	m	1236	499	3
1811	d	1236	497, 501A, 502	3
1811	b	1236	498, 500	3
1811	m	1236	499, 501	3
1812	b	1236	500, 503-505	3
1812	m	1236	501	3
1812	d	1236	501A, 502, 506	3
1813	d	1236	502, 509	3
1813	b	1236	504, 507	3
1814	b	1236	507, 511-512	3
1814	d	1236	509, 513	3
1815	b	1108	21	1
1815	b	1236	511-512	3
1815	d	1236	513, 516-518	3
1815	m	1236	514-515	3
1816	b	1108	15, 21	1
1816	b	1236	15	26
1816	m	1236	16	26
1816	m	1236	514-515, 520	3
1816	d	1236	516-518, 521-522	3
1816	b	1236	519	3
1816	b	1236	523	3
1817	b	1236	15	26
1817	m	1236	16	26
1817	b	1236	519, 523, 525-526, 927, 943, 948	3
1817	m	1236	520, 527	3
1817	d	1236	521-522, 528-529	3
1818	b	1236	37	26
1818	b	1236	530	3
1818	m	1236	531, 636	3
1818	d	1236	532-533	3
1819	b	1236	44	26
1819	d	1236	534, 536-538	3
1819	m	1236	535	3
1819	b	1236	924	3
1820	b	1236	539	3
1820	m	1236	540, 543	3
1820	d	1236	544	3
1820	b	1236	64	26
1821	b	1236	545, 944, 949	3
1821	m	1236	546-547	3
1821	d	1236	548-550	3
1822	b	1108	22	1
1822	b	1236	551, 952	3
1822	m	1236	552, 554	3

Prienai (Pren) continued

Year(s)	Type	Fond	File(s)	Op
1822	d	1236	555-556	3
1822	d	1236	65	26
1823	b	1236	557, 950	3
1823	m	1236	558	3
1823	d	1236	560	3
1824	b	1236	561-562	3
1824	m	1236	563-564, 929	3
1824	d	1236	928, 930	3
1825	m	1236	565-566	3
1825	b	1236	931	3
1825	d	1236	932	3
1826	b	1108	14	1
1826	d	1108	14	1
1826	m	1108	14	1
1827	b	1236	568	3
1827	d	1236	568	3
1827	m	1236	568	3
1828	b	1236	571	3
1828	d	1236	571	3
1828	m	1236	571	3
1835	b	1236	572	3
1835	d	1236	572	3
1835	m	1236	572	3
1836	b	1236	573	3
1836	d	1236	573	3
1836	m	1236	573	3
1837	b	1236	575	3
1837	d	1236	575	3
1837	m	1236	575	3
1839	b	1108	23	1
1839	d	1108	23	1
1839	m	1108	23	1
1840	b	1236	581	3
1840	d	1236	581	3
1840	m	1236	581	3
1841	b	1236	946	3
1841	d	1236	946	3
1841	m	1236	946	3
1842	b	1108	24	1
1842	d	1108	24	1
1842	m	1108	24	1
1843	b	1108	25	1
1843	d	1108	25	1
1843	m	1108	25	1
1844	b	1108	26	1
1844	d	1108	26	1
1844	m	1108	26	1
1845	b	1226	1482	1
1845	d	1226	1482	1
1845	m	1226	1482	1
1846	b	1108	27	1
1846	d	1108	27	1
1846	m	1108	27	1
1847	b	1236	592	3
1847	d	1236	592	3
1847	m	1236	592	3
1848	b	1236	593	3
1848	d	1236	593	3
1848	m	1236	593	3
1849	b	1226	1483	1
1849	d	1226	1483	1
1849	m	1226	1483	1
1852	b	1108	28	1
1852	d	1108	28	1
1852	m	1108	28	1
1855	b	1236	606	3
1855	d	1236	606	3
1855	m	1236	606	3
1856	b	1108	29	1
1856	d	1108	29	1
1856	m	1108	29	1
1857	b	1236	947	3
1857	d	1236	947	3
1857	m	1236	947	3
1858	b	1236	38	26
1858	d	1236	38	26
1858	m	1236	38	26
1860	b	1236	613	3
1860	d	1236	613	3
1860	m	1236	613	3
1861	b	1236	616	3
1861	d	1236	616	3
1861	m	1236	616	3
1862	d	1236	617	3
1862	m	1236	617	3
1863	b	1108	30	1
1863	d	1108	30	1
1863	m	1108	30	1

Prienai (Pren) continued

Year(s)	Type	Fond	File(s)	Op	A	F	Notes
1864	b	1236	622	3			
1864	d	1236	622	3			
1864	m	1236	622	3			
1865	b	1236	623	3			
1865	d	1236	623	3			
1865	m	1236	623	3			
1866	b	1236	625	3			
1866	d	1236	625	3			
1866	m	1236	625	3			
1871	b	728	1125	1			
1871	d	728	1125	1			
1871	m	728	1125	1			
1874	b	728	1126	1			
1874	d	728	1126	1			
1874	m	728	1126	1			
1887	m	1108	16	1			
1888	m	1108	16	1			
1889	m	1108	16	1			
1889	b	1108	17	1			
1890	m	1108	16	1			
1890	b	1108	17	1			
1891	m	1108	16	1			
1891	b	1108	17	1			
1892	m	1108	16	1			
1892	b	1108	17	1			
1893	m	1108	16	1			
1893	b	1108	17	1			
1894	m	1108	16	1			
1894	b	1108	17	1			
1895	m	1108	16	1			
1895	b	1108	17	1			
1896	m	1108	16	1			
1896	b	1108	17	1			
1897	m	1108	16	1			
1897	b	1108	17	1			
1898	d	1108	16	1			
1898	b	1108	17	1			
1899	m	1108	16	1			
1899	b	1108	17	1			
1900	m	1108	16	1			
1900	b	1108	17	1			
1900	b	1226	1404	1			
1900	d	1226	1404	1			
1900	m	1226	1404	1			
1901	m	1108	16	1			
1901	b	1108	17	1			
1902	m	1108	16	1			
1902	b	1108	17-18	1			
1902	d	1108	19	1			
1903	m	1108	16	1			
1903	b	1108	18	1			
1903	d	1108	19	1			
1904	m	1108	16	1			
1904	b	1108	18	1			
1904	d	1108	19	1			
1905	m	1108	16	1			
1905	b	1108	18	1			
1905	d	1108	19	1			
1906	d	1108	16	1			
1906	b	1108	18	1			
1906	d	1108	19	1			
1907	m	1108	16	1			
1907	b	1108	18	1			
1907	d	1108	19	1			
1908	m	1108	16	1			
1908	b	1108	18	1			
1908	d	1108	19	1			
1909	m	1108	16	1			
1909	b	1108	18	1			
1909	d	1108	19	1			
1910	m	1108	16	1			
1910	b	1108	18	1			
1910	d	1108	19	1			
1911	d	1108	16	1			
1911	b	1108	18	1			
1911	d	1108	19	1			
1912	m	1108	16	1			
1912	b	1108	18	1			
1912	d	1108	19	1			
1913	m	1108	16	1			
1913	b	1108	18	1			
1913	d	1108	19	1			
1914	m	1108	16, 20	1			
1914	b	1108	18, 20	1			
1914	d	1108	19-20	1			
1915	b	1108	18	1			

Prienai-Plateliai (Pren-Plotel)

Year(s)	Type	Fond	File(s)	Op	A	F	Notes	Page 88

Prienai-Plateliai (Pren-Plotel) continued

Year(s)	Type	Fond	File(s)	Op	A	F	Notes
1818	b	1236	32	26			
1818	b	1236	635	3			
1818	m	1236	636	3			
1819	b	1236	637	3			
1819	m	1236	638-639	3			
1820	b	1236	637	3			
1820	m	1236	640	3			
1820	d	1236	641	3			
1821	b	1236	33	26			
1821	b	1236	637	3			
1821	m	1236	642-643	3			
1822	b	1236	644	3			
1822	m	1236	645	3			
1823	b	1236	644	3			
1823	m	1236	646	3			
1824	m	1236	647	3			See Mikhaliskis Community.
1824	b	1236	648-649	3			See Mikhaliskis Community.
1825	b	1236	34	26			See Mikhaliskis Community.
1825	b	1236	650	3			See Mikhaliskis Community.
1825	m	1236	651, 935	3			See Mikhaliskis Community.
1825	d	1236	934	3			See Mikhaliskis Community.

Pumpenai (Pumpian)

Year(s)	Type	Fond	File(s)	Op	A	F	Notes
1816	rs						
1818	rs						
1834	rs						
1876	rs	I-215	2	1	K		Alphabetic - Jews
1876	rs	I-215	3	1	K		
1887	rs	I-215	4	1	K		Christians and Jews
1854	d	728	96	1			
1855	m	728	148	1			
1855	v	728	172	1			
1855	d	728	190	1			
1856	d	728	273	1			
1856	v	728	410	1			
1858	b	728	345	1			
1858	v	728	393	1			
1859	b	728	129	1			
1859	d	728	484	1			
1860	m	728	534	1			
1860	v	728	562	1			
1860	d	728	584	1			
1861	d	1226	864	1			
1861	b	728	604	1			
1861	m	728	633	1			
1862	v	728	728, 731	1			
1863	b	728	769	1			
1863	m	728	795	1			
1864	v	1226	1285	1			
1864	b	728	888	1			
1865	b	1226	559	1			
1865	m	1226	560	1			
1865	v	1226	561	1			
1865	d	1226	562	1			
1866	b	1226	563	1			
1866	m	1226	564	1			
1866	v	1226	565	1			
1866	d	1226	566	1			
1867	b	1226	567	1			
1867	m	1226	568	1			
1867	v	1226	569	1			
1867	d	1226	570	1			
1868	b	1226	571	1			
1868	m	1226	572	1			
1868	v	1226	573	1			
1868	d	1226	574	1			
1869	b	1226	575	1			
1869	m	1226	576	1			
1869	v	1226	577	1			
1869	d	1226	578	1			
1870	b	1226	579	1			
1870	m	1226	580	1			
1870	v	1226	581	1			
1870	d	1226	582	1			
1871	b	1226	583	1			
1871	m	1226	584	1			
1871	v	1226	585	1			
1871	d	1226	586	1			
1872	b	1226	587	1			
1872	m	1226	588	1			
1872	v	1226	589	1			
1872	d	1226	590	1			
1873	b	1226	591	1			
1873	m	1226	592	1			
1873	d	1226	593	1			
1874	b	1226	594	1			
1874	m	1226	595	1			
1874	v	1226	596	1			

Pumpenai (Pumpian) continued

Year(s)	Type	Fond	File(s)	Op	A	F	Notes
1874	d	1226	597	1			
1875	b	1226	598	1			
1875	m	1226	599	1			
1875	v	1226	600	1			
1875	d	1226	601	1			
1876	m	1226	1099	1			
1876	v	1226	1103	1			
1876	d	1226	1107	1			
1876	b	1226	2051	1			
1877	m	1226	1100	1			
1877	v	1226	1104	1			
1877	d	1226	1108	1			
1877	b	1226	2051	1			
1878	m	1226	1101	1			
1878	v	1226	1105	1			
1878	d	1226	1109	1			
1878	b	1226	2051	1			
1879	v	1226	1106	1			
1879	d	1226	1110	1			
1879	m	1226	1118	1			
1879	b	1226	2051	1			
1880	m	1226	1102	1			
1880	d	1226	1111	1			
1880	b	1226	2051	1			
1881	b	1226	2051	1			
1881	m	1226	2052	1			
1881	v	1226	2053	1			
1881	d	1226	2054	1			
1882	b	1226	2051	1			
1882	m	1226	2052	1			
1882	v	1226	2053	1			
1882	d	1226	2054	1			
1883	b	1226	2051	1			
1883	m	1226	2052	1			
1883	v	1226	2053	1			
1883	d	1226	2054	1			
1884	b	1226	2051	1			
1884	m	1226	2052	1			
1884	v	1226	2053	1			
1884	d	1226	2054	1			
1885	b	1226	2051	1			
1885	m	1226	2052	1			
1885	v	1226	2053	1			
1885	d	1226	2054	1			
1886	b	1226	2051	1			
1886	m	1226	2052	1			
1886	v	1226	2053	1			
1886	d	1226	2054	1			
1887	b	1226	2051	1			
1887	m	1226	2052	1			
1887	v	1226	2053	1			
1887	d	1226	2054	1			
1888	b	1226	2051	1			
1888	m	1226	2052	1			
1888	v	1226	2053	1			
1888	d	1226	2054	1			
1889	b	1226	2051	1			
1889	m	1226	2052	1			
1889	v	1226	2053	1			
1889	d	1226	2054	1			
1890	b	1226	2051	1			
1890	m	1226	2052	1			
1890	v	1226	2053	1			
1890	d	1226	2054	1			
1891	b	1226	2051	1			
1891	m	1226	2052	1			
1891	v	1226	2053	1			
1891	d	1226	2054	1			
1892	b	1226	2051	1			
1892	m	1226	2052	1			
1892	v	1226	2053	1			
1892	d	1226	2054	1			
1893	b	1226	2051	1			
1893	m	1226	2052	1			
1893	v	1226	2053	1			
1893	d	1226	2054	1			
1894	b	1226	2051	1			
1894	m	1226	2052	1			
1894	v	1226	2053	1			
1894	d	1226	2054	1			
1895	b	1226	2051	1			
1895	m	1226	2052	1			
1895	v	1226	2053	1			
1895	d	1226	2054	1			
1896	b	1226	2051	1			
1896	m	1226	2052	1			
1896	v	1226	2053	1			
1896	d	1226	2054	1			

Pumpenai (Pumpian) continued

Pumpenai (Pumpian) continued

Year(s)	Type	Fond	File(s)	Op	A	F	Notes
1897	b	1226	2051	1			
1897	m	1226	2052	1			
1897	v	1226	2053	1			
1897	d	1226	2054	1			
1898	b	1226	2051	1			
1898	m	1226	2052	1			
1898	v	1226	2053	1			
1898	d	1226	2054	1			
1899	b	1226	2051	1			
1899	m	1226	2052	1			
1899	v	1226	2053	1			
1899	d	1226	2054	1			
1900	b	1226	2051	1			
1900	m	1226	2052	1			
1900	v	1226	2053	1			
1900	d	1226	2054	1			
1901	b	1226	2051	1			
1901	m	1226	2052	1			
1901	v	1226	2053	1			
1901	d	1226	2054	1			
1902	b	1226	2051	1			
1902	m	1226	2052	1			
1902	v	1226	2053	1			
1902	d	1226	2054	1			
1902	d	728	1000	1			
1903	b	1226	2051	1			
1903	m	1226	2052	1			
1903	v	1226	2053	1			
1903	d	1226	2054	1			
1903	d	728	1015-1016	1			
1904	b	1226	2051	1			
1904	m	1226	2052	1			
1904	v	1226	2053	1			
1904	d	1226	2054	1			
1905	b	1226	2051	1			
1905	m	1226	2052	1			
1905	v	1226	2053	1			
1905	d	1226	2054	1			
1905	d	728	1032	1			
1906	b	1226	2051	1			
1906	m	1226	2052	1			
1906	v	1226	2053	1			
1906	d	1226	2054	1			
1906	d	728	1039	1			
1907	b	1226	2051	1			
1907	m	1226	2052	1			
1907	v	1226	2053	1			
1907	d	1226	2054	1			
1907	d	728	1050	1			
1908	b	1226	2051	1			
1908	m	1226	2052	1			
1908	v	1226	2053	1			
1908	d	1226	2054	1			
1909	b	1226	2051	1			
1909	m	1226	2052, 2104	1			
1909	v	1226	2053	1			
1909	d	1226	2054	1			
1910	b	1226	2051	1			
1910	m	1226	2052	1			
1910	v	1226	2053	1			
1910	d	1226	2054	1			
1911	b	1226	2051	1			
1911	m	1226	2052	1			
1911	v	1226	2053	1			
1911	d	1226	2054	1			
1912	b	1226	2051	1			
1912	m	1226	2052, 2104	1			
1912	v	1226	2053	1			
1912	d	1226	2054	1			
1913	b	1226	2051	1			
1913	m	1226	2052, 2104	1			
1913	v	1226	2053	1			
1913	d	1226	2054	1			
1914	b	1226	2051	1			
1914	m	1226	2052	1			
1914	v	1226	2053	1			
1914	d	1226	2054	1			

Punia (Pun)

Year(s)	Type	Fond	File(s)	Op	A	F	Notes
1858-1905	rs	515	110-122	25			
1859	rs	515	123	25			srs, Trakai County
1860	rs	515	124	25			srs, Trakai County
1861	rs	515	124	25			srs, Trakai County
1862	rs	515	124	25			srs, Trakai County
1863	rs	515	124	25			srs, Trakai County
1863	rs	515	124	25			srs, Trakai County
1864	rs	515	125-126	25			srs, Trakai County
1865	rs	515	127	25			srs, Trakai County

Punia (Pun) continued

Year(s)	Type	Fond	File(s)	Op	A	F	Notes
1868	rs	515	128-129	25			srs, Trakai County
1869	rs	515	129-130	25			srs, Trakai County
1870	rs	515	130-131	25			srs, Trakai County
1871	rs	515	132	25			srs, Trakai County
1872	rs	515	133	25			srs, Trakai County
1873	rs	515	133	25			srs, Trakai County
1873	rs	515	133	25			srs, Trakai County
1874	rs	515	133	25			srs, Trakai County
1874	rs	515	133	25			srs, Trakai County
1905	rs	515	144	25			srs, Trakai County
1906	rs	515	144	25			srs, Trakai County
1907	rs	515	144	25			srs, Trakai County
1908	rs	515	144	25			srs, Trakai County
1854	d	728	104	1			
1854	m	728	73	1			
1855	m	728	144	1			
1855	v	728	167	1			
1855	d	728	183	1			
1856	b	728	199	1			
1856	m	728	233	1			
1856	d	728	265	1			
1857	m	728	301	1			
1857	v	728	314	1			
1857	d	728	326	1			
1858	b	728	341	1			
1858	m	728	364	1			
1858	v	728	389	1			
1858	d	728	399	1			
1859	b	728	434	1			
1859	m	728	452	1			
1859	v	728	471	1			
1859	d	728	492	1			
1860	b	728	511	1			
1860	m	728	533	1			
1860	v	728	549	1			
1860	d	728	581	1			
1861	m	728	636	1			
1861	d	728	673	1			
1862	b	728	696	1			
1862	m	728	709	1			
1862	d	728	746	1			
1863	b	728	783	1			
1863	m	728	799	1			
1863	d	728	854	1			
1864	b	728	828	3			
1864	d	728	831	3			
1865	b	728	832	3			
1865	m	728	833	3			
1865	v	728	834	3			
1865	d	728	835	3			
1866	b	728	836-837	3			
1866	d	728	840	3			
1867	b	728	841	3			
1867	m	728	842	3			
1867	d	728	844	3			
1868	b	728	845	3			
1868	m	728	846	3			
1868	d	728	848	3			
1869	b	728	849	3			
1869	m	728	850	3			
1869	d	728	852	3			
1870	b	728	853	3			
1870	m	728	854-855	3			
1870	d	728	857-858	3			
1871	b	728	859	3			
1871	m	728	860-861	3			
1871	d	728	863-864	3			
1872	b	728	865	3			
1872	m	728	866-867	3			
1872	d	728	869	3			
1873	b	728	870	3			
1873	m	728	871-872	3			
1873	d	728	874-875	3			
1874	b	728	876	3			
1874	m	728	877-878	3			
1874	d	728	880-881	3			
1875	b	728	882	3			
1875	d	728	886	3			
1876	d	728	1286-1287	3			
1876	m	728	1293-1294	3			
1876	b	728	1300	3			
1877	d	728	1288-1289	3			
1877	m	728	1295-1296	3			
1878	d	728	1290	3			
1878	m	728	1297	3			
1879	d	728	1291	3			
1879	m	728	1298	3			
1880	d	728	1292	3			

Punia (Pun) continued

Year(s)	Type	Fond	File(s)	Op	A	F	Notes
1880	m	728	1299	3			
1881	b	728	328	4			
1881	d	728	330	4			
1882	d	728	330	4			
1885	d	728	330	4			
1890	d	728	330	4			
1891	d	728	330	4			
1898	b	728	328	4			
1898	d	728	330	4			
1899	b	728	328	4			
1899	d	728	330	4			
1900	b	728	328	4			
1900	d	728	330	4			
1901	b	728	328	4			
1901	m	728	329	4			
1901	d	728	330	4			
1902	b	728	328	4			
1902	m	728	329	4			
1905	d	728	330	4			

Pusalotas (Poshelat)

Year(s)	Type	Fond	File(s)	Op	A	F	Notes
1816	rs						
1818	rs						
1834	rs						
1882	rs	I-217	1	1	K		Jewish Community
1882	m	1226	2056	1			
1882	d	1226	2057	1			
1882	fl	217			K		
1883	m	1226	2056	1			
1883	v	1226	2056	1			
1883	d	1226	2057	1			
1884	m	1226	2056	1			
1884	v	1226	2056	1			
1884	d	1226	2057	1			
1885	b	1226	2055	1			
1885	m	1226	2056	1			
1885	v	1226	2056	1			
1885	d	1226	2057	1			
1886	b	1226	2055	1			
1886	m	1226	2056	1			
1886	v	1226	2056	1			
1886	d	1226	2057	1			
1887	b	1226	2055	1			
1887	m	1226	2056	1			
1887	v	1226	2056	1			
1887	d	1226	2057	1			
1888	b	1226	2055	1			
1888	m	1226	2056	1			
1888	v	1226	2056	1			
1888	d	1226	2057	1			
1889	b	1226	2055	1			
1889	m	1226	2056	1			
1889	v	1226	2056	1			
1889	d	1226	2057	1			
1890	b	1226	2055	1			
1890	m	1226	2056	1			
1890	v	1226	2056	1			
1890	d	1226	2057	1			
1891	b	1226	2055	1			
1891	m	1226	2056	1			
1891	v	1226	2056	1			
1891	d	1226	2057	1			
1892	b	1226	2055	1			
1892	m	1226	2056	1			
1892	v	1226	2056	1			
1892	d	1226	2057	1			
1892	d	728	953	1			
1893	b	1226	2055	1			
1893	m	1226	2056	1			
1893	v	1226	2056	1			
1893	d	1226	2057	1			
1894	b	1226	2055	1			
1894	m	1226	2056	1			
1894	v	1226	2056	1			
1894	d	1226	2057	1			
1895	b	1226	2055	1			
1895	m	1226	2056	1			
1895	v	1226	2056	1			
1895	d	1226	2057	1			
1896	b	1226	2055	1			
1896	m	1226	2056	1			
1896	v	1226	2056	1			
1896	d	1226	2057	1			
1897	b	1226	2055	1			
1897	m	1226	2056	1			
1897	v	1226	2056	1			
1897	d	1226	2057	1			
1898	b	1226	2055	1			

Pusalotas (Poshelat) continued

Year(s)	Type	Fond	File(s)	Op	A	F	Notes
1898	m	1226	2056	1			
1898	v	1226	2056	1			
1898	d	1226	2057	1			
1899	b	1226	2055	1			
1899	m	1226	2056	1			
1899	v	1226	2056	1			
1899	d	1226	2057	1			
1900	b	1226	2055	1			
1900	m	1226	2056	1			
1900	v	1226	2056	1			
1900	d	1226	2057	1			
1900	d	728	982	1			
1901	b	1226	2055	1			
1901	m	1226	2056	1			
1901	v	1226	2056	1			
1901	d	1226	2057	1			
1902	b	1226	2055	1			
1902	m	1226	2056	1			
1902	v	1226	2056	1			
1902	d	1226	2057	1			
1902	d	728	1001	1			
1903	b	1226	2055	1			
1903	m	1226	2056	1			
1903	v	1226	2056	1			
1903	d	1226	2057	1			
1903	d	728	1014	1			
1904	b	1226	2055	1			
1904	m	1226	2056	1			
1904	v	1226	2056	1			
1904	d	1226	2057	1			
1905	b	1226	2055	1			
1905	m	1226	2056	1			
1905	v	1226	2056	1			
1905	d	1226	2057	1			
1905	d	728	1031	1			
1906	b	1226	2055	1			
1906	m	1226	2056	1			
1906	v	1226	2056	1			
1906	d	1226	2057	1			
1906	d	728	1038	1			
1907	b	1226	2055	1			
1907	m	1226	2056	1			
1907	v	1226	2056	1			
1907	d	1226	2057	1			
1907	d	728	1049	1			
1908	b	1226	2055	1			
1908	m	1226	2056	1			
1908	v	1226	2056	1			
1908	d	1226	2057	1			
1908	d	728	1060	1			
1909	b	1226	2055	1			
1909	m	1226	2056	1			
1909	v	1226	2056	1			
1909	d	1226	2057	1			
1910	b	1226	2055	1			
1910	m	1226	2056	1			
1910	v	1226	2056	1			
1910	d	1226	2057	1			
1910	d	728	1074	1			
1911	b	1226	2055	1			
1911	m	1226	2056	1			
1911	v	1226	2056	1			
1911	d	1226	2057	1			
1911	d	728	1082	1			
1912	b	1226	2055	1			
1912	m	1226	2056	1			
1912	d	1226	2057	1			
1912	d	728	1087	1			

Radun, Belarus (Radun)

Year(s)	Type	Fond	File(s)	Op	A	F	Notes
1896	b	728	955	1			Lida County
1897	m	728	1046	1			Lida County
1897	b	728	958	1			Lida County
1898	m	728	1057	1			Lida County
1898	b	728	964	1			Lida County
1899	m	728	1064	1			Lida County
1899	b	728	971	1			Lida County
1900	b	728	975	1			Lida County
1901	b	728	986	1			Lida County
1902	b	728	994	1			Lida County
1903	b	728	1006	1			Lida County
1904	b	728	1018	1			Lida County
1905	b	728	1027	1			Lida County
1906	b	728	1034, 1034A	1			Lida County
1908	b	728	1055	1			Lida County
1909	b	728	1063	1			Lida County
1910	b	728	1070	1			Lida County
1911	b	728	1077	1			Lida County

Year(s)	Type	Fond	File(s)	Op	A	F	Notes
Radun, Belarus (Radun) continued							
1912	b	728	1085	1			Lida County
1913	b	728	1090	1			Lida County
1914	b	728	1094	1			Lida County
Radviliskis (Radvilishok)							
1873	m	1226	1917	1			
1874	m	1226	1917	1			
1912–1916	tpl-r				K		
Raguva							
1851	rs						
1858	rs						
1858	rs						
1866	rs						
1867	rs						
1873	rs						
1874	rs						
1879	rs						
1851							
1867							
1873							
Ramygala (Remigola)							
1816	rs						
1818	rs						
1834	rs						
1875	rs	I-218	1	1	K		Alphabetic – Jews
1875	fl	218			K		
1889	d	728	952	1			
1894	d	728	954	1			
1895	cen						crl
1896	d	728	957	1			
Raseiniai (Rasin)							
1816	rs						
1838	rs						
1842	rs						
1851	rs						
1858	rs						
1863	rs						
1869	rs						
1873	rs						
1876	rs						
1844	m	728	15	1			
1844	d	728	22	1			
1845	m	728	23	1			
1845	b	728	9	1			
1908	dl				K		Mostly Jews
1911	hol				K		Alphabetic – Jews
1911	pib				K		Many Jews
Raseiniai County							
1816	ol				K		
Ratnycia (Rotnitsa)							
1858–1905	rs						
all	bdm	728		4			Some records listed with Merkine (Merech).
Rietavas (Ritova)							
1816	rs						
1839	rs						
1851	rs						
1864	rs						
1869	rs						
1870?	rs						
Rokiskis (Rokishok)							
1864–1871	rs	1262	57	1			
1874	b,m,d	I-210	621	1	K		
1875	b,m,d	I-210	621	1	K		
1876	b,m,d	I-210	621	1	K		
1877	b,m,d	I-210	621	1	K		
1878	b,m,d	I-210	621	1	K		
1879	b,m,d	I-210	621	1	K		
1880	b,m,d	I-210	621	1	K		
1881	b,m,d	I-210	621	1	K		
1882	b,m,d	I-210	621	1	K		
1883	fl	I-210	598	1	K		Alphabetic – Jews
1883	b,m,d	I-210	621	1	K		
1884	b,m,d	I-210	621	1	K		
1885	b,m,d	I-210	621	1	K		
1886	b,m,d	I-210	621	1	K		
1887	fl	210			K		
1887	fl	I-210	599	1	K		Alphabetic – Jews
1887	b,m,d	I-210	621	1	K		
1888	b,m,d	I-210	621	1	K		
1889	b,m,d	I-210	621	1	K		
1890	b,m,d	I-210	621	1	K		

Rokiskis (Rokishok) continued

Year(s)	Type	Fond	File(s)	Op	A	F	Notes
1891	b,m,d	I-210	621	1	K		
1892	b,m,d	I-210	621	1	K		
1893	b,m,d	I-210	621	1	K		
1894	b,m,d	I-210	621	1	K		
1895	b,m,d	I-210	621	1	K		
1896	b,m,d	I-210	621	1	K		
1899	prb				K		
1902-1914	fl	I-210	26-27, 53-569 with gaps	1	K		
1907	el				K		
1908	fl				K		
1909	fl				K		Jews
1909	fl				K		

Rostov-na-Don?

Year(s)	Type	Fond	File(s)	Op	A	F	Notes
1880	b	I-61	1538-1540	3	K		Ukraine?

Rudamina (Rudamin) Items for this town are in the Vilnius County 4th Okrug Registers.

Year(s)	Type	Fond	File(s)	Op	A	F	Notes
1885	m	728	353	4			
1886	m	728	353	4			
1887	d	728	1478	3			
1887	m	728	353	4			
1887	b	728	364	4			
1888	d	728	1478	3			
1888	m	728	353	4			
1888	b	728	364	4			
1889	d	728	1478	3			
1889	m	728	353	4			
1889	b	728	364	4			
1890	d	728	1478	3			
1890	b	728	1479	3			
1890	m	728	1480	3			
1890	m	728	353	4			
1890	b	728	364	4			
1891	b	728	1446	3			
1891	d	728	1478	3			
1891	m	728	1483	3			
1891	m	728	353	4			
1891	b	728	364	4			
1892	d	728	1478	3			
1892	b	728	1486, 1553	3			
1892	m	728	1487, 1488, 1554	3			
1892	v	728	1489	3			
1892	m	728	353	4			
1892	b	728	364	4			
1893	d	728	1478	3			
1893	b	728	1490, 1553	3			
1893	m	728	1494, 1554	3			
1893	v	728	1496	3			
1893	m	728	353	4			
1893	b	728	364	4			
1894	b	728	1499, 1553	3			
1894	m	728	1505, 1554	3			
1894	v	728	1516	3			
1894	m	728	353	4			
1894	b	728	364	4			
1895	b	728	1508, 1553	3			
1895	m	728	1513, 1556	3			
1895	v	728	1519	3			
1895	v	728	3	4			
1895	m	728	353	4			
1895	b	728	364	4			
1896	b	728	13, 364	4			
1896	m	728	14, 353	4			
1896	b	728	1553	3			
1896	m	728	1556	3			
1897	b	728	28-29, 364	4			
1897	m	728	30, 353, 437	4			
1897	d	728	32	4			
1898	b	728	28, 45, 364	4			
1898	d	728	32	4			
1898	m	728	46, 353, 437	4			
1899	b	728	28, 60, 364	4			
1899	v	728	3	4			
1899	d	728	32	4			
1899	m	728	61, 353, 437	4			
1900	v	728	3	4			
1900	b	728	72, 364	4			
1900	m	728	73-74, 353, 437	4			
1900	d	728	75	4			
1901	v	728	3, 88	4			
1901	d	728	75	4			
1901	b	728	86, 364	4			
1901	m	728	87, 353, 437	4			
1902	m	728	102, 353, 438	4			
1902	d	728	103, 439	4			
1902	b	728	364	4			
1903	b	728	114-115, 364	4			

Rudamina (Rudamin) continued

Year(s)	Type	Fond	File(s)	Op	A	F	Notes
1903	m	728	116, 353, 438, 444	4			
1903	d	728	117, 439	4			
1904	b	728	127, 364	4			
1904	m	728	128, 353, 438	4			
1904	d	728	129, 439	4			
1905	b	728	139, 364	4			
1905	m	728	140, 353, 438	4			
1905	d	728	75, 141, 439	4			
1906	b	728	151, 364, 441	4			
1906	m	728	152, 353	4			
1906	d	728	75, 153	4			
1907	b	728	161, 364, 441	4			
1907	m	728	162, 353	4			
1907	v	728	3	4			
1907	d	728	75	4			
1908	b	728	172, 364, 441	4			
1908	v	728	3, 173	4			
1908	m	728	353	4			
1908	d	728	75	4			
1909	b	728	187, 364	4			
1909	v	728	3, 188	4			
1909	m	728	353, 442	4			
1909	d	728	75	4			
1910	b	728	199, 364	4			
1910	v	728	3, 200	4			
1910	m	728	353, 443	4			
1911	b	728	213, 364	4			
1911	m	728	214, 353	4			
1911	v	728	215	4			
1912	b	728	226, 364	4			
1912	m	728	227-228, 353	4			
1913	b	728	239, 364	4			
1913	m	728	240, 353	4			
1914	b	728	253, 364	4			
1914	m	728	253-254, 353	4			
1914	v	728	255	4			
1915	m	728	353	4			
1915	b	728	364	4			
1916	b	728	364	4			
1917	b	728	364	4			
1917	b	728	364	4			
1918	b	728	364	4			
1919	b	728	364	4			
1920	b	728	364	4			
1921	b	728	364	4			

Rumsiskes (Rumshishok)

Year(s)	Type	Fond	File(s)	Op	A	F	Notes
1851	rs						
1874	rs	I-61	1649	1	K		Alphabetic - Jews
1878	rs						
1838	ct						Collection & Distribution List
1838	ml				K		
1843-44	pib				K		
1854	b	1226	1323	1			
1854	m	1226	1324	1			
1854	d	1226	1325	1			
1855	b	1226	1323	1			
1855	m	1226	1324	1			
1855	d	1226	1325	1			
1856	b	1226	1323	1			
1856	m	1226	1324	1			
1856	d	1226	1325	1			
1857	b	1226	1323	1			
1857	m	1226	1324	1			
1857	d	1226	1325	1			
1858	b	1226	1323	1			
1858	m	1226	1324	1			
1858	d	1226	1325-1326	1			
1859	b	1226	1323	1			
1859	m	1226	1324	1			
1859	d	1226	1325-1326	1			
1860	b	1226	1323	1			
1860	m	1226	1324	1			
1860	d	1226	1325-1326	1			
1861	m	1226	1324	1			
1861	d	1226	1325-1326	1			
1861	b	1226	1327	1			
1862	m	1226	1324	1			
1862	d	1226	1325	1			
1862	b	1226	1327	1			
1863	m	1226	1324	1			
1863	d	1226	1325	1			
1863	b	1226	1327	1			
1864	m	1226	1324	1			
1864	d	1226	1325	1			
1864	b	1226	1327	1			
1864	d	728	923	1			
1865	b	1226	208, 1327	1			

Rumsiskes (Rumshishok) continued

Year(s)	Type	Fond	File(s)	Op	A	F	Notes
1865	m	1226	209, 1324	1			
1865	v	1226	210	1			
1865	d	1226	211, 1325	1			
1866	m	1226	1324	1			
1866	d	1226	1325	1			
1866	b	1226	1327	1			
1867	m	1226	1324	1			
1867	d	1226	1325	1			
1867	b	1226	1327	1			
1867	v	1226	1328	1			
1868	b	1226	212, 1327	1			
1868	m	1226	213, 1324	1			
1868	v	1226	214, 1328	1			
1868	d	1226	215, 1325	1			
1869	b	1226	216, 1329	1			
1869	m	1226	217, 1324	1			
1869	v	1226	218, 1328	1			
1869	d	1226	219, 1325	1			
1870	m	1226	1324	1			
1870	d	1226	1325	1			
1870	v	1226	1328	1			
1870	b	1226	1329	1			
1870-74	k				K		
1871	b	1226	220, 1329	1			
1871	m	1226	221, 1324	1			
1871	v	1226	222, 1328	1			
1871	d	1226	223, 1325	1			
1872	b	1226	224, 1329	1			
1872	m	1226	225, 1324	1			
1872	v	1226	226, 1328	1			
1872	d	1226	227	1			
1873	b	1226	228, 1329	1			
1873	m	1226	229, 1324	1			
1873	v	1226	230, 1328	1			
1873	d	1226	231	1			
1874	b	1226	232, 1329	1			
1874	m	1226	233	1			
1874	v	1226	234, 1328	1			
1874	d	1226	235	1			
1874	fl	200			K		
1874	fl	I-200	1	1	K		Index of Jews
1874-78	k				K		
1875	b	1226	236, 1329	1			
1875	m	1226	237, 1330	1			
1875	v	1226	238, 1328	1			
1875	d	1226	239	1			
1876	d	1226	960, 1331	1			
1876	v	1226	971, 1328	1			
1876	m	1226	975, 1330	1			
1876	b	1226	979, 1329	1			
1877	v	1226	1328	1			
1877	b	1226	1329	1			
1877	m	1226	1330	1			
1877	d	1226	961, 1331-1332	1			
1878	d	1226	962, 1331-1332	1			
1878	v	1226	972, 1328	1			
1878	m	1226	976, 1330	1			
1878	b	1226	980, 1329	1			
1879	d	1226	969, 1331-1332	1			
1879	v	1226	973, 1328	1			
1879	m	1226	977, 1330	1			
1879	b	1226	981, 1329	1			
1880	d	1226	970, 1331-1332	1			
1880	v	1226	974, 1328	1			
1880	m	1226	978, 1330	1			
1880	b	1226	982, 1329	1			
1881	v	1226	1328, 2061	1			
1881	b	1226	1329, 2058	1			
1881	m	1226	1330, 2060	1			
1881	d	1226	1331-1332, 2062	1			
1882	v	1226	1328, 2061	1			
1882	b	1226	1329, 2058	1			
1882	m	1226	1330, 2060	1			
1882	d	1226	1331-1332, 2062	1			
1883	v	1226	1328, 2061	1			
1883	m	1226	1330, 2060	1			
1883	d	1226	1331-1332, 2062	1			
1883	b	1226	1333, 2058	1			
1884	v	1226	1328, 2061	1			
1884	m	1226	1330, 2060	1			
1884	d	1226	1331-1332, 2062	1			
1884	b	1226	1333, 2058	1			
1885	v	1226	1328, 2061	1			
1885	m	1226	1330, 2060	1			
1885	d	1226	1331-1332, 2062	1			
1885	b	1226	1333, 2058	1			
1886	v	1226	1328, 2061	1			
1886	m	1226	1330, 2060	1			

Rumsiskes (Rumshishok) continued

Year(s)	Type	Fond	File(s)	Op	A	F	Notes
1886	d	1226	1331–1332, 2062	1			
1886	b	1226	1333, 2058	1			
1887	v	1226	1328, 2061	1			
1887	m	1226	1330, 2060	1			
1887	d	1226	1331–1332, 2062	1			
1887	b	1226	1333, 2058	1			
1888	v	1226	1328, 2061	1			
1888	m	1226	1330, 2060	1			
1888	d	1226	1331, 2062	1			
1888	b	1226	1333, 2058	1			
1889	v	1226	1328, 2061	1			
1889	m	1226	1330, 2060	1			
1889	b	1226	1333, 2058	1			
1889	d	1226	2062	1			
1890	v	1226	1328, 2061	1			
1890	m	1226	1330, 2060	1			
1890	b	1226	1333, 2058	1			
1890	d	1226	2062	1			
1891	v	1226	1328, 2061	1			
1891	b	1226	1333, 2058	1			
1891	d	1226	1334, 2062	1			
1891	m	1226	2060	1			
1892	v	1226	1328, 2061	1			
1892	b	1226	1333, 2058	1			
1892	d	1226	1334, 2062	1			
1892	m	1226	1335, 2060	1			
1893	v	1226	1328, 2061	1			
1893	d	1226	1334, 2062	1			
1893	m	1226	1335, 2060	1			
1893	b	1226	1336, 2058	1			
1894	v	1226	1328, 2061	1			
1894	d	1226	1334, 2062	1			
1894	m	1226	1335, 2060	1			
1894	b	1226	1336, 2058	1			
1895	v	1226	1328, 2061	1			
1895	d	1226	1334, 2062	1			
1895	m	1226	1335, 2060	1			
1895	b	1226	1336, 2058	1			
1896	v	1226	1328, 2061	1			
1896	d	1226	1334, 2062	1			
1896	m	1226	1335, 2060	1			
1896	b	1226	1336, 2058	1			
1897	v	1226	1328, 2061	1			
1897	d	1226	1334, 2062	1			
1897	m	1226	1335, 2060	1			
1897	b	1226	1336, 2058	1			
1898	v	1226	1328, 2061	1			
1898	d	1226	1334, 2062	1			
1898	m	1226	1335, 2060	1			
1898	b	1226	1336, 2058	1			
1899	v	1226	1328, 2061	1			
1899	d	1226	1334, 2062	1			
1899	m	1226	1335, 2060	1			
1899	b	1226	1336, 2059	1			
1900	v	1226	1328, 2061	1			
1900	d	1226	1334, 2062	1			
1900	m	1226	1335, 2060	1			
1900	b	1226	1336, 2059	1			
1901	v	1226	1328, 2061	1			
1901	d	1226	1334, 2062	1			
1901	m	1226	1335, 2060	1			
1901	b	1226	1336, 2059	1			
1902	v	1226	1328, 2061	1			
1902	d	1226	1334, 2062	1			
1902	m	1226	1335, 2060	1			
1902	b	1226	1336, 2059	1			
1903	v	1226	1328, 2061	1			
1903	d	1226	1334, 2062	1			
1903	m	1226	1335, 2060	1			
1903	b	1226	1337, 2059	1			
1904	v	1226	1328, 2061	1			
1904	d	1226	1334, 2062	1			
1904	m	1226	1335, 2060	1			
1904	b	1226	1337, 2059	1			
1905	v	1226	1328, 2061	1			
1905	d	1226	1334, 2062	1			
1905	m	1226	1335, 2060	1			
1905	b	1226	1337, 2059	1			
1906	v	1226	1328, 2061	1			
1906	d	1226	1334, 2062	1			
1906	m	1226	1335, 2060	1			
1906	b	1226	1337, 2059	1			
1907	d	1226	1334, 2062	1			
1907	m	1226	1335, 2060	1			
1907	b	1226	1337, 2059	1			
1907	v	1226	2061	1			
1908	d	1226	1334, 2062	1			
1908	m	1226	1335, 2060	1			

Rumsiskes (Rumshishok) continued

Year(s)	Type	Fond	File(s)	Op	A	F	Notes
1908	b	1226	1337, 2059	1			
1908	v	1226	2061	1			
1909	m	1226	1335, 2060	1			
1909	b	1226	1337, 2059	1			
1909	d	1226	1338, 2062	1			
1909	v	1226	2061	1			
1910	m	1226	1335, 2060	1			
1910	b	1226	1337, 2059	1			
1910	d	1226	1338, 2062	1			
1910	v	1226	2061	1			
1911	m	1226	1335, 2060	1			
1911	b	1226	1337, 2059	1			
1911	d	1226	1338, 2062	1			
1911	v	1226	2061	1			
1912	m	1226	1335, 2060	1			
1912	b	1226	1337, 2059	1			
1912	d	1226	1338, 2062	1			
1912	v	1226	2061	1			
1913	m	1226	1335, 2060	1			
1913	b	1226	1337, 2059	1			
1913	d	1226	1338, 2062	1			
1913	v	1226	2061	1			
1914	m	1226	1335, 2060	1			
1914	b	1226	1337, 2059	1			
1914	d	1226	1338, 2062	1			
1915	b	1226	1337, 2059	1			
1915	m	1226	2060	1			
unclear	dc	61	384	1			K

Sakiai (Shaki)

Year(s)	Type	Fond	File(s)	Op	A	F	Notes
1813	m	1236	760	3			
1814	d	1236	7	6			
1814	m	1236	760, 762	3			
1814	b	1236	761	3			
1815	b	1236	761, 763	3			
1815	m	1236	762, 764, 823	3			
1815	d	1236	765	3			
1816	b	1236	763	3			
1816	m	1236	764, 766, 823	3			
1816	d	1236	765	3			
1817	m	1236	766, 770	3			
1817	b	1236	769	3			
1817	d	1236	772	3			
1818	b	1236	773	3			
1818	m	1236	774	3			
1819	b	1236	775	3			
1820	b	1236	777	3			
1820	m	1236	778	3			
1821	b	1236	780	3			
1821	m	1236	781	3			
1821	d	1236	782	3			
1822	b	1236	783	3			
1822	m	1236	784	3			
1822	d	1236	786	3			
1823	b	1236	787	3			
1823	d	1236	789	3			
1824	b	1236	790	3			
1824	m	1236	791	3			
1824	d	1236	793	3			
1825	b	1236	794	3			
1825	m	1236	795	3			
1825	d	1236	797	3			
1826	b	1236	798	3			
1826	d	1236	798	3			
1826	m	1236	798	3			
1827	d	1236	802	3			
1828	b	1236	802	3			
1828	m	1236	802	3			
1830	d	1236	806	3			
1830	m	1236	806	3			
1832	b	1236	806	3			
1833	b	1236	809	3			
1833	d	1236	809	3			
1833	m	1236	809	3			
1835	b	1236	811	3			
1835	d	1236	811	3			
1835	m	1236	811	3			
1836	b	1236	2	6			
1836	d	1236	2	6			
1836	m	1236	2	6			
1840	b	1236	814	3			
1840	d	1236	814	3			
1840	m	1236	814	3			
1841	b	1236	815	3			
1841	d	1236	815	3			
1841	m	1236	815	3			
1842	b	1108	10	1			
1842	b	1236	816	3			

Sakiai (Shaki) continued

Year(s)	Type	Fond	File(s)	Op	A	F	Notes
1842	d	1236	816	3			
1842	m	1236	816	3			
1843	b	1108	10	1			
1843	b	1236	817	3			
1843	d	1236	817	3			
1843	m	1236	817	3			
1844	b	1108	10	1			
1844	b	1236	819	3			
1844	d	1236	819	3			
1844	m	1236	819	3			
1845	b	1108	10	1			
1845	b	1236	821	3			
1845	d	1236	821	3			
1845	m	1236	821	3			
1846	b	1108	10	1			
1846	b	1236	822	3			
1846	d	1236	822	3			
1846	m	1236	822	3			
1847	b	1108	10	1			
1847	b	1236	825	3			
1847	d	1236	825	3			
1847	m	1236	825	3			
1848	b	1236	827	3			
1848	d	1236	827	3			
1848	m	1236	827	3			
1849	b	1236	829	3			
1849	d	1236	829	3			
1849	m	1236	829	3			
1850	b	1236	831	3			
1850	d	1236	831	3			
1850	m	1236	831	3			
1851	b	1236	833	3			
1851	d	1236	833	3			
1851	m	1236	833	3			
1852	b	1236	835	3			
1852	d	1236	835	3			
1852	m	1236	835	3			
1856	b	1236	842	3			
1856	d	1236	842	3			
1856	m	1236	842	3			
1857	b	1108	11	1			
1858	b	1108	11	1			
1859	b	1108	11	1			
1859	b	1236	846	3			
1859	d	1236	846	3			
1859	m	1236	846	3			
1860	b	1108	11	1			
1861	b	1108	11	1			
1861	b	1236	426	3			
1861	d	1236	426	3			
1861	m	1236	426	3			
1862	b	1108	11	1			
1863	b	1108	11	1			
1864	b	1108	11	1			
1864	b	1108	32	1			
1864	b	1236	432	3			
1864	d	1236	432	3			
1864	m	1236	432	3			
1865	b	1108	32	1			
1866	b	1108	32	1			
1866	b	1236	854	3			
1866	d	1236	854	3			
1866	m	1236	854	3			
1867	b	1108	32	1			
1868	b	1108	32	1			
1868	b	1236	858	3			
1868	d	1236	858	3			
1868	m	1236	858	3			
1869	b	1108	32	1			
1870	b	1108	32	1			
1871	b	1108	32	1			
1872	b	1108	32	1			
1873	b	1108	32	1			
1874	b	1108	32	1			
1875	b	1108	32	1			
1876	b	1108	32	1			
1877	b	1108	32	1			
1878	b	1108	12	1			
1879	b	1108	12	1			
1880	b	1108	12	1			
1881	b	1108	12	1			
1882	b	1108	12	1			
1883	b	1108	12	1			
1884	b	1108	12	1			
1885	b	1108	12	1			
1885	m	1108	13	1			
1886	b	1108	12	1			
1886	m	1108	13	1			

Sakiai (Shaki) continued

Year(s)	Type	Fond	File(s)	Op	A	F	Notes
1887	b	1108	12	1			
1887	m	1108	13	1			
1888	m	1108	13	1			
1889	m	1108	13	1			
1890	m	1108	13	1			
1891	m	1108	13	1			
1892	m	1108	13	1			
1892	d	728	1004	1			
1893	m	1108	13	1			
1893	d	728	1004	1			
1894	m	1108	13	1			
1894	d	728	1004	1			
1895	m	1108	13	1			
1895	d	728	1004	1			
1896	m	1108	13	1			
1896	d	728	1004	1			
1897	m	1108	13	1			
1897	d	728	1004	1			
1898	m	1108	13	1			
1898	d	728	1004	1			
1899	m	1108	13	1			
1899	d	728	1004	1			
1900	m	1108	13	1			
1900	d	728	1004	1			
1901	m	1108	13	1			
1901	d	728	1004	1			
1902	m	1108	13	1			
1902	d	728	1004	1			
1903	m	1108	13	1			
1903	d	728	1004	1			
1904	m	1108	13	1			
1904	d	728	1004	1			
1905	m	1108	13	1			
1905	d	728	1004	1			
1906	m	1108	13	1			
1906	d	728	1004	1			
1907	m	1108	13	1			
1907	d	728	1004	1			
1908	m	1108	13	1			
1909	m	1108	13	1			
1910	m	1108	13	1			
1911	m	1108	13	1			

Salakas

Year(s)	Type	Fond	File(s)	Op	A	F	Notes
1816-27	rs						
1848	rs						
1858	rs						
1860	rs						
1871	rs						
1872-75	rs						
1880-1892	rs	I-211	60	1	K		Jews who moved from other communities.
1876	fl	211			K		
1887	fl				K		
1893	b	I-211	55	1	K		
1894	b	I-211	55	1	K		
1895	b	I-211	55	1	K		
1896	b	I-211	55	1	K		
1897	b	I-211	55	1	K		
1898	b	I-211	55	1	K		
1899	b	I-211	55	1	K		
1900	b	I-211	55	1	K		
1901	d	I-211	53	1	K		
1901	b	I-211	55	1	K		
1902	d	I-211	53	1	K		
1902	b	I-211	55	1	K		
1903	d	I-211	53	1	K		
1903	b	I-211	55	1	K		
1904	d	I-211	53	1	K		
1904	b	I-211	55	1	K		
1905	d	I-211	53	1	K		
1905	b	I-211	55	1	K		
1906	d	I-211	53	1	K		
1906	b	I-211	55	1	K		
1907	d	I-211	53	1	K		
1907	b	I-211	55	1	K		
1908	d	I-211	53	1	K		
1908	m	I-211	54	1	K		
1908	b	I-211	55	1	K		
1909	d	I-211	53	1	K		
1909	m	I-211	54	1	K		
1909	b	I-211	55	1	K		
1909	b	I-211	56	1	K		
1910	d	I-211	53	1	K		
1910	m	I-211	54	1	K		
1910	b	I-211	55	1	K		
1910	b	I-211	56	1	K		
1911	d	I-211	53	1	K		
1911	m	I-211	54	1	K		

Salakas continued

Year(s)	Type	Fond	File(s)	Op	A	F	Notes
1911	b	I-211	56	1	K		
1912	d	I-211	53	1	K		
1912	b	I-211	56	1	K		
1913	d	I-211	53	1	K		
1913	b	I-211	56	1	K		
1913	b?	I-211	57	1	K		
1913-15	resl				K		
1914	d	I-211	53	1	K		
1914	b?	I-211	58	1	K		

Salantai (Salant)

Year(s)	Type	Fond	File(s)	Op	A	F	Notes
1851	rs						
1871	rs						

Salcininkai (Solechniki) Those items with a Flag code of "4" are in the Vilnius County 4th Okrug Registers.

Year(s)	Type	Fond	File(s)	Op	A	F	Notes
1885	m	728	353	4		4	
1886	m	728	353	4		4	
1887	d	728	1478	3		4	
1887	m	728	353	4		4	
1887	b	728	364	4		4	
1888	m	728	353	4		4	
1888	b	728	364	4		4	
1889	d	728	1478	3		4	
1889	m	728	353	4		4	
1889	b	728	364	4		4	
1890	d	728	1478	3		4	
1890	b	728	1479	3		4	
1890	m	728	1480	3		4	
1890	m	728	353	4		4	
1890	b	728	364	4		4	
1891	b	728	1446	3		4	
1891	d	728	1478	3		4	
1891	m	728	1483	3		4	
1891	m	728	353	4		4	
1891	b	728	364	4		4	
1892	d	728	1478	3		4	
1892	b	728	1486, 1553	3		4	
1892	m	728	1487, 1488, 1554	3		4	
1892	v	728	1489	3		4	
1892	m	728	353	4		4	
1892	b	728	364	4		4	
1893	d	728	1478	3		4	
1893	b	728	1490, 1553	3		4	
1893	m	728	1494, 1554	3		4	
1893	v	728	1496	3		4	
1893	m	728	353	4		4	
1893	b	728	364	4		4	
1894	b	728	1499, 1553	3		4	
1894	m	728	1505, 1554	3		4	
1894	v	728	1516	3		4	
1894	m	728	353	4		4	
1894	b	728	364	4		4	
1895	b	728	1508, 1553	3		4	
1895	m	728	1513, 1556	3		4	
1895	v	728	1519	3		4	
1895	v	728	3	4		4	
1895	m	728	353	4		4	
1895	b	728	364	4		4	
1896	b	728	13, 364	4		4	
1896	m	728	14, 353	4		4	
1896	b	728	1553	3		4	
1896	m	728	1556	3		4	
1897	b	728	28-29, 364	4		4	
1897	m	728	30, 353, 437	4		4	
1897	d	728	32	4		4	
1898	b	728	28, 45, 364	4		4	
1898	d	728	32	4		4	
1898	m	728	46, 353, 437	4		4	
1899	b	728	28, 60, 364	4		4	
1899	v	728	3	4		4	
1899	d	728	32	4		4	
1899	m	728	61, 353, 437	4		4	
1900	v	728	3	4		4	
1900	b	728	72, 364	4		4	
1900	m	728	73-74, 353, 437	4		4	
1900	d	728	75	4		4	
1901	v	728	3, 88	4		4	
1901	d	728	75	4		4	
1901	b	728	86, 364	4		4	
1901	m	728	87, 353, 437	4		4	
1902	m	728	102, 353, 438	4		4	
1902	d	728	103, 439	4		4	
1902	b	728	364	4		4	
1903	b	728	114-115, 364	4		4	
1903	m	728	116, 353, 438, 444	4		4	
1903	d	728	117, 439	4		4	
1904	b	728	127, 364	4		4	
1904	m	728	128, 353, 438	4		4	

Salcininkai (Solechniki) continued

Year(s)	Type	Fond	File(s)	Op	A	F	Notes
1904	d	728	129, 439	4		4	
1905	b	728	139, 364	4		4	
1905	m	728	140, 353, 438	4		4	
1905	d	728	75, 141, 439	4		4	
1906	b	728	151, 364, 441	4		4	
1906	m	728	152, 353	4		4	
1906	d	728	75, 153	4		4	
1907	b	728	161, 364, 441	4		4	
1907	m	728	162, 353	4		4	
1907	v	728	3	4		4	
1907	d	728	75	4		4	
1908	b	728	172, 364, 441	4		4	
1908	v	728	3, 173	4		4	
1908	m	728	353	4		4	
1908	d	728	75	4		4	
1909	b	728	187, 364	4		4	
1909	v	728	3, 188	4		4	
1909	m	728	353, 442	4		4	
1909	d	728	75	4		4	
1910	b	728	199, 364	4		4	
1910	v	728	3, 200	4		4	
1910	m	728	353, 443	4		4	
1911	b	728	213, 364	4		4	
1911	m	728	214, 353	4		4	
1911	v	728	215	4		4	
1912	b	728	226, 364	4		4	
1912	m	728	227-228, 353	4		4	
1913	b	728	239, 364	4		4	
1913	m	728	240, 353	4		4	
1914	b	728	253, 364	4		4	
1914	m	728	253-254, 353	4		4	
1914	v	728	255	4		4	
1915	m	728	353	4		4	
1915	b	728	364	4		4	
1916	b	728	364	4		4	
1917	b	728	364	4		4	
1917	b	728	364	4		4	
1918	b	728	364	4		4	
1919	b	728	364	4		4	
1920	b	728	364	4		4	
1921	b	728	364	4		4	

Saukenai

Year(s)	Type	Fond	File(s)	Op	A	F	Notes
1858	rs						
1866-69	rs						
1866-69	rs						
1912-1916	tpl-r				K		

Saukotas

Year(s)	Type	Fond	File(s)	Op	A	F	Notes
1912-1916	tpl-r				K		

Seda

Year(s)	Type	Fond	File(s)	Op	A	F	Notes
1851	rs	1262	89	1			
1866	rs						
1871	rs	1262	95	1			
1895	cen						Township Residents List

Seduva (Shadova)

Year(s)	Type	Fond	File(s)	Op	A	F	Notes
1816	rs						
1818	rs	515	425	25			
1858	rs	1262	99	1			
1866	rs	1262	124	1			
1866	rs	1262	124	1			

Seredzius (Srednik)

Year(s)	Type	Fond	File(s)	Op	A	F	Notes
1816	rs						Kaunas Duma
1834	rs						Kaunas County
1851	rs						
1874	rs	I-61	1650	1	K		Alphabetic - Jews
1844	m	728	17	1			
1844	d	728	18	1			
1844	b	728	6	1			
1850	b	728	7	1			
1854	d	728	108-109	1			
1854	b	728	31-32	1			
1854	m	728	76, 78	1			
1854	v	728	89-90	1			
1855	b	728	140	1			
1855	v	728	175	1			
1855	d	728	178	1			
1856	m	728	155-156, 221	1			
1856	b	728	216, 218	1			
1856	v	728	251-252	1			
1856	d	728	256-257	1			
1857	b	728	292	1			
1857	m	728	311	1			
1857	v	728	321	1			
1857	d	728	335	1			

Seredzius (Srednik) continued

Year(s)	Type	Fond	File(s)	Op	A	F	Notes
1858	b	728	356	1			
1858	m	728	379	1			
1858	v	728	383	1			
1858	d	728	415	1			
1859	b	728	436	1			
1859	m	728	462	1			
1859	v	728	473	1			
1860	b	728	501	1			
1860	m	728	546	1			
1860	v	728	569	1			
1860	d	728	591	1			
1861	b	728	613	1			
1861	m	728	639	1			
1861	v	728	653	1			
1861	d	728	678	1			
1862	b	728	694	1			
1862	m	728	724	1			
1862	v	728	740	1			
1862	d	728	764	1			
1863	b	728	790	1			
1863	m	728	815	1			
1863	d	728	857	1			
1864	b	728	890	1			
1864	m	728	914	1			
1864	d	728	949	1			
1865	b	1226	240	1			
1865	m	1226	241	1			
1865	v	1226	242	1			
1865	d	1226	243	1			
1866	b	1226	244	1			
1866	m	1226	245	1			
1866	v	1226	246	1			
1866	d	1226	247	1			
1867	b	1226	248	1			
1867	m	1226	249	1			
1867	v	1226	250	1			
1867	d	1226	251	1			
1868	b	1226	252	1			
1868	m	1226	253	1			
1868	v	1226	254	1			
1868	d	1226	255	1			
1869	b	1226	256	1			
1869	m	1226	257	1			
1869	v	1226	258	1			
1869	d	1226	259	1			
1870	b	1226	260	1			
1870	m	1226	261	1			
1870	v	1226	262	1			
1870	d	1226	263	1			
1870-74	k				K		
1871	b	1226	264	1			
1871	m	1226	265	1			
1871	v	1226	266	1			
1871	d	1226	267	1			
1872	b	1226	268	1			
1872	m	1226	269	1			
1872	v	1226	270	1			
1872	d	1226	271	1			
1873	b	1226	272	1			
1873	m	1226	273	1			
1873	v	1226	274	1			
1873	d	1226	275	1			
1874	tpl				K		
1874	b	1226	276	1			
1874	m	1226	277	1			
1874	v	1226	278	1			
1874	d	1226	279	1			
1874-78	k				K		
1875	b	1226	280	1			
1875	m	1226	281	1			
1875	v	1226	282	1			
1875	d	1226	283	1			
1876	b	1226	940	1			
1876	m	1226	949	1			
1876	d	1226	950	1			
1876	v	1226	955	1			
1877	b	1226	941	1			
1877	m	1226	945	1			
1877	d	1226	951	1			
1877	v	1226	956	1			
1878	b	1226	942	1			
1878	m	1226	946	1			
1878	d	1226	952	1			
1878	v	1226	957	1			
1879	b	1226	943	1			
1879	m	1226	947	1			
1879	d	1226	953	1			
1879	v	1226	958	1			

Seredzius (Srednik) continued

Year(s)	Type	Fond	File(s)	Op	A	F	Notes
1880	b	1226	944	1			
1880	m	1226	948	1			
1880	d	1226	954	1			
1880	v	1226	959	1			
1881	b	1226	2063	1			
1881	m	1226	2065	1			
1881	v	1226	2065	1			
1881	d	1226	2066	1			
1882	b	1226	2063	1			
1882	m	1226	2065	1			
1882	v	1226	2065	1			
1882	d	1226	2066	1			
1883	b	1226	2063	1			
1883	m	1226	2065	1			
1883	v	1226	2065	1			
1883	d	1226	2066	1			
1884	b	1226	2063	1			
1884	m	1226	2065	1			
1884	v	1226	2065	1			
1884	d	1226	2066	1			
1885	b	1226	2063	1			
1885	m	1226	2065	1			
1885	v	1226	2065	1			
1885	d	1226	2066	1			
1886	b	1226	2063	1			
1886	m	1226	2065	1			
1886	v	1226	2065	1			
1886	d	1226	2066	1			
1887	b	1226	2063	1			
1887	m	1226	2065	1			
1887	v	1226	2065	1			
1887	d	1226	2066	1			
1888	b	1226	2063	1			
1888	m	1226	2065	1			
1888	v	1226	2065	1			
1888	d	1226	2066	1			
1889	b	1226	2063	1			
1889	m	1226	2065	1			
1889	v	1226	2065	1			
1889	d	1226	2066	1			
1890	b	1226	2063	1			
1890	m	1226	2065	1			
1890	v	1226	2065	1			
1890	d	1226	2066	1			
1891	b	1226	2063	1			
1891	m	1226	2065	1			
1891	v	1226	2065	1			
1891	d	1226	2066	1			
1892	b	1226	2063	1			
1892	m	1226	2065	1			
1892	v	1226	2065	1			
1892	d	1226	2066	1			
1893	b	1226	2063	1			
1893	m	1226	2065	1			
1893	v	1226	2065	1			
1893	d	1226	2066	1			
1894	b	1226	2063	1			
1894	m	1226	2065	1			
1894	v	1226	2065	1			
1894	d	1226	2066	1			
1895	b	1226	2063	1			
1895	m	1226	2065	1			
1895	v	1226	2065	1			
1895	d	1226	2066	1			
1896	b	1226	2063	1			
1896	m	1226	2065	1			
1896	v	1226	2065	1			
1896	d	1226	2066	1			
1897	b	1226	2063	1			
1897	m	1226	2065	1			
1897	v	1226	2065	1			
1897	d	1226	2066	1			
1898	b	1226	2063	1			
1898	m	1226	2065	1			
1898	v	1226	2065	1			
1898	d	1226	2066	1			
1899	b	1226	2063	1			
1899	m	1226	2065	1			
1899	v	1226	2065	1			
1899	d	1226	2066	1			
1900	b	1226	2063	1			
1900	m	1226	2065	1			
1900	v	1226	2065	1			
1900	d	1226	2066	1			
1901	b	1226	2064	1			
1901	m	1226	2065	1			
1901	v	1226	2065	1			
1901	d	1226	2066	1			

Seredzius (Srednik) continued

Year(s)	Type	Fond	File(s)	Op	A	F	Notes
1902	b	1226	2064	1			
1902	m	1226	2065	1			
1902	v	1226	2065	1			
1902	d	1226	2066	1			
1902-1905	k	61		1	K		Poor Jews, Recepients
1903	b	1226	2064	1			
1903	m	1226	2065	1			
1903	v	1226	2065	1			
1903	d	1226	2066	1			
1904	b	1226	2064	1			
1904	m	1226	2065	1			
1904	v	1226	2065	1			
1904	d	1226	2066	1			
1905	b	1226	2064	1			
1905	m	1226	2065	1			
1905	v	1226	2065	1			
1905	d	1226	2066	1			
1906	b	1226	2064	1			
1906	m	1226	2065	1			
1906	v	1226	2065	1			
1906	d	1226	2066	1			
1907	b	1226	2064	1			
1907	m	1226	2065	1			
1907	v	1226	2065	1			
1907	d	1226	2066	1			
1908	b	1226	2064	1			
1908	m	1226	2065	1			
1908	v	1226	2065	1			
1908	d	1226	2066	1			
1909	b	1226	2064	1			
1909	m	1226	2065	1			
1909	v	1226	2065	1			
1909	d	1226	2066	1			
1910	b	1226	2064	1			
1910	m	1226	2065	1			
1910	v	1226	2065	1			
1910	d	1226	2066	1			
1911	b	1226	2064	1			
1911	m	1226	2065	1			
1911	v	1226	2065	1			
1911	d	1226	2066	1			
1912	b	1226	2064	1			
1912	m	1226	2065	1			
1912	v	1226	2065	1			
1912	d	1226	2066	1			
1913	b	1226	2064	1			
1913	m	1226	2065	1			
1913	v	1226	2065	1			
1913	d	1226	2066	1			
1914	m	1226	2065	1			
1914	v	1226	2065	1			

Sesuoliai (Sheshol) Items for this town are in the Vilnius County 2nd Okrug Registers.

Year(s)	Type	Fond	File(s)	Op	A	F	Notes
1873	b	728	1030	3			
1873	m	728	142, 144	3			
1873	d	728	146	3			
1874	b	728	148-149	3			
1874	m	728	150-151	3			
1874	d	728	152, 341	3			
1875	b	728	153-154	3			
1875	m	728	155-156	3			
1875	d	728	157-158	3			
1876	b	728	1035	3			
1876	m	728	1074, 1074A	3			
1876	d	728	1124	3			
1877	b	728	1041	3			
1877	m	728	1075-1076	3			
1877	d	728	1128	3			
1878	b	728	1049	3			
1878	m	728	1078	3			
1878	d	728	1134	3			
1890	m	728	1481	3			
1891	b	728	1445	3			
1891	m	728	1482	3			
1892	b	728	1484	3			
1893	b	728	1491	3			
1893	m	728	1495	3			
1894	b	728	1498, 1501	3			
1894	m	728	1504	3			
1895	m	728	1514	3			
1896	m	728	10	4			
1896	b	728	9	4			
1897	b	728	23	4			
1897	m	728	23	4			
1898	b	728	40	4			
1898	m	728	41	4			
1898	v	728	42	4			
1899	b	728	56	4			

Sesuoliai (Sheshol) continued

Year(s)	Type	Fond	File(s)	Op	Notes
1899	m	728	57	4	
1900	b	728	68	4	
1900	m	728	69	4	
1900	d	728	75	4	
1901	d	728	75, 83	4	
1901	b	728	81-82	4	
1902	b	728	96	4	
1902	m	728	97	4	
1902	d	728	98	4	
1903	b	728	109	4	
1903	m	728	110	4	
1903	d	728	111	4	
1904	b	728	122	4	
1904	m	728	123	4	
1904	d	728	124	4	
1905	b	728	135	4	
1905	m	728	136	4	
1905	v	728	137	4	
1905	d	728	75	4	
1906	b	728	147	4	
1906	m	728	148	4	
1906	v	728	149	4	
1906	d	728	75	4	
1907	b	728	159	4	
1907	d	728	75	4	
1908	m	728	170	4	
1908	d	728	75	4	
1909	b	728	181	4	
1909	m	728	182	4	
1909	v	728	183	4	
1909	d	728	75	4	
1910	b	728	195	4	
1910	m	728	196	4	
1911	b	728	209	4	
1911	m	728	210	4	
1912	m	728	223	4	
1913	m	728	236	4	
1914	b	728	249	4	
1914	m	728	250	4	

Seta

Year(s)	Type	Fond	File(s)	Op
1858	rs	1262	16-17	1
1859	rs	1262	17	1
1866	rs			
1867	rs	1262	19	1
1873	rs	1262	20	1
1874	rs	1262	21	1
1878	rs	1262	23	1
1879	rs			

Shchuchin, Belarus (Sciucin)

Year(s)	Type	Fond	File(s)	Op	Notes
1896	b	728	956	1	Lida County
1897	b	728	959	1	Lida County
1897	m	728	960	1	Lida County
1897	d	728	961	1	Lida County
1898	b	728	963	1	Lida County
1898	m	728	966	1	Lida County
1898	d	728	968	1	Lida County
1899	b	728	970	1	Lida County
1899	m	728	972	1	Lida County
1899	d	728	974	1	Lida County
1900	b	728	977	1	Lida County
1900	m	728	979	1	Lida County
1900	d	728	981	1	Lida County
1901	b	728	987	1	Lida County
1901	m	728	989	1	Lida County
1901	d	728	992	1	Lida County
1902	d	728	1003	1	Lida County
1902	b	728	995	1	Lida County
1902	m	728	996	1	Lida County
1903	b	728	1007	1	Lida County
1903	m	728	1009	1	Lida County
1904	b	728	1019	1	Lida County
1904	m	728	1020	1	Lida County
1905	b	728	1026	1	Lida County
1905	m	728	1029	1	Lida County
1906	b	728	1035	1	Lida County
1906	m	728	1037	1	Lida County
1907	b	728	1045	1	Lida County
1907	m	728	1047	1	Lida County
1908	b	728	1056	1	Lida County
1908	m	728	1058	1	Lida County
1909	b	728	1062	1	Lida County
1909	m	728	1065	1	Lida County
1910	b	728	1071	1	Lida County
1910	m	728	1073	1	Lida County
1911	b	728	1076	1	Lida County
1911	m	728	1081	1	Lida County

Year(s)	Type	Fond	File(s)		Op	A	F	Notes
Shchuchin, Belarus (Sciucin) continued								
1912	m	728	1080		1			Lida County
1912	b	728	1083		1			Lida County
1913	b	728	1089		1			Lida County
1913	m	728	1092		1			Lida County
1914	b	728	1093		1			Lida County
1914	m	728	1096		1			Lida County
Siaulenai								
1858	rs							
1866	rs							
Siauliai								
1862	rs							
1865	rs							
1895								
1912–1916	tpl-r					K		
unknown	jh					K		Suspicious Organization
unknown	p					K		Suspicious Organization" – Colonial Union
unknown	p					K		Many Jews, Surveilance List
Siauliai County								
1795	rs	515	436		25	K		Jews
Silale (Shilel)								
1816	rs							
1842	rs							
1858	rs							
1864	rs							
1866–70	rs							
1936	b	1226	1401		1			
Siluva								
1816	rs							
1839	rs							
1851	rs							
1870?	rs							
1847	tpl-r					K		Jews
1886	prb					K		
unknown	fl					K		
Sintautai (Sintoval)								
1815	d	1236	710		3			
1816	d	1236	710, 714		3			
1816	b	1236	711		3			
1816	m	1236	712		3			
1817	b	1236	711		3			
1817	m	1236	712, 715		3			
1817	d	1236	714, 716		3			
1820	b	1236	718		3			
1820	m	1236	719		3			
1821	b	1236	720		3			
1822	m	1236	721		3			
1824	b	1014	192		2			
1824	m	1236	724		3			
1825	b	1236	726		3			
1825	d	1236	728		3			

Sirvintos (Shirvint) Those items with a Flag code of "2" are in the Vilnius County 2nd Okrug Registers. Those with a Flag code of "7" are in the Vilnius County Register.

Year(s)	Type	Fond	File(s)	Op	A	F	Notes
1816–1818	rs	515	288	25	K	7	Jews
1834	rs	515	298	25	K	7	Jews
1843–1849	rs	515	306	25	K	7	Jews
1849	rs	515	312	25	K	7	Jews
1850–1854	rs	515	273	25	K	7	Jews
1858	rs	515	285	25	K	7	Jews
unknown	rs	515	299	25	K	7	Jews
unknown	rs	515	320	25	K	7	Jews
1854	d	728	110–111	1			
1854	b	728	28–29	1			
1854	m	728	69–70	1			
1855	b	728	136	1			
1855	m	728	147	1			
1855	d	728	196	1			
1856	b	728	206	1			
1856	m	728	226	1			
1856	d	728	268	1			
1857	b	728	291	1			
1857	m	728	306	1			
1857	d	728	333	1			
1858	b	728	341–342	1			
1858	m	728	361–362	1			
1858	d	728	396–397	1			
1859	b	728	424–425	1			
1859	m	728	444–445	1			
1859	d	728	482–483	1			
1860	b	728	508–509	1			
1860	m	728	530–531	1			
1860	d	728	580, 588	1			
1861	b	728	611–612	1			

Sirvintos (Shirvint) continued

Year(s)	Type	Fond	File(s)	Op	A	F	Notes
1861	m	728	634–635	1			
1861	d	728	663, 672	1			
1862	b	728	698–699	1			
1862	m	728	706–707	1			
1862	d	728	743–744	1			
1863	b	728	785, 821	1			
1863	m	728	793–794	1			
1863	d	728	849–850	1			
1864	b	728	981–982	3			
1864	m	728	983–984	3			
1864	d	728	985–986	3			
1865	b	728	138, 981A	3			
1865	m	728	987–988	3			
1865	d	728	989–990	3			
1866	b	728	991–992	3			
1866	m	728	993–994	3			
1866	d	728	995–996	3			
1867	d	728	1001–1002	3			
1867	b	728	997–998	3			
1867	m	728	999–1000	3			
1868	b	728	1003–1004	3			
1868	m	728	1005–1006	3			
1868	d	728	1007–1008	3			
1869	b	728	1009–1010	3			
1869	m	728	1011–1012	3			
1869	d	728	1013–1014	3			
1870	b	728	1015–1016	3			
1870	m	728	1017–1018	3			
1870	d	728	1019–1020	3			
1871	b	728	1021	3			
1871	m	728	1022–1023	3			
1871	d	728	1024	3			
1872	b	728	1025–1026	3			
1872	m	728	1027–1028	3			
1872	d	728	1029, 1400	3			
1873	b	728	1030	3		2	
1873	m	728	142, 144	3		2	
1873	d	728	146	3		2	
1874	b	728	148–149	3		2	
1874	m	728	150–151	3		2	
1874	d	728	152, 341	3		2	
1875	b	728	153–154	3		2	
1875	m	728	155–156	3		2	
1875	d	728	157–158	3		2	
1876	b	728	1035	3		2	
1876	m	728	1074	3		2	
1876	d	728	1124	3		2	
1877	b	728	1041	3		2	
1877	m	728	1075–1076	3		2	
1877	d	728	1128	3		2	
1878	b	728	1049	3		2	
1878	m	728	1078	3		2	
1878	d	728	1134	3		2	
1891	b	728	1445	3		2	
1891	m	728	1482	3		2	
1892	b	728	1484	3		2	
1893	b	728	1491	3		2	
1893	m	728	1495	3		2	
1894	b	728	1498, 1501	3		2	
1894	m	728	1504	3		2	
1895	m	728	1481	3		2	
1895	b	728	1510	3		2	
1896	m	728	10	4		2	
1896	b	728	9	4		2	
1897	b	728	23	4		2	
1897	m	728	23	4		2	
1898	b	728	40	4		2	
1898	m	728	41	4		2	
1898	v	728	42	4		2	
1899	b	728	56	4		2	
1899	m	728	57	4		2	
1900	b	728	68	4		2	
1900	m	728	69	4		2	
1900	d	728	75	4		2	
1901	d	728	75, 83	4		2	
1901	b	728	81–82	4		2	
1902	b	728	96	4		2	
1902	m	728	97	4		2	
1902	d	728	98	4		2	
1903	b	728	109	4		2	
1903	m	728	110	4		2	
1903	d	728	111	4		2	
1904	b	728	122	4		2	
1904	m	728	123	4		2	
1904	d	728	124	4		2	
1905	b	728	135	4		2	
1905	m	728	136	4		2	
1905	v	728	137	4		2	

Sirvintos (Shirvint) continued

Year(s)	Type	Fond	File(s)	Op	A	F	Notes
1905	d	728	75	4	2		
1906	b	728	147	4	2		
1906	m	728	148	4	2		
1906	v	728	149	4	2		
1906	d	728	75	4	2		
1907	b	728	159	4	2		
1907	d	728	75	4	2		
1908	m	728	170	4	2		
1908	d	728	75	4	2		
1909	b	728	181	4	2		
1909	m	728	182	4	2		
1909	v	728	183	4	2		
1909	d	728	75	4	2		
1910	b	728	195	4	2		
1910	m	728	196	4	2		
1911	b	728	209	4	2		
1911	m	728	210	4	2		
1912	m	728	223	4	2		
1913	m	728	236	4	2		
1914	b	728	249	4	2		
1914	m	728	250	4	2		

Skaudvile

Year(s)	Type	Fond	File(s)	Op	A	F	Notes
1816	rs						
1851	rs						

Skirsnemune

Year(s)	Type	Fond	File(s)	Op	A	F	Notes
1863	rs						

Skriaudziai (Skravdze)

Year(s)	Type	Fond	File(s)	Op	A	F	Notes
1815	b	1236	234	4			
1816	b	1236	234, 239	4			
1816	d	1236	238	4			
1816	m	1236	28	5			
1817	d	1236	238, 241	4			
1817	b	1236	239-240	4			
1817	m	1236	28	5			
1818	b	1236	242	4			
1818	m	1236	243	4			
1818	d	1236	244	4			
1819	b	1236	245	4			
1819	m	1236	246	4			
1819	d	1236	247	4			
1820	b	1236	1	15			
1820	b	1236	248	4			
1820	m	1236	249	4			
1820	d	1236	250	4			
1821	b	1236	251	4			
1821	m	1236	253	4			
1821	d	1236	254	4			
1821	b	1236	5	15			
1822	b	1236	255	4			
1822	m	1236	256	4			
1822	d	1236	257	4			
1822	b	1236	6	15			
1823	b	1236	258	4			
1823	m	1236	259	4			
1823	d	1236	260	4			
1823	b	1236	7	15			
1824	b	1236	261	4			
1824	m	1236	262	4			
1824	d	1236	263	4			
1824	b	1236	8	15			
1825	b	1236	264	4			
1825	d	1236	265	4			
1825	m	1236	266	4			

Skuodas (Shkud)

Year(s)	Type	Fond	File(s)	Op	A	F	Notes
1851	rs						
1859	rs						
1871	rs						
	p	1384	1	1			

Slavikai (Sloviki)

Year(s)	Type	Fond	File(s)	Op	A	F	Notes
1816	m	1236	654	3			
1817	m	1236	654	3			
1817	b	1236	656	3			
1819	m	1236	660	3			
1819	b	1236	661	3			
1820	m	1236	663	3			
1821	b	1236	665	3			
1821	m	1236	666	3			
1822	m	1236	668	3			
1823	b	1236	670	3			
1824	b	1236	672	3			
1824	m	1236	673	3			
1825	b	1236	675	3			

Snipiskes (Snipishok) Was a suburb of Vilnius. Those items with a Flag code of "7" are in the Vilnius County Register.

Year(s)	Type	Fond	File(s)	Op	A	F	Notes
1816-1818	rs	515	288	25	K	7	Jews
1834	rs	515	298	25	K	7	Jews
1843-1849	rs	515	306	25	K	7	Jews
1849	rs	515	312	25	K	7	Jews
1850-1854	rs	515	273	25	K	7	Jews
1858	rs	515	285	25	K	7	Jews
unknown	rs	515	299	25	K	7	Jews
unknown	rs	515	320	25	K	7	Jews
1854	b	728	888	3			
1855	b	728	94, 129	2			
1855	m	728	95-96	2			
1855	v	728	97	2			
1855	d	728	98	2			
1856	b	728	128, 130	2			
1856	m	728	131	2			
1856	v	728	132	2			
1856	d	728	133	2			
1857	b	728	165-166	2			
1857	m	728	167-168	2			
1857	v	728	169	2			
1857	d	728	170	2			
1858	b	728	209-210	2			
1858	m	728	211-212	2			
1859	b	728	250-251	2			
1859	m	728	252-253	2			
1860	b	728	289-290	2			
1860	m	728	291-292	2			
1861	b	728	320	2			
1861	m	728	321	2			
1861	d	728	322	2			
1862	b	728	345-346	2			
1863	b	728	372-373	2			
1863	m	728	374-375	2			
1864	b	728	393	2			
1864	m	728	394	2			
1864	b	728	889	3			
1864	m	728	890	3			
1865	b	728	891-892	3			
1865	m	728	893-894	3			
1866	b	728	891, 895	3			
1866	m	728	896-897	3			
1867	b	728	891, 898	3			
1867	m	728	899-900	3			
1868	b	728	891, 901	3			
1868	m	728	902-903	3			
1869	m	728	887, 905	3			
1869	b	728	891, 904	3			
1870	b	728	907-907	3			
1870	m	728	908-910	3			
1871	b	728	906, 911	3			
1871	m	728	912-913	3			
1872	b	728	193, 1032	3			
1872	b	728	906, 914	3			
1872	m	728	915-916	3			
1873	b	728	189	3			
1874	b	728	190-191	3			
1874	b	728	362-363	4			
1875	b	728	192	3			
1875	b	728	362-363	4			
1876	b	728	1033	3			
1876	m	728	1072-1073	3			
1876	b	728	362-363	4			
1877	b	728	1040	3			
1877	m	728	1077, 1077A	3			
1877	b	728	362-363	4			
1878	b	728	1048	3			
1878	m	728	1083	3			
1878	b	728	362-363	4			
1879	b	728	1047, 1052	3			
1879	m	728	1079, 1089	3			
1879	b	728	362-363	4			
1880	b	728	1047, 1055	3			
1880	b	728	362-363	4			
1881	b	728	1047, 1062	3			
1881	b	728	1062	3			
1881	b	728	362-363	4			
1882	b	728	1047, 1064	3			
1882	b	728	362-363	4			
1883	b	728	1068	3			
1883	b	728	362-363	4			
1884	b	728	1068, 1165	3			
1884	b	728	362-363	4			
1885	b	728	1068, 1168	3			
1885	b	728	362-363	4			
1886	b	728	1122, 1171	3			
1886	b	728	362-363	4			
1887	b	728	1175, 1421	3			

Snipiskes (Snipishok) continued

Year(s)	Type	Fond	File(s)	Op	A	F	Notes
1887	b	728	362-363	4			
1888	b	728	1421, 1429	3			
1888	b	728	362-363	4			
1889	b	728	1421, 1429	3			
1889	b	728	362-363	4			
1890	b	728	1437, 1439	3			
1890	b	728	362-363	4			
1891	b	728	1447	3			
1891	b	728	362-363	4			
1892	b	728	1453	3			
1892	b	728	362-363	4			
1893	b	728	1459	3			
1893	b	728	362-363	4			
1894	b	728	1466	3			
1894	b	728	362-363, 421	4			
1895	b	728	1473	3			
1895	b	728	362-363, 421	4			
1896	b	728	8, 362-363, 421	4			
1897	b	728	20, 362-363, 422	4			
1898	b	728	38, 362-363, 422	4			
1899	b	728	52, 362-363, 422	4			
1900	b	728	65, 362-363, 423	4			
1901	b	728	80, 362-363, 423	4			
1902	b	728	95, 362-363, 423	4			
1903	b	728	108, 362-363, 424	4			
1904	b	728	108, 362-363, 425	4			
1905	b	728	362-363	4			
1906	b	728	362-363	4			
1907	b	728	362-363	4			
1908	b	728	362-363	4			

Sokolka, Poland (Sokol)

Year(s)	Type	Fond	File(s)	Op	A	F	Notes
1835	b	1108	15	1			
1835	d	1108	15	1			
1835	m	1108	15	1			

Stakliskes (Stoklishok)

Year(s)	Type	Fond	File(s)	Op	A	F	Notes
1858-1905	rs	515		25			
1858-1905	rs	515		25			
1854	b	728	36	1			
1854	m	728	52	1			
1854	v	728	83	1			
1854	d	728	99	1			
1855	b	728	126	1			
1855	d	728	128	1			
1855	m	728	145	1			
1855	v	728	171	1			
1856	d	728	264	1			
1857	b	728	282	1			
1857	d	728	325	1			
1871	b	728	917	3			
1871	m	728	918-919	3			
1871	v	728	920	3			
1871	d	728	921	3			
1872	b	728	922	3			
1872	m	728	923-924	3			
1872	d	728	926	3			
1873	b	728	927	3			
1873	m	728	928-929	3			
1873	d	728	931	3			
1874	b	728	932	3			
1874	m	728	933-934	3			
1874	v	728	935	3			
1874	d	728	936	3			
1875	b	728	937	3			
1875	m	728	938-939	3			
1875	d	728	941	3			
1876	b	728	1362	3			
1876	m	728	1380-1381	3			
1876	d	728	1386	3			
1877	b	728	1363-1364	3			
1877	m	728	1377-1378	3			
1877	d	728	1387	3			
1878	b	728	1365-1366	3			
1878	d	728	1388	3			
1879	b	728	1367-1368	3			
1879	m	728	1373-1374	3			
1879	d	728	1389	3			
1880	b	728	1369-1370	3			
1880	m	728	1371-1372	3			
1880	v	728	1385	3			
1880	d	728	1390	3			

Stundishki (Stundishki)
Items for this town are in the Vilnius County 2nd Okrug Registers. No town by this name could be found. Given its location, it might be Strunaitis.

Year(s)	Type	Fond	File(s)	Op	A	F	Notes
1873	b	728	1030	3			
1873	m	728	142, 144	3			

Stundishki (Stundishki) continued

Year(s)	Type	Fond	File(s)	Op
1873	d	728	146	3
1874	b	728	148-149	3
1874	m	728	150-151	3
1874	d	728	152, 341	3
1875	b	728	153-154	3
1875	m	728	155-156	3
1875	d	728	157-158	3
1876	b	728	1035	3
1876	m	728	1074	3
1876	d	728	1124	3
1877	b	728	1041	3
1877	m	728	1075-1076	3
1877	d	728	1128	3
1878	b	728	1049	3
1878	m	728	1078	3
1878	d	728	1134	3
1891	b	728	1445	3
1891	m	728	1482	3
1892	b	728	1484	3
1893	b	728	1491	3
1893	m	728	1495	3
1894	b	728	1498	3
1894	b	728	1501	3
1894	m	728	1504	3
1895	m	728	1481	3
1895	b	728	1510	3
1896	m	728	10	4
1896	b	728	9	4
1897	b	728	23	4
1897	m	728	23	4
1898	b	728	40	4
1898	m	728	41	4
1898	v	728	42	4
1899	b	728	56	4
1899	m	728	57	4
1900	b	728	68	4
1900	m	728	69	4
1900	d	728	75	4
1901	d	728	75, 83	4
1901	b	728	81-82	4
1902	b	728	96	4
1902	m	728	97	4
1902	d	728	98	4
1903	b	728	109	4
1903	m	728	110	4
1903	d	728	111	4
1904	b	728	122	4
1904	m	728	123	4
1904	d	728	124	4
1905	b	728	135	4
1905	m	728	136	4
1905	v	728	137	4
1905	d	728	75	4
1906	b	728	147	4
1906	m	728	148	4
1906	v	728	149	4
1906	d	728	75	4
1907	b	728	159	4
1907	d	728	75	4
1908	m	728	170	4
1908	d	728	75	4
1909	b	728	181	4
1909	m	728	182	4
1909	v	728	183	4
1909	d	728	75	4
1910	b	728	195	4
1910	m	728	196	4
1911	b	728	209	4
1911	m	728	210	4
1912	m	728	223	4
1913	m	728	236	4
1914	b	728	249	4
1914	m	728	250	4

Sudargas (Sudarg)

Year(s)	Type	Fond	File(s)	Op
1813	b	1236	859	3
1813	m	1236	860	3
1813	d	1236	862	3
1814	b	1236	859, 863	3
1814	d	1236	862, 866	3
1814	m	1236	864	3
1815	d	1236	653, 866	3
1815	b	1236	863	3
1815	m	1236	864	3
1816	d	1236	653, 655, 866, 873	3
1816	m	1236	864	3
1816	b	1236	867	3
1817	d	1236	655, 658, 873-874	3

Sudargas (Sudarg) continued

Year(s)	Type	Fond	File(s)	Op	A	F	Notes
1817	b	1236	867, 870	3			
1817	m	1236	871	3			
1818	d	1236	876	3			
1819	b	1236	877	3			
1819	m	1236	879	3			
1819	d	1236	880	3			
1820	b	1236	881	3			
1820	m	1236	882	3			
1820	d	1236	884	3			
1821	b	1236	885	3			
1821	m	1236	886	3			
1821	d	1236	888	3			
1822	d	1236	669, 891	3			
1822	b	1236	889	3			
1823	m	1236	892	3			
1824	d	1236	674, 894	3			
1825	b	1236	895	3			
1825	m	1236	896	3			
1846	b	1236	700	3			
1846	d	1236	700	3			
1846	m	1236	700	3			
1847	b	1236	701	3			
1847	d	1236	701	3			
1847	m	1236	701	3			
1858	b	1236	704	3			
1858	d	1236	704	3			
1858	m	1236	704	3			
1859	b	1236	707	3			
1859	d	1236	707	3			
1859	m	1236	707	3			

Sumskas (Shumsk)

Year(s)	Type	Fond	File(s)	Op	A	F	Notes
1812	b	1236	114				
1812	b	1236	14-15	5			
1812	d	1236	14-15				
1812	m	1236	16, 114	5			
1812	d	1236	18	5			
1812	d	1236	18				
1812	d	1236	506	3			
1812	d	1236	506				
1813	m	1014	225	2			
1813	d	1236	115				
1813	b	1236	19-20	5			
1813	d	1236	21, 115	5			
1813	b	1236	225				
1814	b	1236	101				
1814	m	1236	101, 364	3			
1814	d	1236	22	5			
1814	b	1236	36	5			
1814	b	1236	364				
1815	b	1236	23	5			
1815	m	1236	24	5			
1815	b	1236	24, 240				
1815	d	1236	25-26	5			
1816	m	1236	102	5			
1816	b	1236	102, 240				
1816	b	1236	27	5			
1816	d	1236	29	5			
1817	b	1236	30	5			
1817	b	1236	31				
1817	m	1236	31	5			
1817	d	1236	32	5			
1818	b	1236	33	5			
1818	b	1236	34				
1818	m	1236	34	5			
1818	d	1236	35	5			
1819	d	1236	37	5			
1820	b	1014	226-227	2			
1820	d	1014	228	2			
1820	b	1236	38				
1820	m	1236	38	5			
1821	b	1014	229-230	2			
1821	d	1014	231-232	2			
1821	b	1236	254				
1821	m	1236	254A	4			
1822	b	1014	233-234	2			
1822	d	1236	103	5			
1822	b	1236	104				
1822	m	1236	104	5			
1823	b	1014	235-236	2			
1823	d	1014	237-238	2			
1823	b	1236	39-40				
1823	m	1236	39-40	5			
1824	b	1014	239	2			
1824	d	1014	240	2			
1824	b	1236	106	5			
1824	b	1236	41-42				
1824	m	1236	41-42	5			

Year(s)	Type	Fond	File(s)	Op	A	F	Notes
Sumskas (Shumsk) continued							
1825	b	1236	107-108	5			
1825	b	1236	43				
1825	m	1236	43	5			
Suvainiskis (Suvinishok)							
1870-74	k				K		
1874-78	k				K		
1904	d	728	1024-1025	1			
1914	k				K		
Svedasai							
1858	rs						
1874	rs						
Sveksna							
1816	rs						
1875?	rs						
1909	ct	220			K		Contents Unclear
Taurage (Tavrig)							
1816	rs	1262		1			
1835?	rs						
1851-1869	rs	1262	76,83,84,86,127	1			
1858	rs						
1864	rs						
1874	rs						
Tauragnai							
1816-27	rs						
Telsiai (Telz)							
1851	rs						
1871	rs						
1854	b	1226	754-755	1			
1854	m	728	61-62	2			
1854	v	728	64-65	2			
1854	d	728	66-67	2			
1855	b	1226	756-757	1			
1855	v	728	100	2			
1855	d	728	101-102	2			
1855	m	728	99, 109	2			
1856	b	1226	758	1			
1856	m	728	134	2			
1856	v	728	135	2			
1856	d	728	136-137	2			
1857	b	1226	759-760	1			
1857	d	728	136, 171-172	2			
1857	m	728	173-174	2			
1857	v	728	175-176	2			
1858	b	1226	761-762	1			
1858	d	728	136, 216	2			
1858	m	728	213	2			
1858	v	728	214-215	2			
1859	b	1226	763	1			
1859	m	1226	764	1			
1859	d	728	136, 258-259	2			
1859	b	728	254	2			
1859	m	728	255	2			
1859	v	728	256-257	2			
1860	b	1226	765	1			
1860	d	728	136, 298-299	2			
1860	b	728	293	2			
1860	m	728	294-295	2			
1860	v	728	296-297	2			
1861	b	1226	766-767	1			
1861	d	728	136, 318-319	2			
1861	m	728	314-315	2			
1861	v	728	316-317	2			
1862	b	1226	768	1			
1862	v	1226	769-770	1			
1862	d	728	136, 350-351	2			
1862	b	728	347	2			
1862	m	728	348-349	2			
1863	b	1226	771	1			
1863	v	1226	772	1			
1863	d	728	136, 378	2			
1863	m	728	377	2			
1864	b	1226	773-774	1			
1864	v	1226	775-776	1			
1864	m	728	376, 395	2			
1864	d	728	396-397	2			
1865	b	1226	777-778	1			
1865	m	1226	779-780	1			
1865	v	1226	781-782	1			
1865	d	1226	783-784	1			
1866	m	1226	785-786	1			
1866	v	1226	787-788	1			
1866	d	728	399	2			

Telsiai (Telz) continued

Year(s)	Type	Fond	File(s)	Op	A	F	Notes
1867	b	1226	789-790	1			
1867	m	1226	791-792	1			
1867	v	1226	793-794	1			
1867	d	1226	795	1			
1867	d	728	400	2			
1868	b	1226	796-797	1			
1868	m	1226	798-799	1			
1868	v	1226	800-801	1			
1868	d	1226	802	1			
1868	d	728	401	2			
1869	b	1226	803-804	1			
1869	m	1226	805-806	1			
1869	v	1226	807-808	1			
1869	d	1226	809	1			
1869	d	728	402	2			
1870	b	1226	810-811	1			
1870	m	1226	812-813	1			
1870	v	1226	814-815	1			
1870	d	1226	816-817	1			
1871	b	1226	818-819	1			
1871	m	1226	820-821	1			
1871	v	1226	823	1			
1871	d	1226	824-825	1			
1872	b	1226	826-827	1			
1872	m	1226	828-829	1			
1872	v	1226	830-831	1			
1872	d	1226	832-833	1			
1873	b	1226	834-835	1			
1873	m	1226	836-837	1			
1873	v	1226	838-839	1			
1873	d	1226	840-841	1			
1874	b	1226	842-843	1			
1874	m	1226	844-845	1			
1874	v	1226	846-847	1			
1874	d	1226	848-849	1			
1875	b	1226	850-851	1			
1875	m	1226	852-853	1			
1875	v	1226	854-855	1			
1875	d	1226	856-857	1			
1876	b	1226	1167-1168	1			
1876	m	1226	1173-1174	1			
1876	v	1226	1181-1182	1			
1876	d	1226	858, 1191	1			
1877	v	1226	1183, 1190	1			
1877	d	1226	1192-1193	1			
1877	b	1226	859, 1318	1			
1877	m	1226	860, 1175	1			
1878	v	1226	1184-1885	1			
1878	d	1226	1194-1195	1			
1878	b	1226	861, 1169	1			
1878	m	1226	862, 1176	1			
1879	m	1226	1177-1178	1			
1879	v	1226	1186-1187	1			
1879	d	1226	1196-1197	1			
1879	b	1226	863, 1170	1			
1880	b	1226	1171-1172	1			
1880	m	1226	1179-1180	1			
1880	v	1226	1188-1189	1			
1880	d	1226	1198-1199	1			
1881	b	1226	1315	1			
1881	m	1226	1316	1			
1881	d	1226	1317	1			
1882	b	1226	1315	1			
1882	m	1226	1316	1			
1882	d	1226	1317	1			
1883	b	1226	1315	1			
1883	m	1226	1316	1			
1883	d	1226	1317	1			
1884	b	1226	1315, 1318	1			
1884	m	1226	1316	1			
1884	d	1226	1317	1			
1885	b	1226	1315, 1318	1			
1885	m	1226	1316	1			
1885	d	1226	1317	1			
1886	b	1226	1315, 1318	1			
1886	m	1226	1316	1			
1886	d	1226	2071	1			
1887	b	1226	1315, 1318	1			
1887	m	1226	1316	1			
1887	d	1226	2071	1			
1888	b	1226	1315	1			
1888	m	1226	1316	1			
1888	d	1226	2071	1			
1889	m	1226	2069	1			
1889	d	1226	2071-2072	1			
1890	m	1226	2069	1			
1890	d	1226	2071-2072, 2092	1			
1891	b	1226	2067	1			

Telsiai (Telz) continued

Year(s)	Type	Fond	File(s)	Op	A	F	Notes
1891	m	1226	2069	1			
1891	d	1226	2071-2072, 2092	1			
1892	m	1226	2069	1			
1892	d	1226	2071-2072, 2092	1			
1893	m	1226	2069	1			
1893	d	1226	2071-2072, 2092	1			
1894	m	1226	2069	1			
1894	d	1226	2071-2072, 2092	1			
1895	b	1226	2067	1			
1895	m	1226	2069	1			
1895	d	1226	2071-2072, 2092	1			
1896	b	1226	2067	1			
1896	m	1226	2069	1			
1896	d	1226	2071-2072, 2092	1			
1897	b	1226	2067	1			
1897	m	1226	2069	1			
1897	d	1226	2071-2072, 2092	1			
1898	b	1226	2067	1			
1898	m	1226	2069	1			
1898	d	1226	2071-2072, 2092	1			
1899	b	1226	2067	1			
1899	m	1226	2069	1			
1899	d	1226	2071, 2092	1			
1900	b	1226	2068	1			
1900	m	1226	2069	1			
1900	d	1226	2071, 2092	1			
1901	b	1226	2068	1			
1901	m	1226	2070	1			
1901	d	1226	2071, 2092	1			
1902	b	1226	2068	1			
1902	m	1226	2070	1			
1902	d	1226	2071, 2092	1			
1903	b	1226	2068	1			
1903	m	1226	2070	1			
1903	d	1226	2071, 2093	1			
1904	b	1226	2068	1			
1904	m	1226	2070	1			
1904	d	1226	2071, 2093	1			
1905	b	1226	2068	1			
1905	m	1226	2070	1			
1905	d	1226	2071, 2093	1			
1906	b	1226	2068	1			
1906	m	1226	2070	1			
1906	d	1226	2093	1			
1907	b	1226	2068	1			
1907	m	1226	2070	1			
1907	d	1226	2093	1			
1908	b	1226	2068	1			
1908	m	1226	2070	1			
1908	d	1226	2093	1			
1909	b	1226	2068	1			
1909	m	1226	2070	1			
1909	d	1226	2093	1			
1909	p	1384	1	1			
1910	b	1226	2068	1			
1910	m	1226	2070	1			
1910	d	1226	2093	1			
1911	m	1226	2070	1			
1911	d	1226	2093	1			
1912	m	1226	2070	1			
1912	d	1226	2093	1			
1913	m	1226	2070	1			
1913	d	1226	2093	1			
1914	m	1226	2070	1			
1915	m	1226	2070	1			
unknown	ml	1251					Jewish Residents, Military Commander of Telsiai County
unknown	p	J-42			K		

Trakai (Troki)

Year(s)	Type	Fond	File(s)	Op	A	F	Notes
1858	rs	515	110-122	25			
1858-1908	rs						
1859	rs	515	123	25			srs, Trakai County
1860	rs	515	124	25			srs, Trakai County
1861	rs	515	124	25			srs, Trakai County
1862	rs	515	124	25			srs, Trakai County
1863	rs	515	124	25			srs, Trakai County
1864	rs	515	125	25			srs, Trakai County
1864	rs	515	126	25			srs, Trakai County
1865	rs	515	127	25			srs, Trakai County
1867	rs	515	128	25			srs, Trakai County
1868	rs	515	128-129	25			srs, Trakai County
1869	rs	515	129-130	25			srs, Trakai County
1870	rs	515	130-131	25			srs, Trakai County
1871	rs	515	132	25			srs, Trakai County
1872	rs	515	133	25			srs, Trakai County
1873	rs	515	133	25			srs, Trakai County
1874	rs	515	133	25			srs, Trakai County

Year(s)	Type	Fond	File(s)	Op	A	F	Notes
Trakai (Troki) continued							
1905	rs	515	144	25			srs, Trakai County
1906	rs	515	144	25			srs, Trakai County
1907	rs	515	144	25			srs, Trakai County
1908	rs	515	144	25			srs, Trakai County
1870	b	728	943	3			
1870	d	728	945	3			
1872	b	728	946	3			
1872	m	728	948	3			
1872	v	728	949	3			
1872	d	728	950	3			
1873	b	728	952	3			
1873	d	728	953	3			
1874	d	728	955	3			
1875	b	728	956	3			
1875	d	728	958	3			
1876	v	728	1326	3			
1876	d	728	1333	3			
1878	m	728	1321	3			
1878	d	728	1334-1335	3			
1879	m	728	1322-1323	3			
1879	v	728	1330-1331	3			
1879	d	728	1336-1337	3			
1880	m	728	1324-1325	3			
1881	m	728	334	4			
1881	d	728	336	4			
1882	m	728	334	4			
1882	d	728	336	4			
1883	m	728	334	4			
1883	d	728	336	4			
1884	m	728	334	4			
1884	d	728	336	4			
1885	m	728	334	4			
1886	m	728	334	4			
1886	d	728	336	4			
1887	m	728	334	4			
1887	d	728	336	4			
1888	m	728	334	4			
1888	d	728	336	4			
1889	m	728	334	4			
1889	d	728	336	4			
1890	m	728	334	4			
1890	d	728	336	4			
1891	m	728	334	4			
1891	d	728	336	4			
1892	d	728	336	4			
1893	m	728	334	4			
1893	d	728	336	4			
1894	m	728	334	4			
1894	d	728	336	4			
1895	m	728	334	4			
1895	d	728	336	4			
1896	m	728	334	4			
1896	d	728	336	4			
1897	m	728	334	4			
1897	d	728	336	4			
1898	m	728	335	4			
1898	d	728	336	4			
1899	m	728	335	4			
1899	d	728	336	4			
1900	m	728	335	4			
1901	m	728	335	4			
1902	m	728	335	4			
1903	m	728	335	4			
1904	m	728	335	4			
1905	m	728	335	4			
1906	m	728	335	4			
1907	m	728	335	4			
1908	m	728	335	4			
Trakai County							
1859-1908	rs	515	123-144	25			
Troskunai							
1891	fl	206			K		
1891	fl	I-206	8	1			
Tryskiai (Trishik)							
1858	rs						
1866	rs						
1912-1916	tpl-r				K		

Turgeliai (Turgeli) Items for this town are in the Vilnius County 4th Okrug Registers.

Year(s)	Type	Fond	File(s)	Op	A	F	Notes
1885	m	728	353	4			
1886	m	728	353	4			
1887	d	728	1478	3			
1887	m	728	353	4			
1887	b	728	364	4			
1888	d	728	1478	3			

Turgeliai (Turgeli) continued

Year(s)	Type	Fond	File(s)	Op	A	F	Notes
1888	m	728	353	4			
1888	b	728	364	4			
1889	d	728	1478	3			
1889	m	728	353	4			
1889	b	728	364	4			
1890	d	728	1478	3			
1890	b	728	1479	3			
1890	m	728	1480	3			
1890	m	728	353	4			
1890	b	728	364	4			
1891	b	728	1446	3			
1891	d	728	1478	3			
1891	m	728	1483	3			
1891	m	728	353	4			
1891	b	728	364	4			
1892	d	728	1478	3			
1892	b	728	1486, 1553	3			
1892	m	728	1487, 1488, 1554	3			
1892	v	728	1489	3			
1892	m	728	353	4			
1892	b	728	364	4			
1893	d	728	1478	3			
1893	b	728	1490, 1553	3			
1893	m	728	1494, 1554	3			
1893	v	728	1496	3			
1893	m	728	353	4			
1893	b	728	364	4			
1894	b	728	1499, 1553	3			
1894	m	728	1505, 1554	3			
1894	v	728	1516	3			
1894	m	728	353	4			
1894	b	728	364	4			
1895	b	728	1508, 1553	3			
1895	m	728	1513, 1556	3			
1895	v	728	1519	3			
1895	v	728	3	4			
1895	m	728	353	4			
1895	b	728	364	4			
1896	b	728	13, 364	4			
1896	m	728	14, 353	4			
1896	b	728	1553	3			
1896	m	728	1556	3			
1897	b	728	28-29, 364	4			
1897	m	728	30, 353, 437	4			
1897	d	728	32	4			
1898	b	728	28, 45, 364	4			
1898	d	728	32	4			
1898	m	728	46, 353, 437	4			
1899	b	728	28, 60, 364	4			
1899	v	728	3	4			
1899	d	728	32	4			
1899	m	728	61, 353, 437	4			
1900	v	728	3	4			
1900	b	728	72, 364	4			
1900	m	728	73-74, 353, 437	4			
1900	d	728	75	4			
1901	v	728	3, 88	4			
1901	d	728	75	4			
1901	b	728	86, 364	4			
1901	m	728	87, 353, 437	4			
1902	m	728	102, 353, 438	4			
1902	d	728	103, 439	4			
1902	b	728	364	4			
1903	b	728	114-115, 364	4			
1903	m	728	116, 353, 438, 444	4			
1903	d	728	117, 439	4			
1904	b	728	127, 364	4			
1904	m	728	128, 353, 438	4			
1904	d	728	129, 439	4			
1905	b	728	139, 364	4			
1905	m	728	140, 353, 438	4			
1905	d	728	75, 141, 439	4			
1906	b	728	151, 364, 441	4			
1906	m	728	152, 353	4			
1906	d	728	75, 153	4			
1907	b	728	161, 364, 441	4			
1907	m	728	162, 353	4			
1907	v	728	3	4			
1907	d	728	75	4			
1908	b	728	172, 364, 441	4			
1908	v	728	3, 173	4			
1908	m	728	353	4			
1908	d	728	75	4			
1909	b	728	187, 364	4			
1909	v	728	3, 188	4			
1909	m	728	353, 442	4			
1909	d	728	75	4			
1910	b	728	199, 364	4			

Turgeliai (Turgeli) continued

Year(s)	Type	Fond	File(s)	Op	A	F	Notes
1910	v	728	3, 200	4			
1910	m	728	353, 443	4			
1911	b	728	213, 364	4			
1911	m	728	214, 353	4			
1911	v	728	215	4			
1912	b	728	226, 364	4			
1912	m	728	227-228, 353	4			
1913	b	728	239, 364	4			
1913	m	728	240, 353	4			
1914	b	728	253, 364	4			
1914	m	728	253-254, 353	4			
1914	v	728	255	4			
1915	m	728	353	4			
1915	b	728	364	4			
1916	b	728	364	4			
1917	b	728	364	4			
1918	b	728	364	4			
1919	b	728	364	4			
1920	b	728	364	4			
1921	b	728	364	4			

Ukmerge (Vilkomir)

Year(s)	Type	Fond	File(s)	Op	A	F	Notes
1795-1831	rs	515	1032	15	K		All Social Classes including Jews
1851	rs						
1858	rs	1262	16	1			
1859	rs	1262	17	1			
1866-1894	rs	1262	19	1			
1872-1874	rs	1262	21	1			
1878-1879	rs	1262	23	1			
1893-1894	rs	1262	24	1			
1919	rs	I-517	28	1	K		
	fin	525					State Property Management Committee
1809-1813?	ml	497					Ukmerge County Draft Commission Records
1827-1918	fin	715					Property
1865-1917	p	I-223			K		Ukmerge County Police Headquarters, 900 files
1878	rs?	1262	23	1			
1895	fl						
1895	b	1226	1484	1			
1895	cen	768					Used in 1897 Census.
1900-1914	p	J-34	34	1	K		Ukmerge Okrug Police Heaquarters
1908	crl	I-517	19	1	K		
1918	crl				K		

Ukmerge & Surrounding Area

Year(s)	Type	Fond	File(s)	Op	A	F	Notes
ca. WWI	var				K		Regarding Jews

Ukmerge County

Year(s)	Type	Fond	File(s)	Op	A	F	Notes
	fin	715					Financial Records
1809-1813?	ml	497					Draft Commission Records
1863-1870	ml	1252					Ukmerge County Military Commander

Upyna

Year(s)	Type	Fond	File(s)	Op	A	F	Notes
1816	rs						
1851	rs						

Utena

Year(s)	Type	Fond	File(s)	Op	A	F	Notes
1858	rs						
1866	rs						
1874	rs						
1879	rs						
1895	rs						
1893	fl	I-207	1	1	K		

Uzpaliai

Year(s)	Type	Fond	File(s)	Op	A	F	Notes
1851	rs						
1858	rs						
1874	rs						
1879	rs						

Uzventis

Year(s)	Type	Fond	File(s)	Op	A	F	Notes
1795	rs						
1858	rs						
1912-1916	tpl-r				K		

Vabalninkas (Vabolnik)

Year(s)	Type	Fond	File(s)	Op	A	F	Notes
1816	rs						
1818	rs						
1834	rs						
1872	b	1226	419	1			
1872	m	1226	420	1			
1872	v	1226	421	1			
1872	d	1226	422	1			
1873	b	1226	423	1			
1873	m	1226	424	1			
1873	v	1226	425	1			
1873	d	1226	426	1			
1874	b	1226	427	1			

Vabalninkas (Vabolnik) continued

Year(s)	Type	Fond	File(s)	Op
1874	m	1226	428	1
1874	v	1226	429	1
1874	d	1226	430	1
1875	b	1226	431	1
1875	m	1226	432	1
1875	v	1226	433	1
1875	d	1226	434	1
1876	b	1226	1042	1
1876	m	1226	1046	1
1876	v	1226	1051	1
1876	d	1226	1055	1
1877	b	1226	1043	1
1877	m	1226	1047	1
1877	d	1226	1056	1
1878	m	1226	1048	1
1878	v	1226	1052	1
1878	d	1226	1057	1
1879	b	1226	1044	1
1879	m	1226	1049	1
1879	v	1226	1053	1
1880	b	1226	1045	1
1880	m	1226	1050	1
1881	b	1226	1978	1
1882	b	1226	1978	1
1882	m	1226	1979	1
1882	v	1226	1980	1
1882	d	1226	1981	1
1883	b	1226	1978	1
1883	m	1226	1979	1
1883	v	1226	1980	1
1883	d	1226	1981	1
1884	b	1226	1978	1
1884	m	1226	1979	1
1884	v	1226	1980	1
1884	d	1226	1981	1
1885	b	1226	1978	1
1885	m	1226	1979	1
1885	v	1226	1980	1
1885	d	1226	1981	1
1886	b	1226	1978	1
1886	m	1226	1979	1
1886	v	1226	1980	1
1886	d	1226	1981	1
1887	b	1226	1978	1
1887	m	1226	1979	1
1887	v	1226	1980	1
1887	d	1226	1981	1
1888	b	1226	1978	1
1888	m	1226	1979	1
1888	v	1226	1980	1
1888	d	1226	1981	1
1889	b	1226	1978	1
1889	m	1226	1979	1
1889	v	1226	1980	1
1889	d	1226	1981	1
1890	b	1226	1978	1
1890	m	1226	1979	1
1890	v	1226	1980	1
1890	d	1226	1981	1
1891	b	1226	1978	1
1891	m	1226	1979	1
1891	v	1226	1980	1
1891	d	1226	1981	1
1892	b	1226	1978	1
1892	m	1226	1979	1
1892	v	1226	1980	1
1892	d	1226	1981	1
1893	b	1226	1978	1
1893	m	1226	1979	1
1893	v	1226	1980	1
1893	d	1226	1981	1
1894	b	1226	1978	1
1894	m	1226	1979	1
1894	v	1226	1980	1
1894	d	1226	1981	1
1895	b	1226	1978	1
1895	m	1226	1979	1
1895	v	1226	1980	1
1895	d	1226	1981	1
1896	b	1226	1978	1
1896	m	1226	1979	1
1896	v	1226	1980	1
1896	d	1226	1981	1
1897	b	1226	1978	1
1897	m	1226	1979	1
1897	v	1226	1980	1
1897	d	1226	1981	1
1898	b	1226	1978	1

Vabalninkas (Vabolnik) continued

Year(s)	Type	Fond	File(s)	Op
1898	m	1226	1979	1
1898	v	1226	1980	1
1898	d	1226	1981	1
1899	b	1226	1978	1
1899	m	1226	1979	1
1899	v	1226	1980	1
1899	d	1226	1981	1
1900	b	1226	1978	1
1900	m	1226	1979	1
1900	v	1226	1980	1
1900	d	1226	1981	1
1901	b	1226	1978	1
1901	m	1226	1979	1
1901	v	1226	1980	1
1901	d	1226	1981	1
1902	b	1226	1978	1
1902	m	1226	1979	1
1902	v	1226	1980	1
1902	d	1226	1981	1
1903	b	1226	1978	1
1903	m	1226	1979	1
1903	v	1226	1980	1
1903	d	1226	1981	1
1903	d	728	1013	1
1904	b	1226	1978	1
1904	m	1226	1979	1
1904	v	1226	1980	1
1904	d	1226	1981	1
1904	d	728	1023	1
1905	b	1226	1978	1
1905	m	1226	1979	1
1905	v	1226	1980	1
1905	d	1226	1981	1
1906	b	1226	1978	1
1906	m	1226	1979	1
1906	v	1226	1980	1
1906	d	1226	1981	1
1907	b	1226	1978	1
1907	m	1226	1979	1
1907	v	1226	1980	1
1907	d	1226	1981	1
1908	b	1226	1978	1
1908	m	1226	1979	1
1908	v	1226	1980	1
1908	d	1226	1981	1
1909	b	1226	1978	1
1909	m	1226	1979	1
1909	v	1226	1980	1
1909	d	1226	1981	1
1909	d	728	1067-1067A	1
1910	b	1226	1978	1
1910	m	1226	1979	1
1910	v	1226	1980	1
1910	d	1226	1981	1
1911	b	1226	1978	1
1911	m	1226	1979	1
1911	v	1226	1980	1
1911	d	1226	1981	1
1912	b	1226	1978	1
1912	m	1226	1979	1
1912	v	1226	1980	1
1912	d	1226	1981	1
1913	b	1226	1978	1
1913	m	1226	1979	1
1913	v	1226	1980	1
1913	d	1226	1981	1
1914	m	1226	1979	1
1914	v	1226	1980	1
1914	d	1226	1981	1

Vainutas

Year(s)	Type
1816	rs
1851	rs
1858	rs

Valkininkai (Olkenik)

Year(s)	Type	Fond	File(s)	Op
1858-1905	rs			
1856	v	728	247	1
1857	b	728	293	1
1860	v	728	561	1
1865	v	728	756	3
1869	m	728	757	3
1870	b	728	758	3
1870	m	728	759	3
1870	v	728	760	3
1870	d	728	761	3
1871	b	728	762-763	3
1871	m	728	764	3

Valkininkai (Olkenik) continued

Year(s)	Type	Fond	File(s)	Op	A	F	Notes
1871	v	728	765	3			
1871	d	728	766	3			
1872	b	728	767, 947	3			
1872	d	728	768	3			
1873	b	728	769, 951	3			
1873	m	728	770-771	3			
1873	v	728	772	3			
1874	b	728	773	3			
1874	m	728	774-775	3			
1874	v	728	776	3			
1875	b	728	777	3			
1875	m	728	778	3			
1875	d	728	779-780	3			
1876	b	728	1260	3			
1876	m	728	1265	3			
1876	d	728	1274	3			
1877	b	728	1261	3			
1877	m	728	1266-1267	3			
1877	d	728	1275	3			
1877	v	728	1280	3			
1878	b	728	1262	3			
1878	m	728	1268-1269	3			
1878	d	728	1276	3			
1879	b	728	1263	3			
1879	m	728	1270-1271	3			
1879	d	728	1277-1278	3			
1880	b	728	1264	3			
1880	m	728	1272-1273	3			
1880	d	728	1279	3			
1881	m	728	323	4			
1886	m	728	323	4			
1887	m	728	323	4			
1888	m	728	323	4			
1889	m	728	323	4			
1890	m	728	323	4			
1891	m	728	323	4			
1893	m	728	323	4			
1894	m	728	323	4			
1896	m	728	323	4			
1897	m	728	323	4			
1898	m	728	323	4			
1899	m	728	323	4			
1900	m	728	323	4			
1901	m	728	323	4			
1902	m	728	323	4			
1903	m	728	323	4			
1904	m	728	323	4			
1905	m	728	323	4			

Vandziogala (Vendzhigola)

Year(s)	Type	Fond	File(s)	Op	A	F	Notes
1874	rs	I-61	1654	1	K		Index of Jews
1856	b	1226	1347	1			
1856	d	1226	1348	1			
1856	d	1226	1349	1			
1857	b	1226	1347	1			
1857	d	1226	1348	1			
1857	d	1226	1349	1			
1858	b	1226	1347	1			
1858	d	1226	1348	1			
1858	d	1226	1349	1			
1859	b	1226	1347	1			
1859	d	1226	1348	1			
1859	d	1226	1349	1			
1860	b	1226	1347	1			
1860	d	1226	1348	1			
1860	d	1226	1349	1			
1861	b	1226	1347	1			
1861	d	1226	1348	1			
1861	d	1226	1349	1			
1862	b	1226	1347	1			
1862	d	1226	1348	1			
1862	d	1226	1349	1			
1863	b	1226	1347	1			
1863	d	1226	1348	1			
1863	d	1226	1349	1			
1864	b	1226	1347	1			
1864	d	1226	1348	1			
1864	d	1226	1349	1			
1865	b	1226	1347	1			
1865	d	1226	1348	1			
1865	d	1226	1349	1			
1865	v	1226	49	1			
1866	d	1226	1348	1			
1866	b	1226	50, 1347	1			
1866	v	1226	51	1			
1866	d	1226	52, 1349	1			
1867	b	1226	1347	1			
1867	d	1226	1348	1			

Vandziogala (Vendzhigola) continued

Year(s)	Type	Fond	File(s)	Op	A	F	Notes
1867	d	1226	1349	1			
1868	b	1226	1347	1			
1868	d	1226	1348	1			
1868	d	1226	1349	1			
1869	b	1226	1347	1			
1869	d	1226	1348	1			
1869	d	1226	1349	1			
1870	b	1226	1347	1			
1870	d	1226	1348	1			
1870	d	1226	1349	1			
1870-74	k				K		
1871	b	1226	1347	1			
1871	d	1226	1348	1			
1871	d	1226	1349	1			
1872	b	1226	1347	1			
1872	d	1226	1348	1			
1872	d	1226	1349	1			
1873	b	1226	53, 1347	1			
1873	d	1226	54, 1348	1			
1873	v	1226	55	1			
1873	d	1226	56, 1349	1			
1874	b	1226	1347	1			
1874	d	1226	1348	1			
1874	d	1226	1349	1			
1875	b	1226	1347	1			
1875	d	1226	1348	1			
1875	d	1226	1349	1			
1876	b	1226	1347	1			
1876	d	1226	1348	1			
1876	d	1226	1349	1			
1877	d	1226	1348	1			
1877	d	1226	1349	1			
1877	b	1226	1350	1			
1878	d	1226	1348	1			
1878	d	1226	1349	1			
1878	b	1226	1350	1			
1879	d	1226	1348	1			
1879	d	1226	1349	1			
1879	b	1226	1350	1			
1880	d	1226	1348	1			
1880	d	1226	1349	1			
1880	b	1226	1350	1			
1881	b	1226	1350	1			
1882	b	1226	1350	1			
1883	b	1226	1350	1			
1884	b	1226	1350	1			
1885	b	1226	1350	1			
1886	b	1226	1350	1			
1887	b	1226	1350	1			
1888	b	1226	1350	1			
1889	b	1226	1350	1			
1890	b	1226	1350	1			
1891	b	1226	1350	1			
1892	b	1226	1350	1			
1928-1939	bdmv	1226	1351	1			Extracts
1928-1940	bdmv	1226	1352	1			Extracts

Varena (Oran)

Year(s)	Type	Fond	File(s)	Op	A	F	Notes
1858-1905	rs						
1857	b	728	281	1			
1857	m	728	300	1			
1858	b	728	344	1			
1870	b	728	781	3			
1871	m	728	783	3			
1872	m	728	785	3			
1873	m	728	787	3			
1874	m	728	789	3			
1875	m	728	791	3			
1876	m	728	1307	3			
1877	m	728	1305-1306	3			
1877	v	728	1310-1311	3			
1877	d	728	1312	3			
1878	m	728	1304	3			
1878	v	728	1309	3			
1879	m	728	1303	3			
1880	v	1226	1054	1			
1880	m	728	1302	3			
1881	m	728	325	4			
1882	m	728	325	4			
1883	m	728	325	4			
1884	m	728	325	4			
1885	m	728	325	4			
1886	m	728	325	4			
1886	v	728	326	4			
1887	m	728	325	4			
1888	b	728	324	4			
1888	m	728	325	4			
1889	b	728	324	4			

Varena (Oran) continued

Year(s)	Type	Fond	File(s)	Op
1889	m	728	325	4
1889	d	728	327	4
1890	b	728	324	4
1890	m	728	325	4
1890	d	728	327	4
1891	b	728	324	4
1891	m	728	325	4
1891	d	728	327	4
1892	b	728	324	4
1892	m	728	325	4
1892	d	728	327	4
1893	b	728	324	4
1893	m	728	325	4
1894	b	728	324	4
1894	m	728	325	4
1894	v	728	326	4
1894	d	728	327	4
1895	b	728	324	4
1895	m	728	325	4
1895	d	728	327	4
1896	b	728	324	4
1896	m	728	325	4
1896	v	728	326	4
1896	d	728	327	4
1897	b	728	324	4
1897	v	728	326	4
1897	d	728	327	4
1898	b	728	324	4
1898	m	728	325	4
1898	d	728	327	4
1899	b	728	324	4
1899	m	728	325	4
1900	b	728	324	4
1900	m	728	325	4
1900	v	728	326	4
1900	d	728	327	4
1901	b	728	324	4
1901	m	728	325	4
1901	v	728	326	4
1902	b	728	324	4
1902	m	728	325	4
1903	b	728	324	4
1903	m	728	325	4
1904	m	728	325	4
1904	d	728	327	4
1905	b	728	324	4
1905	m	728	325	4
1906	b	728	324	4
1906	m	728	325	4
1906	d	728	327	4
1907	b	728	324	4
1907	m	728	325	4
1908	b	728	324	4
1908	m	728	325	4
1908	d	728	327	4
1909	b	728	324	4
1909	m	728	325	4
1909	d	728	327	4
1910	m	728	325	4
1910	v	728	326	4
1911	b	728	324	4
1911	m	728	325	4
1911	d	728	327	4
1912	b	728	324	4
1912	m	728	325	4
1912	d	728	327	4
1913	b	728	324	4
1913	m	728	325	4
1913	v	728	326	4
1913	d	728	327	4
1914	b	728	324	4
1914	m	728	325	4
1915	b	728	324	4
1915	m	728	325	4
1915	d	728	327	4

Varnenai (Vorniany) Items for this town are in the Vilnius County 4th Okrug Registers.

Year(s)	Type	Fond	File(s)	Op
1885	m	728	353	4
1886	m	728	353	4
1887	d	728	1478	3
1887	m	728	353	4
1887	b	728	364	4
1888	d	728	1478	3
1888	m	728	353	4
1888	b	728	364	4
1889	d	728	1478	3
1889	m	728	353	4
1889	b	728	364	4
1890	d	728	1478	3
1890	b	728	1479	3

Varnenai (Vorniany) continued

Year(s)	Type	Fond	File(s)	Op	A	F	Notes
1890	m	728	1480	3			
1890	m	728	353	4			
1890	b	728	364	4			
1891	b	728	1446	3			
1891	d	728	1478	3			
1891	m	728	1483	3			
1891	m	728	353	4			
1891	b	728	364	4			
1892	d	728	1478	3			
1892	b	728	1486, 1553	3			
1892	m	728	1487, 1488, 1554	3			
1892	v	728	1489	3			
1892	m	728	353	4			
1892	b	728	364	4			
1893	d	728	1478	3			
1893	b	728	1490, 1553	3			
1893	m	728	1494, 1554	3			
1893	v	728	1496	3			
1893	m	728	353	4			
1893	b	728	364	4			
1894	b	728	1499, 1553	3			
1894	m	728	1505, 1554	3			
1894	v	728	1516	3			
1894	m	728	353	4			
1894	b	728	364	4			
1895	b	728	1508, 1553	3			
1895	m	728	1513, 1556	3			
1895	v	728	1519	3			
1895	v	728	3	4			
1895	m	728	353	4			
1895	b	728	364	4			
1896	b	728	13, 364	4			
1896	m	728	14, 353	4			
1896	b	728	1553	3			
1896	m	728	1556	3			
1897	b	728	28-29, 364	4			
1897	m	728	30, 353, 437	4			
1897	d	728	32	4			
1898	b	728	28, 45, 364	4			
1898	d	728	32	4			
1898	m	728	46, 353, 437	4			
1899	b	728	28, 60, 364	4			
1899	v	728	3	4			
1899	d	728	32	4			
1899	m	728	61, 353, 437	4			
1900	v	728	3	4			
1900	b	728	72, 364	4			
1900	m	728	73-74, 353, 437	4			
1900	d	728	75	4			
1901	v	728	3, 88	4			
1901	d	728	75	4			
1901	b	728	86, 364	4			
1901	m	728	87, 353, 437	4			
1902	m	728	102, 353, 438	4			
1902	d	728	103, 439	4			
1902	b	728	364	4			
1903	b	728	114-115, 364	4			
1903	m	728	116, 353, 438, 444	4			
1903	d	728	117, 439	4			
1904	b	728	127, 364	4			
1904	m	728	128, 353, 438	4			
1904	d	728	129, 439	4			
1905	b	728	139, 364	4			
1905	m	728	140, 353, 438	4			
1905	d	728	75, 141, 439	4			
1906	b	728	151, 364, 441	4			
1906	m	728	152, 353	4			
1906	d	728	75, 153	4			
1907	b	728	161, 364, 441	4			
1907	m	728	162, 353	4			
1907	v	728	3	4			
1907	d	728	75	4			
1908	b	728	172, 364, 441	4			
1908	v	728	3, 173	4			
1908	m	728	353	4			
1908	d	728	75	4			
1909	b	728	187, 364	4			
1909	v	728	3, 188	4			
1909	m	728	353, 442	4			
1909	d	728	75	4			
1910	b	728	199, 364	4			
1910	v	728	3, 200	4			
1910	m	728	353, 443	4			
1911	b	728	213, 364	4			
1911	m	728	214, 353	4			
1911	v	728	215	4			
1912	b	728	226, 364	4			
1912	m	728	227-228, 353	4			
1913	b	728	239, 364	4			
1913	m	728	240, 353	4			

Varnenai (Vorniany) continued

Year(s)	Type	Fond	File(s)	Op
1914	b	728	253, 364	4
1914	m	728	253-254, 353	4
1914	v	728	255	4
1915	m	728	353	4
1915	b	728	364	4
1916	b	728	364	4
1917	b	728	364	4
1918	b	728	364	4
1919	b	728	364	4
1920	b	728	364	4
1921	b	728	364	4

Varniai (Vorna)

Year(s)	Type	Fond	File(s)	Op
1848	rs			
1859	rs			
1865	rs			
1852	b	728	31	2
1852	m	728	32	2
1852	v	728	33	2
1852	d	728	34	2
1853	b	728	35	2
1853	m	728	36	2
1853	v	728	37	2
1853	d	728	38	2
1854	b	728	47	2
1854	m	728	48	2
1854	v	728	63	2
1854	d	728	86	2
1855	b	728	82	2
1855	m	728	83	2
1855	v	728	84	2
1855	d	728	85	2
1856	b	728	116	2
1856	m	728	117	2
1856	v	728	118	2
1856	d	728	119	2
1857	b	728	154	2
1857	d	728	155	2
1857	m	728	156	2
1857	v	728	157	2
1858	b	728	192	2
1858	m	728	193	2
1858	v	728	194	2
1858	d	728	195	2
1859	b	728	234	2
1859	v	728	235	2
1859	m	728	236	2
1859	d	728	237	2
1860	b	728	276	2
1860	m	728	277	2
1860	v	728	278	2
1860	d	728	279	2
1861	b	728	304	2
1861	m	728	305	2
1861	v	728	306	2
1861	d	728	307	2
1862	b	728	334	2
1862	m	728	335	2
1862	v	728	336	2
1862	d	728	337	2
1863	v	728	362	2
1863	m	728	363	2
1863	b	728	364	2
1864	d	728	365	2
1865	b	1226	666	1
1865	m	1226	667	1
1865	v	1226	668	1
1865	d	1226	669	1
1866	b	1226	670	1
1866	m	1226	671	1
1866	v	1226	672	1
1866	d	1226	673	1
1868	b	1226	674	1
1868	m	1226	675	1
1868	v	1226	676	1
1868	d	1226	677	1
1869	b	1226	678	1
1869	m	1226	679	1
1869	v	1226	680	1
1869	d	1226	681	1
1870	b	1226	682	1
1870	m	1226	683	1
1870	v	1226	684	1
1870	d	1226	685	1
1871	b	1226	686	1
1871	m	1226	687	1
1871	v	1226	688	1
1871	d	1226	689	1
1872	b	1226	690	1
1872	m	1226	691	1

Varniai (Vorna) continued

Year(s)	Type	Fond	File(s)	Op
1872	v	1226	692	1
1872	d	1226	693	1
1873	b	1226	694	1
1873	m	1226	695	1
1873	v	1226	696	1
1873	d	1226	697	1
1874	b	1226	698	1
1874	m	1226	699	1
1874	v	1226	700	1
1874	d	1226	701	1
1875	b	1226	702	1
1875	m	1226	703	1
1875	v	1226	704	1
1875	d	1226	705	1
1876	v	1226	1157	1
1876	d	1226	1162	1
1876	b	1226	706, 1149	1
1876	m	1226	707	1
1877	m	1226	1153	1
1877	v	1226	1158	1
1877	d	1226	1163	1
1877	b	1226	707	1
1878	b	1226	1150	1
1878	m	1226	1154	1
1878	v	1226	1159	1
1878	d	1226	1164	1
1879	b	1226	1151	1
1879	m	1226	1155	1
1879	v	1226	1160	1
1879	d	1226	1165	1
1880	b	1226	1152	1
1880	m	1226	1156	1
1880	v	1226	1161	1
1880	d	1226	1166	1
1881	b	1226	1320	1
1881	m	1226	1321	1
1881	v	1226	1984	1
1881	d	1226	1985	1
1882	b	1226	1320	1
1882	m	1226	1321	1
1882	v	1226	1984	1
1882	d	1226	1985	1
1883	b	1226	1320	1
1883	m	1226	1321	1
1883	v	1226	1984	1
1883	d	1226	1985	1
1884	b	1226	1320	1
1884	m	1226	1321	1
1884	v	1226	1984	1
1884	d	1226	1985	1
1885	b	1226	1320	1
1885	m	1226	1321	1
1885	v	1226	1984	1
1885	d	1226	1985	1
1886	b	1226	1320	1
1886	m	1226	1321	1
1886	v	1226	1984	1
1886	d	1226	1985	1
1887	b	1226	1320	1
1887	m	1226	1321	1
1887	v	1226	1984	1
1887	d	1226	1985	1
1888	b	1226	1320	1
1888	m	1226	1321	1
1888	v	1226	1984	1
1888	d	1226	1985	1
1889	b	1226	1320	1
1889	m	1226	1321	1
1889	v	1226	1984	1
1889	d	1226	1985	1
1890	b	1226	1320	1
1890	m	1226	1321	1
1890	v	1226	1984	1
1890	d	1226	1985	1
1891	b	1226	1320	1
1891	m	1226	1983	1
1891	v	1226	1984	1
1891	d	1226	1985	1
1892	b	1226	1320, 1916	1
1892	m	1226	1983	1
1892	v	1226	1984	1
1892	d	1226	1985	1
1893	b	1226	1982	1
1893	m	1226	1983	1
1893	v	1226	1984	1
1893	d	1226	1985	1
1894	b	1226	1982	1
1894	m	1226	1983	1
1894	v	1226	1984	1
1894	d	1226	1985	1

Varniai (Vorna) continued

Year(s)	Type	Fond	File(s)	Op	A	F	Notes
1895	b	1226	1982	1			
1895	m	1226	1983	1			
1895	v	1226	1984	1			
1895	d	1226	1985	1			
1896	b	1226	1982	1			
1896	m	1226	1983	1			
1896	v	1226	1984	1			
1896	d	1226	1985	1			
1897	b	1226	1982	1			
1897	m	1226	1983	1			
1897	v	1226	1984	1			
1897	d	1226	1985	1			
1898	b	1226	1982	1			
1898	m	1226	1983	1			
1898	v	1226	1984	1			
1898	d	1226	1985	1			
1899	b	1226	1982	1			
1899	m	1226	1983	1			
1899	v	1226	1984	1			
1899	d	1226	1985	1			
1900	b	1226	1982	1			
1900	m	1226	1983	1			
1900	v	1226	1984	1			
1900	d	1226	1985	1			
1901	b	1226	1982	1			
1901	m	1226	1983	1			
1901	v	1226	1984	1			
1901	d	1226	1985	1			
1902	b	1226	1982	1			
1902	m	1226	1983	1			
1902	v	1226	1984	1			
1902	d	1226	1985	1			
1903	b	1226	1982	1			
1903	m	1226	1983	1			
1903	v	1226	1984	1			
1903	d	1226	1985	1			
1904	b	1226	1982	1			
1904	m	1226	1983	1			
1904	v	1226	1984	1			
1904	d	1226	1985	1			
1905	b	1226	1982	1			
1905	m	1226	1983	1			
1905	v	1226	1984	1			
1905	d	1226	1985	1			
1906	b	1226	1982	1			
1906	m	1226	1983	1			
1906	v	1226	1984	1			
1906	d	1226	1985	1			
1907	b	1226	1982	1			
1907	m	1226	1983	1			
1907	v	1226	1984	1			
1907	d	1226	1985	1			
1908	b	1226	1982	1			
1908	m	1226	1983	1			
1908	v	1226	1984	1			
1908	d	1226	1985	1			
1909	b	1226	1982	1			
1909	m	1226	1983	1			
1909	v	1226	1984	1			
1909	d	1226	1985	1			
1910	b	1226	1982	1			
1910	m	1226	1983	1			
1910	v	1226	1984	1			
1910	d	1226	1985	1			
1911	b	1226	1982	1			
1911	m	1226	1983	1			
1911	v	1226	1984	1			
1911	d	1226	1985	1			
1912	b	1226	1982	1			
1912	m	1226	1983	1			
1912	v	1226	1984	1			
1912	d	1226	1985	1			
1913	b	1226	1982	1			
1913	m	1226	1983	1			
1913	v	1226	1984	1			
1913	d	1226	1985	1			

Vegeriai (Veger)

Year(s)	Type	Fond	File(s)	Op	A	F	Notes
1858	rs	1262	99	1			
1864-1869	rs						
1864	rs?						

Veivirzenai

Year(s)	Type	Fond	File(s)	Op	A	F	Notes
1816	rs						
1851	rs						
1870?	rs						

Veliuona (Vilon)

Year(s)	Type	Fond	File(s)	Op	A	F	Notes
1816	rs						
1869	rs	I-197	1-2	1	K		Jews

Veliuona (Vilon) continued

Year(s)	Type	Fond	File(s)	Op	A	F	Notes
1874	rs	I-61	1640	1	K		Alphabetic - Jews
1887	rs	I-197	1-2	1	K		Jews
1844	b	728	11	1			
1844	m	728	16	1			
1844	d	728	19	1			
1844	v	728	8	1			
1862	b	728	703	1			
1862	m	728	712	1			
1862	v	728	734	1			
1862	d	728	749	1			
1863	b	728	780	1			
1863	m	728	792	1			
1863	v	728	826	1			
1863	d	728	841	1			
1864	b	728	873	1			
1864	m	728	899	1			
1864	d	728	946	1			
1865	b	1226	1	1			
1865	m	1226	2	1			
1865	v	1226	3	1			
1865	d	1226	4	1			
1866	b	1226	5	1			
1866	m	1226	6	1			
1866	v	1226	7	1			
1866	d	1226	8	1			
1867	m	1226	10	1			
1867	v	1226	11	1			
1867	d	1226	12	1			
1867	b	1226	9	1			
1868	b	1226	13	1			
1868	m	1226	14	1			
1868	v	1226	15	1			
1868	d	1226	16	1			
1869	b	1226	17-18	1			
1869	m	1226	19-20	1			
1869	v	1226	21-22	1			
1869	d	1226	23-24	1			
1869	jcl	I-197	1-2	1	K		
1870	b	1226	25	1			
1870	m	1226	26	1			
1870	v	1226	27	1			
1870	d	1226	28	1			
1870-74	k				K		
1871	b	1226	29	1			
1871	m	1226	30	1			
1871	v	1226	31	1			
1871	d	1226	32	1			
1872	b	1226	33	1			
1872	m	1226	34	1			
1872	v	1226	35	1			
1872	d	1226	36	1			
1873	b	1226	37	1			
1873	m	1226	38	1			
1873	v	1226	39	1			
1873	d	1226	40	1			
1874	b	1226	41	1			
1874	m	1226	42	1			
1874	v	1226	43	1			
1874	d	1226	44	1			
1874-78	k				K		
1875	b	1226	45	1			
1875	m	1226	46	1			
1875	v	1226	47	1			
1875	d	1226	48	1			
1876	b	1226	987	1			
1876	m	1226	988	1			
1876	d	1226	993	1			
1876	v	1226	998	1			
1877	b	1226	986	1			
1877	m	1226	989	1			
1877	d	1226	994	1			
1877	v	1226	999	1			
1878	v	1226	1000	1			
1878	b	1226	985	1			
1878	m	1226	990	1			
1878	d	1226	995	1			
1879	v	1226	1001	1			
1879	b	1226	984	1			
1879	m	1226	991	1			
1879	d	1226	996	1			
1880	v	1226	1002	1			
1880	b	1226	983	1			
1880	m	1226	992	1			
1880	d	1226	997	1			
1881	b	1226	1963	1			
1881	m	1226	1964	1			
1881	v	1226	1965	1			
1881	d	1226	1966	1			
1882	b	1226	1963	1			
1882	m	1226	1964	1			

Veliuona (Vilon) continued

Year(s)	Type	Fond	File(s)	Op	A	F	Notes
1882	v	1226	1965	1			
1882	d	1226	1966	1			
1883	b	1226	1963	1			
1883	m	1226	1964	1			
1883	v	1226	1965	1			
1883	d	1226	1966	1			
1884	b	1226	1963	1			
1884	m	1226	1964	1			
1884	v	1226	1965	1			
1884	d	1226	1966	1			
1885	b	1226	1963	1			
1885	m	1226	1964	1			
1885	v	1226	1965	1			
1885	d	1226	1966	1			
1886	b	1226	1963	1			
1886	m	1226	1964	1			
1886	v	1226	1965	1			
1886	d	1226	1966	1			
1887	fl				K		
1887	b	1226	1963	1			
1887	m	1226	1964	1			
1887	v	1226	1965	1			
1887	d	1226	1966	1			
1887	jcl	I-197	1-2	1	K		
1888	b	1226	1963	1			
1888	m	1226	1964	1			
1888	v	1226	1965	1			
1888	d	1226	1966	1			
1889	b	1226	1963	1			
1889	m	1226	1964	1			
1889	v	1226	1965	1			
1889	d	1226	1966	1			
1890	b	1226	1963	1			
1890	m	1226	1964	1			
1890	v	1226	1965	1			
1890	d	1226	1966	1			
1891	b	1226	1963	1			
1891	m	1226	1964	1			
1891	v	1226	1965	1			
1891	d	1226	1966	1			
1892	b	1226	1963	1			
1892	m	1226	1964	1			
1892	v	1226	1965	1			
1892	d	1226	1966	1			
1893	b	1226	1963	1			
1893	m	1226	1964	1			
1893	v	1226	1965	1			
1893	d	1226	1966	1			
1894	b	1226	1963	1			
1894	m	1226	1964	1			
1894	v	1226	1965	1			
1894	d	1226	1966	1			
1895	b	1226	1963	1			
1895	m	1226	1964	1			
1895	v	1226	1965	1			
1895	d	1226	1966	1			
1896	b	1226	1963	1			
1896	m	1226	1964	1			
1896	v	1226	1965	1			
1896	d	1226	1966	1			
1897	m	1226	1964	1			
1897	v	1226	1965	1			
1897	d	1226	1966	1			
1898	b	1226	1963	1			
1898	m	1226	1964	1			
1898	v	1226	1965	1			
1898	d	1226	1966	1			
1899	b	1226	1963	1			
1899	m	1226	1964	1			
1899	v	1226	1965	1			
1899	d	1226	1966	1			
1900	b	1226	1963	1			
1900	m	1226	1964	1			
1900	v	1226	1965	1			
1900	d	1226	1966	1			
1901	b	1226	1963	1			
1901	m	1226	1964	1			
1901	v	1226	1965	1			
1901	d	1226	1966	1			
1902	b	1226	1963	1			
1902	m	1226	1964	1			
1902	v	1226	1965	1			
1902	d	1226	1966	1			
1903	b	1226	1963	1			
1903	m	1226	1964	1			
1903	v	1226	1965	1			
1903	d	1226	1966	1			
1904	b	1226	1963	1			
1904	m	1226	1964	1			
1904	v	1226	1965	1			

Veliuona (Vilon) continued

Year(s)	Type	Fond	File(s)	Op	A	F	Notes
1904	d	1226	1966	1			
1905	b	1226	1963	1			
1905	m	1226	1964	1			
1905	v	1226	1965	1			
1905	d	1226	1966	1			
1906	b	1226	1963	1			
1906	m	1226	1964	1			
1906	v	1226	1965	1			
1906	d	1226	1966	1			
1907	b	1226	1963	1			
1907	b	1226	1963	1			
1907	m	1226	1964	1			
1907	v	1226	1965	1			
1907	d	1226	1966	1			
1908	b	1226	1963	1			
1908	m	1226	1964	1			
1908	v	1226	1965	1			
1908	d	1226	1966	1			
1909	b	1226	1963	1			
1909	m	1226	1964	1			
1909	v	1226	1965	1			
1909	d	1226	1966	1			
1910	b	1226	1963	1			
1910	m	1226	1964	1			
1910	v	1226	1965	1			
1910	d	1226	1966	1			
1911	b	1226	1963	1			
1911	m	1226	1964	1			
1911	v	1226	1965	1			
1911	d	1226	1966	1			
1912	b	1226	1963	1			
1912	m	1226	1964	1			
1912	v	1226	1965	1			
1912	d	1226	1966	1			
1913	b	1226	1963	1			
1913	m	1226	1964	1			
1913	v	1226	1965	1			
1913	d	1226	1966	1			
1914	b	1226	1963	1			
1914	m	1226	1964	1			
1914	v	1226	1965	1			
1914	d	1226	1966	1			

Vidukle

Year(s)	Type	Fond	File(s)	Op	A	F	Notes
1816	rs						
1839	rs						
1870?	rs						
1873	rs						

Vidzy, Belarus

Year(s)	Type	Fond	File(s)	Op	A	F	Notes
1816-27	rs						Novo-Aleksandrovsk (Zarasai) County
1871	rs						Novo-Aleksandrovsk (Zarasai) County
1882	rs						Novo-Aleksandrovsk (Zarasai) County
1892-94	ta	208			K		Novo-Aleksandrovsk (Zarasai) County

Vieksniai

Year(s)	Type	Fond	File(s)	Op	A	F	Notes
1845	rs	I-223	32	1	K		Alphabetic - Jews
1858	rs	1262	99	1			
1858	rs	I-223	32	1	K		40 files
1858 1862-1876?	rs	I-223	31	1	K		
1858, 1862-1876?	rs	I-223	31	1	K		
1858-66	rs						
1866	rs						
1908	rs	I-223	34	1	K		Alphabetic - Jews
1845	al				K		40 files
1874	ta						
1895	cen						
1912-1916	tpl-r				K		

Vievis (Veviya)

Year(s)	Type	Fond	File(s)	Op	A	F	Notes
1858-1905	rs						
1864	m	728	398	2			
1870	b	728	412-413	3			
1870	m	728	414	3			
1870	v	728	415, 944	3			
1870	d	728	416	3			
1871	b	728	417-418	3			
1871	m	728	419	3			
1871	d	728	421	3			
1872	b	728	422-423	3			
1872	m	728	424	3			
1872	d	728	426	3			
1873	b	728	427-428	3			
1873	m	728	429	3			
1873	d	728	431	3			
1874	b	728	432	3			
1874	m	728	433	3			
1874	d	728	435	3			

Vievis (Veviya) continued

Year(s)	Type	Fond	File(s)	Op	A	F	Notes
1875	b	728	436-437	3			
1875	m	728	438	3			
1875	v	728	439	3			
1876	b	728	1313	3			
1876	m	728	1316	3			
1876	b	728	301	4			
1877	m	728	1317	3			
1877	b	728	1319A	3			
1877	d	728	1320	3			
1877	b	728	301	4			
1878	b	728	301	4			
1879	b	728	1314	3			
1879	b	728	301	4			
1880	b	728	1315	3			
1882	b	728	301	4			
1883	b	728	301	4			
1884	b	728	301	4			
1885	b	728	301	4			
1885	d	728	440	3			
1886	b	728	301	4			
1887	b	728	301	4			
1887	m	728	302	4			
1888	b	728	301	4			
1889	b	728	301	4			
1892	b	728	301	4			
1893	b	728	301	4			
1893	m	728	302	4			
1894	b	728	301	4			
1894	m	728	302	4			
1895	b	728	301	4			
1895	d	728	302	4			
1895	m	728	302	4			
1896	b	728	301	4			
1896	d	728	302	4			
1896	m	728	302	4			
1897	b	728	301	4			
1897	d	728	302	4			
1898	b	728	301	4			
1898	d	728	302	4			
1898	m	728	302	4			
1899	b	728	301	4			
1899	d	728	302	4			
1900	b	728	301	4			
1901	b	728	301	4			
1901	m	728	302	4			
1902	b	728	301	4			
1902	m	728	302	4			
1904	b	728	301	4			
1904	m	728	302	4			
1905	b	728	301	4			
1905	m	728	302	4			
1906	b	728	301	4			
1906	m	728	302	4			
1907	m	728	302	4			
1908	b	728	301	4			
1908	m	728	302	4			
1909	b	728	301	4			
1909	m	728	302	4			
1910	b	728	301	4			
1911	b	728	301	4			
1911	m	728	302	4			
1912	b	728	301	4			
1913	b	728	301	4			
1914	m	728	302	4			

Vileika

Year(s)	Type	Fond	File(s)	Op	A	F	Notes
1795-1831	rs	515	1032	15	K		All Social Classes including Jews

Vilijampole (Slobodka)

Year(s)	Type	Fond	File(s)	Op	A	F	Notes
1834	rs						Kaunas Duma
1854	b	728	30	1			
1854	v	728	92	1			
1855	b	728	123	1			
1855	m	728	143	1			
1855	v	728	164	1			
1855	d	728	179	1			
1856	b	728	200	1			
1856	m	728	222	1			
1856	v	728	242	1			
1857	d	1226	2090	1			
1857	b	728	287	1			
1857	m	728	303	1			
1857	v	728	319	1			
1858	m	728	370	1			
1858	v	728	388	1			
1859	b	728	418	1			
1859	v	728	477	1			
1860	d	1226	2091	1			

Vilijampole (Slobodka) continued

Year(s)	Type	Fond	File(s)	Op	A	F	Notes
1860	b	728	504	1			
1861	m	728	442	1			
1861	b	728	595	1			
1862	d	1226	2105	1			
1862	b	728	700	1			
1863	b	1226	101	1			
1863	v	728	818, 824	1			
1863	m	728	904	1			
1864	b	728	877	1			
1864	m	728	904	1			
1864	d	728	945	1			
1865	b	1226	102-103	1			
1865	v	1226	104	1			
1866	b	1226	105	1			
1866	d	1226	106	1			
1866	m	1226	107	1			
1866	v	1226	108	1			
1867	b	1226	109	1			
1867	v	1226	110	1			
1867	d	1226	111	1			
1868	b	1226	112	1			
1868	m	1226	113	1			
1868	v	1226	114	1			
1868	d	1226	115	1			
1869	b	1226	116	1			
1869	m	1226	117	1			
1869	v	1226	118	1			
1869	d	1226	119	1			
1870	b	1226	120	1			
1870	m	1226	121	1			
1870	v	1226	122	1			
1870-74	k				K		
1871	b	1226	123	1			
1871	m	1226	124	1			
1871	d	1226	125	1			
1872	b	1226	126	1			
1872	m	1226	127	1			
1872	v	1226	128	1			
1873	b	1226	129	1			
1873	v	1226	130	1			
1873	d	1226	131	1			
1874	fl				K		
1874	b	1226	132	1			
1874	m	1226	133	1			
1874	v	1226	134	1			
1874	fl	I-61	1627-1628	1	K		
1874	fl	I-61	1638, 1652	1	K		Alphabetic List
1874	fl	I-61	1641	1	K		Alphabetic - Jews
1874-78	k				K		
1875	b	1226	135	1			
1875	m	1226	136	1			
1875	d	1226	137	1			
1876	fl						
1876	b	1226	924, 1858	1			
1876	m	1226	928	1			
1876	v	1226	933	1			
1876	d	1226	938	1			
1877	b	1226	1859	1			
1877	v	1226	934	1			
1878	b	1226	925, 1860	1			
1878	m	1226	929	1			
1878	v	1226	935	1			
1878	d	1226	939	1			
1879	b	1226	926, 1861	1			
1879	m	1226	930	1			
1879	v	1226	936	1			
1880	b	1226	1286, 1864	1			
1880	d	1226	927	1			
1880	m	1226	931	1			
1880	v	1226	937	1			
1881	b	1226	1287	1			
1881	d	1226	1303	1			
1881	v	1226	1975	1			
1882	b	1226	1287	1			
1882	d	1226	1303	1			
1882	m	1226	1974	1			
1882	v	1226	1975	1			
1882	b	728	1114	3			
1883	d	1226	1303	1			
1883	m	1226	1974	1			
1883	v	1226	1975	1			
1884	d	1226	1303	1			
1884	b	1226	1972	1			
1884	m	1226	1974	1			
1884	v	1226	1975	1			
1885	d	1226	1303	1			
1885	b	1226	1871	1			
1885	m	1226	1974	1			

Vilijampole (Slobodka) continued

Year(s)	Type	Fond	File(s)		Op	A	F	Notes
1885	m	1226	1974		1			
1885	v	1226	1975		1			
1885	b	728	1119		3			
1886	d	1226	1303		1			
1886	b	1226	1873		1			
1886	m	1226	1974		1			
1886	v	1226	1975		1			
1886	b	728	1121		3			
1887	d	1226	1303		1			
1887	b	1226	1318, 1875		1			In File #1318, see pages 204-273.
1887	m	1226	1974		1			
1887	v	1226	1975		1			
1887-1893	fl	I-61	1629		1	K		
1887-1893	fl	I-61	1630		1	K		
1888	d	1226	1303		1			
1888	b	1226	1315, 1877		1			In File #1315, see pages 222-274.
1888	m	1226	1974		1			
1888	v	1226	1975		1			
1889	d	1226	1303		1			
1889	b	1226	1318, 1881		1			In File #1318, see pages 305-335.
1889	m	1226	1974		1			
1889	v	1226	1975		1			
1890	b	1226	1304, 1883		1			
1890	m	1226	1974		1			
1890	v	1226	1975		1			
1890	d	1226	1976		1			
1891	b	1226	1305, 1885-1886		1			
1891	m	1226	1974		1			
1891	v	1226	1975		1			
1891	d	1226	1976		1			
1892	b	1226	1887		1			
1892	m	1226	1974		1			
1892	v	1226	1975		1			
1892	d	1226	1976		1			
1893	b	1226	1891, 1973		1			
1893	m	1226	1974		1			
1893	v	1226	1975		1			
1893	d	1226	1976		1			
1894	b	1226	1892		1			
1894	m	1226	1974		1			
1894	v	1226	1975		1			
1894	d	1226	1976		1			
1894	b	728	1502		3			
1895	b	1226	1306, 1894		1			
1895	m	1226	1974		1			
1895	v	1226	1975		1			
1895	d	1226	1976		1			
1896	m	1226	1974		1			
1896	v	1226	1975		1			
1896	d	1226	1976-1977		1			
1897	m	1226	1974		1			
1897	v	1226	1975		1			
1897	d	1226	1976-1977		1			
1898	m	1226	1974		1			
1898	v	1226	1975		1			
1898	d	1226	1976-1977		1			
1898	d	1226	1976-1977		1			
1899	m	1226	1974		1			
1899	v	1226	1975		1			
1899	d	1226	1976-1977		1			
1900	m	1226	1974		1			
1900	v	1226	1975		1			
1900	d	1226	1976-1977		1			
1901	m	1226	1974		1			
1901	v	1226	1975		1			
1901	d	1226	1976-1977		1			
1902	m	1226	1974		1			
1902	v	1226	1975		1			
1902	d	1226	1976-1977		1			
1903	b	1226	1973		1			
1903	m	1226	1974		1			
1903	v	1226	1975		1			
1903	d	1226	1976-1977		1			
1904	b	1226	1972-1973, 2008		1			
1904	m	1226	1974		1			
1904	v	1226	1975		1			
1904	d	1226	1976-1977		1			
1905	b	1226	1972		1			
1905	m	1226	1974		1			
1905	v	1226	1975		1			
1905	d	1226	1976-1977		1			
1906	b	1226	1972		1			
1906	m	1226	1974		1			
1906	v	1226	1975		1			
1906	d	1226	1976-1977		1			
1907	b	1226	1972		1			
1907	m	1226	1974		1			
1907	v	1226	1975		1			

Vilijampole (Slobodka) continued

Year(s)	Type	Fond	File(s)	Op	A	F	Notes
1907	d	1226	1976-1977	1			
1908	b	1226	1972	1			
1908	m	1226	1974	1			
1908	v	1226	1975	1			
1908	d	1226	1976-1977	1			
1909	b	1226	1972, 2018	1			
1909	m	1226	1974	1			
1909	v	1226	1975	1			
1909	d	1226	1976-1977	1			
1909	d	1226	1976-1977	1			
1910	b	1226	1972	1			
1910	m	1226	1974	1			
1910	v	1226	1975	1			
1910	d	1226	1976-1977	1			
1911	b	1226	1972	1			
1911	m	1226	1974	1			
1911	v	1226	1975	1			
1911	d	1226	1976-1977	1			
1912	b	1226	1972	1			
1912	m	1226	1974	1			
1912	v	1226	1975	1			
1912	d	1226	1976-1977	1			
1913	b	1226	1972	1			
1913	m	1226	1974	1			
1913	v	1226	1975	1			
1913	d	1226	1976-1977	1			
1914	b	1226	1972	1			
1914	m	1226	1974	1			
1914	v	1226	1975	1			
1914	d	1226	1977	1			

Vilkaviskis (Vilkovishk)

Year(s)	Type	Fond	File(s)	Op	A	F	Notes
1810	b	1236	7	5			
1810	m	1236	8	5			
1810	d	1236	9	5			
1811	b	1236	7, 10	5			
1811	m	1236	8, 11	5			
1811	d	1236	9, 12-13	5			
1912	hol	1035	108	1			
1914	tpl-a	697	656	1			
1914-15	dl	57			K		Many Jews

Vilkija (Vilki)

Year(s)	Type	Fond	File(s)	Op	A	F	Notes
1816	rs						
1834	rs						Kaunas Duma
1851	rs						
1890	rs	I-198	2	1	K		
1838	b	728	1	1			
1840	b	728	5	1			
1844	m	728	13	1			
1844	d	728	20	1			
1847	b	728	24	1			
1854	d	728	107	1			
1854	b	728	50	1			
1854	m	728	51	1			
1854	v	728	91	1			
1855	b	728	120	1			
1855	m	728	141	1			
1855	v	728	163	1			
1855	d	728	189	1			
1856	b	728	213-214	1			
1856	m	728	237	1			
1856	d	728	259-260	1			
1857	b	728	295	1			
1857	v	728	312	1			
1857	d	728	336	1			
1858	b	728	337-338	1			
1858	m	728	380	1			
1858	d	728	412	1			
1859	b	728	417	1			
1859	m	728	439	1			
1859	v	728	474	1			
1859	d	728	498	1			
1860	b	728	523	1			
1860	m	728	526	1			
1860	v	728	568	1			
1860	d	728	592	1			
1861	b	728	594	1			
1861	m	728	640	1			
1861	d	728	677	1			
1862	b	728	701	1			
1862	m	728	723	1			
1862	d	728	742	1			
1863	b	728	789	1			
1863	m	728	791	1			
1863	d	728	858	1			
1864	b	728	891	1			
1864	m	728	892	1			

Vilkija (Vilki) continued

Year(s)	Type	Fond	File(s)	Op	A	F	Notes
1864	d	728	929	1			
1865	b	1226	57	1			
1865	m	1226	58	1			
1865	v	1226	59	1			
1865	d	1226	60	1			
1866	b	1226	61	1			
1866	m	1226	62	1			
1866	v	1226	63	1			
1866	d	1226	64	1			
1867	b	1226	65	1			
1867	m	1226	66, 1291	1			
1867	v	1226	67	1			
1867	d	1226	68	1			
1868	b	1226	69	1			
1868	m	1226	70	1			
1868	v	1226	71	1			
1868	d	1226	72	1			
1869	b	1226	73	1			
1869	m	1226	74	1			
1869	v	1226	75	1			
1869	d	1226	76	1			
1870	b	1226	77	1			
1870	m	1226	78	1			
1870	v	1226	79	1			
1870	d	1226	80	1			
1870-74	k					K	
1871	b	1226	81	1			
1871	m	1226	82	1			
1871	v	1226	83	1			
1871	d	1226	84	1			
1871	dl	198				K	Includes Jews
1872	b	1226	85	1			
1872	m	1226	86	1			
1872	v	1226	87	1			
1872	d	1226	88	1			
1873	b	1226	89	1			
1873	m	1226	90	1			
1873	v	1226	91	1			
1873	d	1226	92	1			
1874	b	1226	93	1			
1874	m	1226	94	1			
1874	v	1226	95	1			
1874	d	1226	96	1			
1874-78	k					K	
1875	d	1226	100	1			
1875	b	1226	97	1			
1875	m	1226	98	1			
1875	v	1226	99	1			
1876	b	1226	904	1			
1876	m	1226	909	1			
1876	d	1226	914	1			
1876	v	1226	919	1			
1877	b	1226	905	1			
1877	m	1226	910	1			
1877	d	1226	915	1			
1877	v	1226	920	1			
1878	b	1226	906	1			
1878	m	1226	911	1			
1878	d	1226	916	1			
1878	v	1226	921	1			
1879	b	1226	907	1			
1879	m	1226	912	1			
1879	d	1226	917	1			
1879	v	1226	922	1			
1880	b	1226	908	1			
1880	m	1226	913	1			
1880	d	1226	918	1			
1880	v	1226	923	1			
1881	m	1226	1307	1			
1881	b	1226	1967	1			
1881	v	1226	1970	1			
1881	d	1226	1971	1			
1882	m	1226	1307	1			
1882	b	1226	1967	1			
1882	v	1226	1970	1			
1882	d	1226	1971	1			
1883	m	1226	1307	1			
1883	b	1226	1967	1			
1883	v	1226	1970	1			
1883	d	1226	1971	1			
1884	m	1226	1307	1			
1884	b	1226	1967	1			
1884	v	1226	1970	1			
1884	d	1226	1971	1			
1885	m	1226	1307	1			
1885	b	1226	1967	1			
1885	v	1226	1970	1			
1885	d	1226	1971	1			

Vilkija (Vilki) continued

Year(s)	Type	Fond	File(s)	Op	A	F	Notes
1886	b	1226	1292, 1967	1			
1886	m	1226	1307	1			
1886	v	1226	1970	1			
1886	d	1226	1971	1			
1887	b	1226	1289, 1967	1			
1887	m	1226	1307	1			
1887	v	1226	1970	1			
1887	d	1226	1971	1			
1888	b	1226	1290, 1967	1			
1888	m	1226	1307	1			
1888	v	1226	1970	1			
1888	d	1226	1971	1			
1889	m	1226	1307	1			
1889	b	1226	1967	1			
1889	v	1226	1970	1			
1889	d	1226	1971	1			
1890	resl				K		
1890	m	1226	1307	1			
1890	b	1226	1967	1			
1890	v	1226	1970	1			
1890	d	1226	1971	1			
1890	jcl	I-198	2	1	K		
1891	m	1226	1307	1			
1891	b	1226	1967	1			
1891	v	1226	1970	1			
1891	d	1226	1971	1			
1892	m	1226	1307	1			
1892	b	1226	1967	1			
1892	v	1226	1970	1			
1892	d	1226	1971	1			
1893	m	1226	1307	1			
1893	b	1226	1967	1			
1893	v	1226	1970	1			
1893	d	1226	1971	1			
1894	m	1226	1307	1			
1894	b	1226	1967	1			
1894	v	1226	1970	1			
1894	d	1226	1971	1			
1895	b	1226	1967	1			
1895	m	1226	1969	1			
1895	v	1226	1970	1			
1895	d	1226	1971	1			
1895	b	728	1511	3			
1896	b	1226	1967	1			
1896	m	1226	1969	1			
1896	v	1226	1970	1			
1896	d	1226	1971	1			
1897	b	1226	1967	1			
1897	m	1226	1969	1			
1897	v	1226	1970	1			
1897	d	1226	1971	1			
1898	b	1226	1967	1			
1898	m	1226	1969	1			
1898	v	1226	1970	1			
1898	d	1226	1971	1			
1899	b	1226	1968	1			
1899	m	1226	1969	1			
1899	v	1226	1970	1			
1899	d	1226	1971	1			
1900	b	1226	1968	1			
1900	m	1226	1969	1			
1900	v	1226	1970	1			
1900	d	1226	1971	1			
1901	b	1226	1968	1			
1901	m	1226	1969	1			
1901	v	1226	1970	1			
1901	d	1226	1971	1			
1902	b	1226	1968	1			
1902	m	1226	1969	1			
1902	v	1226	1970	1			
1902	d	1226	1971	1			
1903	b	1226	1968	1			
1903	m	1226	1969	1			
1903	v	1226	1970	1			
1903	d	1226	1971	1			
1904	b	1226	1968	1			
1904	m	1226	1969	1			
1904	v	1226	1970	1			
1904	d	1226	1971	1			
1905	b	1226	1968	1			
1905	m	1226	1969	1			
1905	v	1226	1970	1			
1905	d	1226	1971	1			
1906	b	1226	1968	1			
1906	m	1226	1969	1			
1906	v	1226	1970	1			
1906	v	1226	1970	1			
1906	d	1226	1971	1			

Vilkija (Vilki) continued

Year(s)	Type	Fond	File(s)	Op	A	F	Notes
1907	b	1226	1968	1			
1907	m	1226	1969	1			
1907	v	1226	1970	1			
1907	d	1226	1971	1			
1908	b	1226	1968	1			
1908	m	1226	1969	1			
1908	v	1226	1970	1			
1908	d	1226	1971	1			
1909	b	1226	1968	1			
1909	m	1226	1969	1			
1909	v	1226	1970	1			
1909	d	1226	1971	1			
1910	b	1226	1968	1			
1910	m	1226	1969	1			
1910	v	1226	1970	1			
1910	d	1226	1971	1			
1911	b	1226	1968	1			
1911	m	1226	1969	1			
1911	v	1226	1970	1			
1911	d	1226	1971	1			
1912	b	1226	1968	1			
1912	m	1226	1969	1			
1912	v	1226	1970	1			
1912	d	1226	1971	1			
1912-1916	tpl-r				K		
1913	b	1226	1968	1			
1913	m	1226	1969	1			
1913	v	1226	1970	1			
1913	d	1226	1971	1			
1914	b	1226	1968	1			
1914	m	1226	1969	1			
1914	v	1226	1970	1			
1914	d	1226	1971	1			
unknown	tpl				K		

Vilna Governorship

Year(s)	Type	Fond	File(s)	Op	A	F	Notes
	var	380					Vilnius Governor Heaquaters

Vilnius (Vilno)

Year(s)	Type	Fond	File(s)	Op	A	F	Notes
1795	rs	515	6	15	K		Kahal rs
1795-1858-1915	rs	515	1-177	26	K		
1816	rs	515	286-323				
1858	rs						
1837	b	728	1	2			
1837	m	728	2	2			
1837	d	728	3	2			
1838	b	728	4, 5	2			
1838	v	728	6	2			
1838	d	728	7	2			
1838	d	728	8	2			
1839	m	728	10	2			
1839	v	728	11	2			
1839	d	728	12	2			
1839	b	728	9	2			
1840	b	728	13	2			
1840	m	728	14	2			
1840	v	728	15	2			
1840	d	728	16	2			
1841	b	728	17	2			
1841	m	728	18	2			
1841	v	728	19	2			
1841	d	728	20	2			
1842	b	728	21	2			
1842	m	728	22	2			
1842	v	728	23	2			
1842	d	728	25	2			
1843	b	728	21	2			
1843	m	728	22	2			
1843	v	728	24	2			
1843	d	728	25	2			
1844	b	728	26	2			
1844	m	728	27	2			
1844	v	728	28	2			
1844	d	728	29	2			
1845	b	728	26	2			
1845	m	728	27	2			
1845	v	728	28	2			
1845	d	728	29	2			
1846	d	728	1	3			
1846	b	728	26	2			
1846	m	728	27	2			
1846	v	728	28	2			
1846	d	728	29	2			
1847	d	728	1	3			
1847	b	728	2	3			
1847	m	728	3-4	3			
1847	b	728	30	2			
1847	v	728	5	3			

Vilkija (Vilki) continued

Year(s)	Type	Fond	File(s)	Op	A	F	Notes
1848	d	728	1	3			
1848	b	728	2	3			
1848	m	728	3-4	3			
1848	b	728	30	2			
1848	v	728	5	3			
1849	d	728	1	3			
1849	b	728	2	3			
1849	m	728	3-4	3			
1849	b	728	30	2			
1849	v	728	5	3			
1850	d	728	1	3			
1850	b	728	2	3			
1850	m	728	3-4, 6	3			
1850	b	728	30	2			
1850	v	728	5	3			
1851	m	728	6	3			
1851	b	728	7	3			
1851	v	728	8	3			
1851	d	728	9	3			
1852	m	728	6	3			
1852	b	728	7	3			
1852	v	728	8	3			
1852	d	728	9	3			
1853	d	728	39	2			
1853	m	728	6	3			
1853	b	728	7	3			
1853	v	728	8	3			
1853	d	728	9	3			
1854	b	728	10, 1045	3			
1854	m	728	11	3			
1854	m	728	43	2			
1854	v	728	44, 77	2			
1854	d	728	45	2			
1854	b	728	46	2			
1855	b	728	1045	3			
1855	b	728	75	2			
1855	m	728	76	2			
1855	v	728	78-79	2			
1855	d	728	80, 81	2			
1856	b	728	1045	3			
1856	b	728	110	2			
1856	m	728	111	2			
1856	v	728	112-113	2			
1856	d	728	114, 115	2			
1857	b	728	1045	3			
1857	b	728	146-147	2			
1857	m	728	148-150	2			
1857	v	728	151-152	2			
1857	d	728	153, 185	2			
1858	b	728	1045	3			
1858	b	728	147, 184	2			
1858	m	728	186	2			
1858	v	728	187-188,190	2			
1858	d	728	189, 191	2			
1859	b	728	1045	3			
1859	b	728	224-226	2			
1859	m	728	227, 228	2			
1859	v	728	229-231	2			
1859	d	728	232-233	2			
1860	b	728	267-269	2			
1860	m	728	270-272	2			
1860	v	728	273, 275A	2			
1860	d	728	274-275	2			
1861	b	728	300, 320	2			
1861	m	728	301, 321	2			
1861	v	728	302	2			
1861	d	728	303, 322	2			
1862	v	728	14	3			
1862	b	728	327-329	2			
1862	m	728	330	2			
1862	v	728	331	2			
1862	d	728	332, 333	2			
1863	b	728	1046	3			
1863	v	728	14	3			
1863	b	728	355-357	2			
1863	m	728	358	2			
1863	v	728	359	2			
1863	d	728	360-361	2			
1864	b	728	1046	3			
1864	m	728	12-13	3			
1864	v	728	14-15	3			
1864	d	728	16	3			
1864	b	728	382-384	2			
1864	d	728	385	2			
1865	b	728	1046	3			
1865	v	728	14, 29	3			
1865	b	728	17-18	3			
1865	m	728	19-20	3			

Vilkija (Vilki) continued

Year(s)	Type	Fond	File(s)	Op	A	F	Notes
1865	d	728	21-23	3			
1865	m	728	353	4			
1866	b	728	1046	3			
1866	v	728	14, 33-34	3			
1866	b	728	24-28	3			
1866	m	728	30-32	3			
1866	d	728	35-38	3			
1866	m	728	353	4			
1867	v	728	14, 47	3			
1867	m	728	353	4			
1867	b	728	39-42	3			
1867	m	728	43-46	3			
1867	d	728	48-50	3			
1868	v	728	14, 57	3			
1868	m	728	353	4			
1868	b	728	51-54	3			
1868	m	728	55-56	3			
1868	d	728	58-60	3			
1869	v	728	14, 68	3			
1869	m	728	353	4			
1869	b	728	61-63	3			
1869	m	728	64-67	3			
1869	d	728	69-72	3			
1870	m	728	353	4			
1870	b	728	73-76	3			
1870	m	728	77, 79-81	3			
1870	d	728	78, 83-85	3			
1870	v	728	82, 1176	3			
1871	m	728	353	4			
1871	b	728	86-88	3			
1871	m	728	89-91	3			
1871	v	728	92-93, 1176	3			
1871	d	728	94-95, 140	3			
1872	v	728	100-101, 1176	3			
1872	d	728	102-104	3			
1872	m	728	353	4			
1872	b	728	96-97	3			
1872	m	728	98-99	3			
1873	m	728	107-108	3			
1873	v	728	109-110, 1176	3			
1873	d	728	111-113, 145	3			
1873	m	728	353	4			
1873	b	728	96, 105, 106, 141	3			
1874	b	728	114-116	3			
1874	m	728	117-119	3			
1874	v	728	121-122, 1176	3			
1874	d	728	123-126	3			
1874	b	728	343	4			
1874	m	728	354	4			
1875	v	728	1176	3			
1875	b	728	127-130, 1036	3			
1875	m	728	131-132	3			
1875	d	728	133-137	3			
1875	b	728	343	4			
1875	m	728	354	4			
1876	b	728	1036-39	3			
1876	m	728	131, 1070-1071	3			
1876	m	728	131, 1070-1071, 1552	3			
1876	d	728	133, 1125-1127	3			
1876	v	728	14A, 1176	3			
1876	b	728	343	4			
1876	m	728	354	4			
1877	b	728	1043-1044, 1057	3			
1877	d	728	1129-1131, 1140	3			
1877	v	728	1176-1177	3			
1877	m	728	131, 1080	3			
1877	b	728	343	4			
1877	m	728	354	4			
1878	b	728	1050, 1057, 1057A	3			
1878	m	728	1081-1082, 1089	3			
1878	d	728	1132-1133	3			
1878	v	728	1178, 1410	3			
1878	b	728	343	4			
1878	m	728	354	4			
1879	b	728	1053-1054, 1058	3			
1879	m	728	1085-1086	3			
1879	d	728	1135-1137, 1139	3			
1879	v	728	1179, 1410	3			
1879	b	728	343	4			
1879	m	728	354	4			
1880	b	728	1056, 1059, 1060, 1061, 1105	3			
1880	m	728	1087-1089	3			
1880	d	728	1138, 1141-1144	3			
1880	v	728	1181-1182, 1410	3			
1880	b	728	343	4			
1880	m	728	354	4			
1880	d	728	356	4			

Vilkija (Vilki) continued

Year(s)	Type	Fond	File(s)	Op	A	F	Notes
1881	m	728	1090-1093	3			
1881	b	728	1107-1110, 1538	3			
1881	d	728	1145-1150	3			
1881	v	728	1410-1411	3			
1881	b	728	343	4			
1881	m	728	354	4			
1881	d	728	356	4			
1882	b	728	1063, 1111, 1113, 1115, 1116	3			
1882	m	728	1094-1096	3			
1882	d	728	1151-1155	3			
1882	v	728	1410, 1412-1413	3			
1882	b	728	344	4			
1882	m	728	354	4			
1882	d	728	356	4			
1883	b	728	1065-1067	3			
1883	m	728	1097-1099	3			
1883	b	728	1097A	1			
1883	d	728	1097A	1			
1883	m	728	1097A	1			
1883	d	728	1157, 1541	3			
1883	v	728	1410, 1414	3			
1883	b	728	344	4			
1883	m	728	354	4			
1883	d	728	356	4			
1884	b	728	1069, 1166	3			
1884	b	728	1097A	1			
1884	d	728	1097A	1			
1884	m	728	1097A	1			
1884	m	728	1098-1099	3			
1884	d	728	1158, 1160	3			
1884	v	728	1410, 1415	3			
1884	b	728	344	4			
1884	m	728	354	4			
1884	d	728	356	4			
1885	b	728	1097A	1			
1885	d	728	1097A	1			
1885	m	728	1097A	1			
1885	m	728	1100-1101	3			
1885	d	728	1159, 1161	3			
1885	b	728	1167, 1169	3			
1885	v	728	1416-1417	3			
1885	b	728	344	4			
1885	m	728	354	4			
1885	d	728	356	4			
1886	b	728	1097A	1			
1886	d	728	1097A	1			
1886	m	728	1097A	1			
1886	m	728	1102, 1422	3			
1886	d	728	1162-1163	3			
1886	b	728	1170, 1172	3			
1886	v	728	1418	3			
1886	b	728	344	4			
1886	m	728	354	4			
1886	d	728	356	4			
1887	b	728	1097A	1			
1887	d	728	1097A	1			
1887	m	728	1097A	1			
1887	m	728	1103, 1422	3			
1887	d	728	1164, 1542	3			
1887	b	728	1173, 1174, 1477	3			
1887	v	728	1419	3			
1887	b	728	344	4			
1887	m	728	354	4			
1887	d	728	357	4			
1888	b	728	1097A	1			
1888	d	728	1097A	1			
1888	m	728	1097A	1			
1888	m	728	1422, 1426	3			
1888	b	728	1423, 1425, 1477	3			
1888	v	728	1427	3			
1888	d	728	1428, 1543	3			
1888	b	728	345	4			
1888	m	728	354	4			
1888	d	728	357	4			
1889	b	728	1097A	1			
1889	d	728	1097A	1			
1889	m	728	1097A	1			
1889	m	728	1422, 1432	3			
1889	b	728	1430-1431, 1477	3			
1889	v	728	1433-1434	3			
1889	d	728	1435, 1544	3			
1889	b	728	345	4			
1889	m	728	354	4			
1889	d	728	357	4			
1890	b	728	1	4			
1890	b	728	1097A	1			
1890	d	728	1097A	1			

Vilkija (Vilki) continued

Year(s)	Type	Fond	File(s)	Op	A	F	Notes
1890	m	728	1097A	1			
1890	v	728	1434, 1442	3			
1890	b	728	1436, 1438, 1477	3			
1890	m	728	1440-1441	3			
1890	d	728	1443, 1545	3			
1890	b	728	345	4			
1890	m	728	354	4			
1890	d	728	357	4			
1891	b	728	1097A	1			
1891	d	728	1097A	1			
1891	m	728	1097A	1			
1891	v	728	1434, 1458?	3			
1891	b	728	1444, 1449, 1477	3			
1891	m	728	1449	3			
1891	d	728	1451, 1546	3			
1891	b	728	345	4			
1891	m	728	354	4			
1891	d	728	357	4			
1892	b	728	1097A	1			
1892	d	728	1097A	1			
1892	m	728	1097A	1			
1892	v	728	1434, 1457	3			
1892	m	728	1436, 1455	3			
1892	b	728	1452, 1454	3			
1892	d	728	1458, 1547	3			
1892	b	728	345	4			
1892	m	728	354	4			
1892	d	728	357	4			
1893	b	728	1	4			
1893	b	728	1097A	1			
1893	d	728	1097A	1			
1893	m	728	1097A	1			
1893	b	728	1460	3			
1893	m	728	1461	3			
1893	v	728	1462-1463	3			
1893	d	728	1466?, 1548	3			
1893	b	728	345-346	4			
1893	m	728	354	4			
1893	d	728	358	4			
1894	b	728	1097A	1			
1894	d	728	1097A	1			
1894	m	728	1097A	1			
1894	b	728	1465, 1539	3			
1894	m	728	1467	3			
1894	v	728	1468	3			
1894	d	728	1469, 1470	3			
1894	b	728	2, 345, 346	4			
1894	m	728	354	4			
1894	d	728	358, 366	4			
1895	b	728	1097A	1			
1895	d	728	1097A	1			
1895	m	728	1097A	1			
1895	d	728	1470, 1476	3			
1895	b	728	1471-1472	3			
1895	m	728	1474	3			
1895	v	728	1475	3			
1895	b	728	2, 346, 347	4			
1895	m	728	355	4			
1895	m	728	355	4			
1895	d	728	358, 369	4			
1895	m	728	367	4			
1895	v	728	368	4			
1896	b	728	1097A	1			
1896	d	728	1097A	1			
1896	m	728	1097A	1			
1896	d	728	1470	3			
1896	d	728	15, 358, 371?	4			
1896	b	728	2, 4, 346, 347, 360	4			
1896	m	728	355	4			
1896	m	728	5, 367	4			
1896	v	728	6, 368	4			
1897	b	728	1097A	1			
1897	d	728	1097A	1			
1897	m	728	1097A	1			
1897	m	728	17-18	4			
1897	v	728	19, 368	4			
1897	b	728	2, 16, 346, 347, 372	4			
1897	d	728	31, 358, 371?	4			
1897	m	728	355	4			
1898	b	728	1097A	1			
1898	d	728	1097A	1			
1898	m	728	1097A	1			
1898	b	728	33, 346-348, 374	4			
1898	m	728	34, 375	4			
1898	v	728	35, 376	4			
1898	m	728	355	4			
1898	d	728	47, 359	4			
1899	b	728	1097A	1			

Vilkija (Vilki) continued

Year(s)	Type	Fond	File(s)	Op
1899	d	728	1097A	1
1899	m	728	1097A	1
1899	m	728	355,	4
1899	b	728	48, 346, 348, 377	4
1899	m	728	49, 378	4
1899	v	728	50?, 376	4
1899	d	728	51, 359	4
1900	b	728	1, 62, 349-350, 379	4
1900	b	728	1097A	1
1900	d	728	1097A	1
1900	m	728	1097A	1
1900	m	728	355	4
1900	m	728	63-64, 380-381	4
1900	d	728	76, 359, 382	4
1901	b	728	1, 349-350	4
1901	b	728	1097A	1
1901	d	728	1097A	1
1901	m	728	1097A	1
1901	m	728	355	4
1901	m	728	63, 384-385	4
1901	b	728	77, 383	4
1901	v	728	78, 376	4
1901	d	728	79, 359, 386	4
1902	b	728	1097A	1
1902	d	728	1097A	1
1902	m	728	1097A	1
1902	m	728	355	4
1902	b	728	89, 351, 387	4
1902	m	728	90-91, 388	4
1902	v	728	92, 389	4
1902	d	728	93, 360, 390	4
1903	b	728	104, 351, 391	4
1903	m	728	105, 392, 395	4
1903	v	728	106, 389	4
1903	d	728	107, 360, 394	4
1903	b	728	1097A	1
1903	d	728	1097A	1
1903	m	728	1097A	1
1903	m	728	355	4
1904	b	728	1097A	1
1904	d	728	1097A	1
1904	m	728	1097A	1
1904	b	728	118, 352, 395	4
1904	m	728	119, 396	4
1904	v	728	120, 389	4
1904	d	728	121, 360, 397	4
1904	m	728	355	4
1905	b	728	1097A	1
1905	d	728	1097A	1
1905	m	728	1097A	1
1905	b	728	130, 348, 352, 398	4
1905	m	728	131, 399-400	4
1905	d	728	132, 360	4
1905	m	728	355	4
1906	b	728	1097A	1
1906	d	728	1097A	1
1906	m	728	1097A	1
1906	b	728	142, 348, 352, 401	4
1906	m	728	143, 402-403	4
1906	v	728	144, 389, 402	4
1906	d	728	145, 360, 405	4
1906	m	728	355	4
1907	b	728	1097A	1
1907	d	728	1097A	1
1907	m	728	1097A	1
1907	b	728	154, 348, 352, 406	4
1907	m	728	155, 407	4
1907	v	728	156, 402	4
1907	d	728	157, 360, 408	4
1907	m	728	355	4
1908	b	728	1097A	1
1908	d	728	1097A	1
1908	m	728	1097A	1
1908	b	728	163, 409	4
1908	m	728	164, 410-411	4
1908	v	728	165, 402	4
1908	d	728	166, 361, 412	4
1909	b	728	1097A	1
1909	d	728	1097A	1
1909	m	728	1097A	1
1909	b	728	174, 413	4
1909	m	728	175-176, 414	4
1909	v	728	177-178	4
1909	d	728	179, 361, 415	4
1910	b	728	1097A	1
1910	d	728	1097A	1
1910	m	728	1097A	1
1910	v	728	178, 191	4

Vilkija (Vilki) continued
1910	b	728	189, 416	4			
1910	m	728	190, 417-418	4			
1910	d	728	192, 361, 419	4			
1911	b	728	1097A	1			
1911	d	728	1097A	1			
1911	m	728	1097A	1			
1911	b	728	201	4			
1911	m	728	202-203, 420	4			
1911	v	728	204-205	4			
1911	d	728	206	4			
1912	b	728	1097A	1			
1912	d	728	1097A	1			
1912	m	728	1097A, 1098	1			
1912	b	728	216	4			
1912	m	728	217-218	4			
1912	v	728	219	4			
1912	d	728	220	4			
1913	b	728	1097A	1			
1913	d	728	1097A	1			
1913	m	728	1097A, 1098	1			
1913	b	728	229	4			
1913	m	728	230-232	4			
1913	v	728	233	4			
1913	d	728	234	4			
1914	b	728	1097A	1			
1914	d	728	1097A	1			
1914	m	728	1097A, 1098	1			
1914	b	728	241	4			
1914	m	728	242-244	4			
1914	v	728	245	4			
1914	d	728	246	4			
1915	b	728	1097A	1			
1915	d	728	1097A	1			
1915	m	728	1097A, 1098	1			
1915	b	728	256	4			
1915	m	728	257	4			
1915	v	728	258	4			
1915	d	728	259-260	4			
1916	b	728	1097A	1			
1916	d	728	1097A	1			
1916	m	728	1097A, 1098	1			
1917	b	728	1097A	1			
1917	d	728	1097A	1			
1917	m	728	1097A, 1098	1			
1918	b	728	1097A	1			
1918	d	728	1097A	1			
1918	m	728	1097A, 1098	1			
1919	b	728	1097A	1			
1919	d	728	1097A	1			
1919	m	728	1097A	1			
1920	b	728	1097A	1			
1920	d	728	1097A	1			
1920	m	728	1097A	1			
1921	b	728	1097A	1			
1921	d	728	1097A	1			
1921	m	728	1097A	1			
1922	b	728	1097A	1			
1922	d	728	1097A	1			
1922	m	728	1097A	1			
1923	b	728	1097A	1			
1923	d	728	1097A	1			
1923	m	728	1097A	1			

Vilnius County (Vilna County)
1795-1796	rs	515	7	15	K		Community & Subcommunity lists
1816-1818	rs	515	288	25	K		Jews
1834	rs	515	298	25	K		Jews
1843-1849	rs	515	306	25	K		Jews
1849	rs	515	312	25	K		Jews
1850-1854	rs	515	273	25	K		Jews
1858	rs	515	285	25	K		Jews
unknown	rs	515	299	25	K		Jews
unknown	rs	515	320	25	K		Jews
1873	b	728	141	3			Unspecified Localities
1873	d	728	145	3			Unspecified Localities
1887	b	728	1477	3			Unspecified Localities
1888	b	728	1477	3			Unspecified Localities
1889	b	728	1477	3			Unspecified Localities
1890	b	728	1	4			Unspecified Localities
1890	b	728	1477	3			Unspecified Localities
1891	b	728	1477	3			Unspecified Localities
1893	b	728	1	4			Unspecified Localities
1894	d	728	1470	3			Unspecified Localities
1895	d	728	1470	3			Unspecified Localities
1896	d	728	1470	3			Unspecified Localities
1897	d	728	31	4			Unspecified Localities
1898	d	728	47	4			Unspecified Localities
1899	d	728	51	4			Unspecified Localities

Vilnius County (Vilna County) continued

Year(s)	Type	Fond	File(s)	Op	A	F	Notes
1900	b	728	1	4			Unspecified Localities
1900	d	728	76	4			Unspecified Localities
1901	b	728	1	4			Unspecified Localities
1902	d	728	93	4			Unspecified Localities

Zagare (Zhagory)

Year(s)	Type	Fond	File(s)	Op	A	F	Notes
1852	rs						
1858	rs	1262	99				
1864-1869	rs	1262	124				
1866	rs						residents short list
1895	cen						Used in 1897 Census.

Zapyskis (Sapizishok)

Year(s)	Type	Fond	File(s)	Op	A	F	Notes
1900	b	728	978	1			
1901	b	728	978	1			
1902	b	728	978	1			
1903	b	728	978	1			
1904	b	728	978	1			
1905	b	728	978	1			
1906	b	728	978	1			
1907	b	728	978	1			
1908	b	728	978	1			
1909	b	728	978	1			
1910	b	728	978	1			
1911	b	728	978	1			
1912	b	728	978	1			
1913	b	728	978	1			

Zarasai (Novo-Aleksandrovsk)

Year(s)	Type	Fond	File(s)	Op	A	F	Notes
1816-27	rs						
1840-42	rs						
1863-64	rs						
1883	rs						
	fin	715					District Treasury Documents
1864-66	crl				K		New

Zarasai Area (Novo-Aleksandrovsk area)

Year(s)	Type	Fond	File(s)	Op	A	F	Notes
1900	pib				K		
1903-1917	prb				K		40 files
1908	crl				K		New

Zaskevichi, Belarus (Zaskevichi)

Year(s)	Type	Fond	File(s)	Op	A	F	Notes
1855	b	728	1103	1			
1856	b	728	1104	1			
1857	b	728	1105	1			
1857	m	728	1106	1			
1858	b	728	1107	1			
1859	b	728	1108	1			
1860	v	728	1109	1			
1861	d	728	1110	1			
1862	v	728	1111	1			
1863	b	728	1113	1			
1863	d	728	1114	1			
1864	b	728	1112	1			
1864	v	728	1115	1			
1865	b	728	1116	1			
1871	b	728	1117	1			
1871	m	728	1118	1			
1871	d	728	1119	1			
1871	v	728	1120	1			
1872	b	728	1121	1			
1872	m	728	1122	1			

Zasliai (Zhusli)

Year(s)	Type	Fond	File(s)	Op	A	F	Notes
1858-1905	rs						
1871	b	728	1340	3			
1871	m	728	1343	3			
1872	m	728	451	3			
1873	b	728	452	3			
1873	m	728	453	3			
1874	d	728	1348	3			
1874	m	728	454	3			
1875	d	728	1347	3			
1877	b	728	1340	3			
1878	b	728	1341	3			
1878	m	728	1346	3			
1879	b	728	1342	3			
1879	m	728	1344	3			
1880	m	728	1345	3			
1885	b	728	1118	3			
1886	b	728	1120	3			
1916	m	728	1551	3			

Zeimelis (Zhaimel)

Year(s)	Type	Fond	File(s)	Op	A	F	Notes
1816	rs						
1818-19	rs						
1834	rs						
1850	rs						

Zeimelis (Zhaimel) continued

Year(s)	Type	Fond	File(s)	Op	A	F	Notes
1857	v	728	317	1			
1858	m	728	369	1			
1859	d	728	478	1			
1860	b	728	503	1			
1860	m	728	542	1			
1860	v	728	564	1			
1860	d	728	593	1			
1861	b	728	603	1			
1861	m	728	629	1			
1861	v	728	650	1			
1861	d	728	668	1			
1862	b	728	691	1			
1862	v	728	742	1			
1862	d	728	762	1			
1863	m	728	796	1			
1864	b	728	872	1			
1864	m	728	903	1			
1864	d	728	939	1			
1865	b	1226	435	1			
1865	m	1226	436	1			
1865	d	1226	437	1			
1865	v	1226	438	1			
1866	b	1226	439	1			
1866	v	1226	440	1			
1866	d	1226	441	1			
1867	b	1226	442	1			
1867	m	1226	443	1			
1867	v	1226	444	1			
1867	d	1226	445	1			
1868	b	1226	446	1			
1868	m	1226	447	1			
1868	v	1226	448	1			
1868	d	1226	449	1			
1869	b	1226	450	1			
1869	m	1226	451	1			
1869	v	1226	452	1			
1869	d	1226	453	1			
1870	b	1226	454	1			
1870	m	1226	455	1			
1870	d	1226	456	1			
1871	m	1226	457	1			
1871	v	1226	458	1			
1871	d	1226	459	1			
1872	m	1226	460	1			
1873	b	1226	461	1			
1873	m	1226	462	1			
1873	v	1226	463	1			
1873	d	1226	464	1			
1874	b	1226	465	1			
1874	m	1226	466	1			
1874	v	1226	467	1			
1874	d	1226	468	1			
1875	b	1226	469	1			
1875	m	1226	470	1			
1875	v	1226	471	1			
1875	d	1226	472	1			
1876	b	1226	1224	1			
1876	m	1226	1229	1			
1876	d	1226	1234	1			
1876	v	1226	1238	1			
1877	b	1226	1225	1			
1877	m	1226	1230	1			
1877	d	1226	1235	1			
1877	v	1226	1239	1			
1878	b	1226	1226	1			
1878	m	1226	1231	1			
1878	d	1226	1237	1			
1878	v	1226	1240	1			
1879	b	1226	1227	1			
1879	m	1226	1232	1			
1879	d	1226	1236	1			
1879	v	1226	1241	1			
1880	b	1226	1228	1			
1880	m	1226	1233	1			
1880	v	1226	1242	1			
1880	d	1226	1243	1			
1882	m	1226	1990	1			
1883	m	1226	1990	1			
1884	m	1226	1990	1			
1885	m	1226	1990	1			
1886	m	1226	1990	1			
1887	m	1226	1990	1			
1888	m	1226	1990	1			
1889	m	1226	1990	1			
1890	m	1226	1990	1			
1891	m	1226	1990	1			
1892	m	1226	1990	1			
1893	m	1226	1990	1			

Zeimelis (Zhaimel) continued

Year(s)	Type	Fond	File(s)	Op	A	F	Notes
1894	m	1226	1990	1			
1895	m	1226	1990	1			
1896	m	1226	1990	1			
1897	m	1226	1990	1			
1898	m	1226	1990	1			
1899	m	1226	1990	1			
1900	m	1226	1990	1			
1901	m	1226	1990	1			
1902	m	1226	1990	1			
1903	m	1226	1990	1			
1904	m	1226	1990	1			
1905	m	1226	1990	1			
1906	m	1226	1990	1			
1907	m	1226	1990	1			
1908	m	1226	1990	1			
1909	m	1226	1990	1			
1910	m	1226	1990	1			
1911	m	1226	1990	1			
1912	m	1226	1990	1			
1913	m	1226	1990	1			
1914	m	1226	1990	1			
1914	b	1226	2088	1			
1914	d	1226	2088	1			
1915	m	1226	2087-2088	1			

Zeimena

Year(s)	Type	Fond	File(s)	Op	A	F	Notes
1874	rs	I-61	1648	1	K		Alphabetic - Jews

Zeimiai

Year(s)	Type	Fond	File(s)	Op	A	F	Notes
1851	rs						
1874	rs				K		Index of Jews
1870-74	k				K		
1874-78	k				K		

Zeizmariai

Year(s)	Type	Fond	File(s)	Op	A	F	Notes
1858-1905	rs						

Zelva (Pazhelva)

Year(s)	Type	Fond	File(s)	Op	A	F	Notes
1858	rs						
1874	rs						
1879	rs						
unknown	ta	204			K		Documents send & received

Zemaiciu Naumiestis

Year(s)	Type	Fond	File(s)	Op	A	F	Notes
1816	rs						
1836-40	rs						
1851	rs						
1858	rs						
1870-75	rs						
1873	rs						

Zidikiai

Year(s)	Type	Fond	File(s)	Op	A	F	Notes
1859	rs						

Ziezmariai (Zhezmir)

Year(s)	Type	Fond	File(s)	Op	A	F	Notes
1854	m	728	72	1			
1855	v	728	168	1			
1855	d	728	184	1			
1856	m	728	220	1			
1865	m	728	441	3			
1866	m	728	443	3			
1866	d	728	444	3			
1870	m	728	445	3			
1871	m	728	446	3			
1872	m	728	447-448	3			
1873	m	728	448	3			
1874	m	728	449	3			
1875	m	728	450	3			
1876	m	728	1353	3			
1876	m	728	1353A	3			
1878	b	728	1350	3			
1878	m	728	1354-1354A	3			
1878	d	728	1359	3			
1879	b	728	1351	3			
1879	m	728	1355-1356	3			
1879	d	728	1360	3			
1880	b	728	1352	3			
1880	m	728	1357-1358	3			
1880	d	728	1361	3			
1880	v	728	310	4			
1881	b	728	304	4			
1881	m	728	309-310	4			
1881	v	728	310	4			
1881	d	728	311	4			
1882	b	728	304	4			
1882	m	728	309-310	4			
1882	d	728	311	4			
1883	b	728	304	4			

Ziezmariai (Zhezmir) continued

Year(s)	Type	Fond	File(s)	Op
1883	m	728	309-310	4
1883	v	728	310	4
1883	d	728	311	4
1884	b	728	304	4
1884	m	728	309-310	4
1884	v	728	310	4
1884	d	728	311	4
1885	b	728	304	4
1885	m	728	309-310	4
1886	m	728	309	4
1886	d	728	311	4
1887	b	728	304	4
1887	m	728	309	4
1887	d	728	311	4
1888	b	728	304	4
1888	m	728	309	4
1888	d	728	311	4
1889	m	728	309	4
1889	d	728	311	4
1890	b	728	304	4
1890	m	728	310	4
1890	d	728	311	4
1891	b	728	304	4
1891	m	728	309	4
1891	v	728	310	4
1891	d	728	311	4
1892	b	728	304	4
1892	m	728	309	4
1893	b	728	1520	3
1893	b	728	304	4
1893	m	728	309	4
1893	v	728	310	4
1893	d	728	311	4
1894	b	728	1520	3
1894	d	728	311	4
1895	m	728	309-310	4
1895	v	728	310	4
1895	d	728	311	4
1896	b	728	305	4
1896	m	728	309-310	4
1896	d	728	311	4
1897	b	728	306	4
1897	m	728	309-310	4
1898	m	728	309-310	4
1899	b	728	307	4
1899	m	728	309-310	4
1900	b	728	308	4
1900	m	728	309-310	4
1900	d	728	311	4
1901	b	728	304	4
1901	d	728	311	4
1902	b	728	304	4
1902	d	728	311	4
1903	b	728	304	4
1903	d	728	311	4
1904	b	728	304	4
1904	d	728	311	4
1905	d	728	311	4
1906	b	728	304	4
1906	d	728	311	4
1907	b	728	304	4
1907	v	728	310	4
1908	b	728	304	4
1908	v	728	310	4
1909	b	728	304	4
1909	d	728	311	4
1910	b	728	304	4
1910	d	728	311	4
1911	b	728	304	4
1912	b	728	304	4
1912	d	728	311	4
1913	b	728	304	4
1913	d	728	311	4
1914	b	728	304	4
1914	d	728	311	4
1915	b	728	304	4